ELITE FAMILIES

SUNY SERIES IN THE SOCIOLOGY OF WORK
RICHARD H. HALL, EDITOR

ELITE FAMILIES

Class and Power in Nineteenth-Century Boston

BETTY G. FARRELL

STATE UNIVERSITY OF NEW YORK PRESS

The following publishers have generously given permission to use extended quotations from copyrighted works: excerpts from *To Be Young Was Very Heaven* by Marian Lawrence Peabody. Copyright © 1967 by Marian Lawrence Peabody. Reprinted by permission of Houghton Mifflin Company. All rights reserved; permission from Dun and Bradstreet and Baker Library, Harvard University Graduate School of Business Administration to cite from the R. G. Dun and Co. collection.

Published by
State University of New York Press, Albany

© 1993 State University of New York

For information, address State University of New York
Press, State University Plaza, Albany, N.Y., 12246

Production by E. Moore
Marketing by Lynne Lekakis

Library of Congress Cataloging-in-Publication Data

Farrell, Betty, 1949-
    Elite families : class and power in nineteenth-century Boston /
Betty Farrell.
        p.   cm. — (SUNY series in the sociology of work)
    Includes bibliographical references (p.   ) and index.
    ISBN 0-7914-1593-7 (hard : alk. paper). — ISBN 0-7914-1594-5
(pbk. : alk. paper)
    1. Elite (Social sciences)—Massachusetts—Boston—History—19th
century. 2. Upper class families—Massachusetts—Boston-
-History—19th century. 3. Textile industry—Social aspects-
-Massachusetts—Boston—History—19th century. I. Title.
II. Series.
HN80.B7F37 1993
305.5'2'09446109034—dc20   92-30978
                                                            CIP

10 9 8 7 6 5 4 3 2 1

HN
80
.B7
F37
1993

CONTENTS

ACKNOWLEDGMENTS

This book, true to its subject, has been produced with the help and support of several overlapping networks of family, friends, and professional colleagues. I am fortunate indeed to count among my kin a social historian of nineteenth-century America, an editor, and a researcher/drafter par excellence. I thank Janet Farrell Brodie for her sustained sisterly support through every stage of this project and for her invaluable close readings of the manuscript with a historian's critical eye more times than she may care to remember. Deborah Farrell has provided editorial help and an unflagging interest in this project over its long duration. Patricia Farrell was instrumental in locating important sources for me during one season as a researcher in the Boston archives. Her artistic skills as a landscape architect were also engaged in the drawings of Boston's Back Bay in chapter two. Others in my extended family are too numerous to thank individually, but their example has been particularly important in shaping my understanding of how families can work effectively to nurture and support what appears to be an individual effort.

I have benefited from the thoughtful comments and critical advice of many friends and professional colleagues who have read versions of this manuscript. My earliest searches in the historical archives were supported by Lee Rainwater, Ezra Vogel, Stephan Thernstrom, Tamara Hareven, and Theda Skocpol. Paul DiMaggio has read a recent version with more care and critical insight than most authors are privileged to receive. Daniel Horowitz and Helena Wall gave the manuscript particularly astute historical readings. Thanks to my Claremont colleagues Don Brenneis, Pieter Judson, Lucian Marquis, Stuart McConnell, Daniel

Segal, Ann Stromberg for their thoughtful comments, and to Rena Fraden and Joanna Worthley for making writing a weekly pleasure.

Special thanks also to Britta Fischer, Sylvia Freed, Terry Littleton, and Maureen Mahoney whose long-term friendship and scholarly camraderie have stretched over many years in Boston and beyond. My greatest intellectual debts are to Sam Kaplan, who taught me the pleasures of thinking sociologically, and to Moune Charrad, whose critical advice I have valued over many years and at every stage of my work.

Institutional support from Pitzer College and the National Endowment for the Humanities came at crucial times during my research on this project. The help of reference librarians at the Massachusetts Historical Society and the New England Historic Genealogical Society was invaluable. I am grateful to the Massachusetts Historical Society, to the Department of Special Collections at Baker Library, the Harvard Graduate School of Business Administration, to the Museum of Fine Arts, Boston, and to Houghton Mifflin Publishers for permission to quote from their sources.

INTRODUCTION

This is a book about families and the process of social change. More specifically, it is about economically prominent Boston families during the era of industrialization in nineteenth-century America and the ways in which they helped shape the direction of change while preserving their own social and economic position over time.

My focus is on a group of Bostonians whose centrality in developing the textile industry of the early nineteenth century identified them as an important regional economic elite. More than a set of individual economic leaders, however, the men who founded the New England textile industry were embedded in extended families, or broad kinship networks. These networks were laced together by strong personal ties that provided the structural basis for group solidarity amid the diffuse economic activities of a newly industrializing society. A central concern of this study is to trace how effectively these kinship networks were able to mediate the process of social change. What were the mechanisms of families' economic continuity or decline? Were these members of the Boston economic elite in the early nineteenth century the core of an emergent economic upper class with intergenerational continuity?[1] To what extent were they able to shape some of the economic changes with which they were faced to their long-term family interests, thus preserving economic position, wealth, and status over several generations?

The group of families appropriate to this study were those known collectively as the Boston Brahmins. Given the label "the Brahmin Caste of New England" in a novel by Oliver Wendell Holmes,[2] the families constituting Boston's social aristocracy have been widely known as statesmen, men and women of letters, and, often, puritanical moralists. In a society that celebrates social mobility and an egalitarian ethos, the Brahmins have been noted for their closure and insularity. People who otherwise know little about Boston's history and culture can readily quote the verse: "And this is good old Boston, the home of the bean and the cod, where the Lowells talk to the Cabots and the Cabots talk only to God."[3]

Thus branded an American aristocracy, anachronistic and socially exclusive, Boston Brahmins have only rarely been identified as key economic innovators of the early nineteenth century. My study traces the most economically central of these families. A small core group of the Brahmin establishment, they were nevertheless disproportionately influential in developing the textile industry in New England and the foundation of a modern economic infrastructure in Boston. It is the history of the original textile entrepreneurs in these families and their lineal and collateral descendants traced over the course of the nineteenth century that forms the basis for this book.

As the site of early industrial development in the United States, Boston is a particularly appropriate area for the study of family, social change, and economic persistence. The Boston textile industry represented the first modern corporate enterprise and constituted a key center of entrepreneurial activity in the period following the American Revolution. Throughout the nineteenth and into the early twentieth century, Boston capital was instrumental in funding large-scale investment projects, including railroads and western mining ventures.

Despite the fact that it was surpassed by other cities both in terms of wealth and diversity of industry, Boston continued to be an important center of finance and the site of new corporate business in the first decades of the twentieth century. This book focuses on a single location, but the particular configuration of Boston's history—first as an early center of economic development and later as a city renowned for its vintage wealth and established Brahmin cultural institutions—makes it an important setting for the study of family and economic persistence.

Studying families as significant economic units is by definition a historical project, since it is a common understanding that families in the United States declined in their economic functions with the advent of industrialization. My orientation is indeed historical: a study set in the nineteenth century when the shift in the family's functions from economic control to emotional support was supposed to have occurred as a consequence of industrialization. It is even more broadly sociological in its goal of questioning the conventional wisdom about the inevitable privatization of family life in the face of this economic and social change. Assumptions about the changing role of the family have been critical in shaping sociological theories about class, power, and social change. This study addresses these broader sociological questions through the focus on a specific historical setting and group.

My case study of prominent and privileged Boston families emerges out of two concerns. One is to bring the family back to the center of macrosociological analysis: to the study of political economy, social stratification, and social change. As a key institution that places individuals in the larger social order by establishing the socially recognized lines of descent, succession, inheritance, and socialization, the family would appear to be central to the tasks of theory building and societal analysis. Yet, in American sociology, more attention has been given to the internal dynamics of family behavior than to the place of this institution in the structure of power or to its role in effecting or resisting social change.

In addition to bringing the study of the family back to a more central role in macrosociology, a related concern behind this project is to redress the balance of class analysis in the social history literature. Two decades of research by labor historians, community and family historians, and women's historians, in particular, have accumulated a wealth of information about specific locales, groups, and institutions during the important period of social, economic, and cultural transformation in nineteenth-century America. Much of the focus has been on working-class or middle-class experience, with the accumulated findings pointing to the varied and complex nature of intraclass social experience.[4] The wealthy, privileged, and powerful have been left out of social historical analysis, both because new methodological techniques made it possible to include new groups in the historical record, and because of a concern by social historians for studying those formerly ignored and forgotten instead of the wealthy and powerful who were overrepresented in traditional historical sources.

Study of the upper class is thus in a peculiar state. On the one hand there is considerable popular interest in the intimate details of upper-class family life and social experience;[5] on the other, scholarly interest in the upper class has almost always been posed in terms of general group characteristics, rather than a particular set of families who make it up.[6] There has been very little systematic study of the ways in which particular upper-class families succeeded in maintaining their position or failed by losing their footing in an era of great change in American history.

Even more unusual in the literature is the recognition that an upper-class family is not just a social institution, but a group of interacting people. Men and women shared many collective stakes in the larger family enterprise of which they were a part, but they also experienced family life in quite different, gender-specific ways. While men's business activities drew on family ties to coordinate their economic interests, women's familial relationships were often primarily personal and social in nature. But rather than constituting separate spheres of experience, the family ties of men and women were overlapping and mutually reinforcing. Charting the intersection of gendered experiences within the family is an important part of correcting the historical sociological record, and it involves shifting between different kinds of sources.

Reconstruction of kinship networks as economic entities in this project was aided by the use of varied sources: genealogies, business records, city and business directories. I received fuller information about individual histories and family relations within kin networks from personal memoirs, family papers, wills, obituaries, and the biographical accounts in Harvard class reunion reports. While these sources provided a rich store of information on men's lives and the interconnections between family and business activities, they rarely allowed a glimpse into the family lives of Boston Brahmin women. For such a perspective, diaries, journals, and women's personal letters in family collections have been important source materials. Although constituting a dramatic shift in tone and style from the business records of men, these documents capture the domestic side of the kinship networks in which women were important actors. The variety of sources tapped for this study not only addresses both male and female experiences in families, but the way in which the family simultaneously had individual and social structural significance.

The interdisciplinary orientation of this project, finally, deserves note. While the distinction between the work of social historians and historical sociologists is always a fine one, I define my task as bringing the specific data of a historical case study to bear on more general sociological questions. This is therefore a study of a segment of the nineteenth-century Boston upper class, with an analysis intended to illustrate one facet of the relationship between family and social change. It is hoped that this book will contribute both to a revived interest in the family as a social institution with macrosociological consequences and to the growing social historical literature on family systems and experiences that must include elites among other community, institutional, and group studies before the broader picture of cross-class patterns can fully emerge.

Chapter one begins with an overview of the ways family and economy have been juxtaposed in the interdisciplinary literature. The purpose of this overview is to expose the underlying premises in the fields of economic history, political sociology, and family and gender history, which have shaped the perspective and research agenda dominating family studies. A new orientation to the study of elite or upper-class families—one that promotes the family's macrostructural concern with alliance-building and its longer-term interest in maintaining economic continuity—is proposed here as a theoretical contribution to family sociology and as an organizing framework for this study.

Chapter two describes the geography and culture of Boston as the setting for this project. The particular cohesion of Brahmin Boston is revealed both in its unique residential patterns and in the dominant cultural institutions established during the nineteenth century. But a debate over the continued economic vitality of Brahmin families captures the issue for further study.

The remaining chapters are organized around the dual themes of economic alliance-building and maintaining family continuity. Chapter three begins to address the structural underpinnings of economic alliance-building with a discussion of the new financial infrastructure built by the Boston Associate textile entrepreneurs in the period between 1820 and 1840, and the kinship networks that laced them together. A central focus of my general argument is to show how men used their families to help coordinate economic interests. The kin network provided individual businessmen with a structure that more effectively allowed the mobilization of capital and the coordination of economic activities.

But the structure of networks describes only one facet of the family as an economic institution. How family solidarity was developed and maintained is another facet worth investigating. An additional concern in this study is to expand the analysis of the structure of kin networks with an understanding of the dynamic processes that maintained them. To a large extent, women were the central nodes of the kinship network.

Chapter four presents the argument that women's role in kin-keeping was the ongoing process through which family alliances were sustained. In their domestic lives and social activities, women, as well as men, worked to preserve the family as an economic institution. Because intermarriage was one of the key means though which kinship net-works were extended, this chapter also explores the engagements and marriages of four young Boston Brahmin women from the 1830s to the turn of the twentieth century. These case studies provide individual accounts of the process through which marriage was contracted. They suggest that while there was substantial individual choice over mar-riage partners among the Boston Brahmins, marital alliances within the upper class continued to have significant structural outcomes for the family and group.

The analysis in chapter five shifts from individual case histories to longitudinal group patterns. Both marriage patterns and occupational patterns among descendants of the original textile entrepreneurs are traced to the early twentieth century, when key records cease. Different patterns of intermarriage characterized the experience of Boston upper-class descendants over the course of the nineteenth century, suggesting that Brahmin families pursued multiple strategies for preserving their economic continuity into the early twentieth century.

Chapter six concludes this study with a look at the changing insti-tutional context of Boston's economy in the first decades of the twenti-eth century. Although this was another period of fundamental social structural change in the transition to an advanced industrial economy, lessons from an earlier era could be applied to this period as well. Boston Brahmins, who had been adept at turning the personalistic ties of family to new economic ends in the early nineteenth century, were still enmeshed in overlapping networks of family and business by the early twentieth. Against this background, I suggest that the family's modern economic functions need to be reassessed, with some implica-tions for further sociological analysis.

Chapter 1

FAMILY AND ECONOMY

Social theorists recognize the central role of the family in organizing the social structure, not because the family is the prototype for all other social institutions as has often been assumed, but because it is so effective an institution in mobilizing two key resources: strategic alliances and the basis for longer-term political and economic continuity. It is in the process of establishing both alliances and continuity that the core of a political economy is formed. The family, in its most fundamental social interactions, is organized around the central macrosociological tasks of securing political power and long-term social and economic placement.

Claude Lévi-Strauss was one of the theorists who noted that the key universal feature of the family was not its structure or internal organization, on which there is great cultural variation, but its rule prohibiting incest. Two socially significant consequences follow directly from the incest taboo: the restriction of sexual relations within the family of origin and the push to establish marital alliances outside the boundaries of the original family unit, through the formation of new families of procreation. The key universal feature of the family, then, is its capacity to build strategic alliances through the process of intermarriage, an act that in undifferentiated societies created a dense social web based on reciprocal obligation, personalistic loyalty, and political bonds of solidarity.[1]

Besides forming an intricate network of political rights and obligations through family alliances, there were also other macrostructural consequences of marriage. The marital bond defined an elementary family unit and thus created the basis for family continuity by defining sexual and material property rights of the marital pair, by establishing the basis for the socially recognized legitimacy of children, and by charting the lines of inheritance. Wealth and position could flow through family lines that were drawn by birth and marriage. Particularly in societies without other forms of social organization, the family was an effective institutional means of structuring and regulating the social order.

Developing and expanding this insight about the centrality of the family into a broader comparative-historical theoretical framework, Max Weber has been the primary theorist of the stages of societal development that link the family, economy, and state. While pre-state tribal societies relied on the kind of formal and complex marital exchanges described by Lévi-Strauss to create political and economic alliances, a new kind of family-based political economy emerged in feudal and agrarian societies. Under conditions of greater social stratification, the patrimonial household of the aristocracy brought both military power and property-holding under the control of the extended family.[2] Building political alliances and securing a basis for political authority and economic continuity were central goals of patrimonial households. To this end, the rules of intermarriage were less formalized than in tribal, more kin-based societies, but were just as important a means of political strategy. While marital alliances provided aristocratic families with a means of accruing political power, the emphasis on producing heirs to ensure succession and property transmission was also a central economic concern.

For Weber, the development of modern capitalism and the rise of the modern bureaucratic state involved the most radical rupture of the family as a central institution of the political economy. This undermining of the family's macrostructural role occurred early in Western Europe, as the Church began to compete for an expanded share of inherited wealth and political power.[3] The rise of a state bureaucracy— based on more formalized rules than the personal loyalties embedded in the patrimonial household—and the development of a paid professional army as an extrafamilial military force effectively stripped the family of its political centrality.[4] Where once the family had regulated the flow of political power, the bureaucratized state now rapidly developed the means to usurp this role.

In economic terms as well, Weber's theoretical model accounts for the decline of the centrality of the family in the modern era. The rise of modern capitalism required many preconditions: a stable money economy, an accessible market, a dependable and motivated labor force. But, above all, it required predictability in work behavior and economic exchange. The household economy of the precapitalist era had drawn a sharp distinction between "brother" and "other"—those trusted insiders bound by personalistic ties of family and community as distinguished from outsiders who were not to be trusted and who were therefore prey for exploitation and piracy. Modern capitalism dissolved that distinction, turning all—even brothers—into others. It did so by introducing a more rationalized and predictable standard of behavior, which served to regulate economic life and thereby ensure repeated economic exchange. The personalistic ties of family were no longer privileged in such transactions, and the result was the increasing privatization of family life as the realm of personal relationships in contrast to the spread of a more rationalized, bureaucratized political economy.[5]

Such a theoretical model of the role of the family in the process of societal development and historical change offers a sweeping picture of the family's centrality and subsequent decline in the development of modern society. While this picture is convincing in its broadest strokes, the finer details of historical change and the more intricate dynamics of the family's relationship to the political economy have hardly begun to be filled in. Nevertheless, historians and sociologists have often accepted the outlines of the theoretical model as concrete historical fact, rather than as a question for further investigation.

In American sociology, in particular, the study of the dynamics of interpersonal relationships within contemporary families—issues relating to the private nature of modern family life—have preempted more macrostructural and historically-based concerns.[6] Few questions have been posed about the extent to which traditional economic and political functions of families might have been carried into the modern era. Instead, it has largely been assumed, based on theoretical premises but little concrete historical data, that the family's economic functions, while appropriate to a domestic economy, were subsumed by larger, more corporate enterprises as the demand for greater rationalization became the imperative of an industrial society.

Outside the subfield of family sociology, such assumptions have had striking consequences for scholarly inquiry within the discipline. When it comes to understanding the processes of institutional development and social change, or the dynamics of social class and power, implicit assumptions about the family and its macrostructural demise have provided the starting point for explanations about the nature of power and social organization in American society. While in other societies studies of family dynasties, business patterns, and economic change are well documented, even after the development of industrial capitalism,[7] in the United States the idea of the family's economic decline has been taken for granted as a social fact.

Because several kinds of literature help contribute to this perspective, it is important to look at the way separate disciplinary premises have overlapped to produce a set of shared assumptions guiding interdisciplinary investigation. Premises about the nature and importance of the family in economic history, political sociology, family history, and gender studies are addressed here through three interrelated topics: the family and economic change; the family, power, and social class; and the privatization of the family and the separation of spheres. All these are central to the ways family and economy have been juxtaposed and understood. By making explicit the assumptions about the relationship between family and economy in each of these areas of historical and sociological research, I mean to suggest new ways in which the family's macrostructural concerns with building alliances and maintaining economic continuity might be reinterpreted in the context of a modern society.

THE FAMILY AND ECONOMIC CHANGE

A particular chronology of economic development in the United States dominates much of the work of economists, economic historians, and political sociologists. According to this standard chronology, the American economy has passed through a series of developmental stages corresponding to the degree of complexity of the business firm and, most importantly, to the separation of ownership from management control within the modern corporation.

Between the 1790s and the 1840s, entrepreneurial or family capitalism predominated, with firms traditionally organized as single-unit enterprises, owned and controlled by individuals, family members, and their close associates. Virtually no multiunit business enterprises existed in this period, nor was there a managerial class differentiated from the entrepreneurial owners. The period of transition in which an agrarian and rural economy became industrial and urban occurred between 1840 and 1920, a transition that also spelled the demise of a family-based system of capitalism.[8]

Expanded economic activity over the second half of the nineteenth century is widely assumed to have undermined the effectiveness of the single-unit family firm in a number of significant ways. Larger and more complex organizations with distinct operating units evolved to meet higher production standards and more dispersed distribution needs. Entrepreneurial founders and their families were no longer capable of staffing such multiunit business enterprises. In their place, a trained, salaried, career staff of middle managers could work more effectively to monitor and coordinate economic activities. A rational economic strategy of long-term growth and stability over short-term profit guided management decisions in this modern business enterprise.[9]

In short, the personalistic ties of family were replaced by the impersonal hierarchy of a management bureaucracy in American business by the early twentieth century. The dominance of this new organizational form was so complete and sweeping as to constitute an economic revolution. In the words of one of the leading American economic historians, "rarely in the history of the world has an institution grown to be so important and so pervasive in so short a period of time."[10]

While business historians have charted the decline of the family firm and the rise of the large corporation in the United States, sociologists have used the same model of economic growth to argue for the transformation of power in American society. Along with the change in the social organization of the firm, there appeared an even more significant shift in power relations that signaled the further erosion of the family from its traditional economic base: that of the separation of ownership from managerial control within the large corporation, with the consequence of a redistribution of power in American society.

In an important review of the literature on corporate ownership and the question of economic control, published in 1974, sociologist Maurice Zeitlin argued that the widespread and uncritical acceptance of the separation of ownership and control constituted a pseudofact with an "astonishing consensus" among social scientists.[11] The source of this consensus was Berle and Means's classic study, *The Modern Corporation and Private Property*, originally published in 1932, in which the authors argued that the spread of ownership among widely dispersed stockholders within the large corporation effectively undermined the foundation of private property on which a system of family capitalism had been based.

Despite challenges to the Berle and Means analysis by various critics, on the grounds both of a reassessment of the original data and subsequent study of the persistence of family control within the corporation,[12] the theory of managerial capitalism has carried great weight in the debate about the distribution of power in American sociology. In general, even critics of the managerial revolution hypothesis have tended to accept the premise of the family's decline as an economic institution, while focusing their attention on interlocking directorates or other structural means through which power has been coalesced.[13] In adopting the premises about family and business organization contained in this chronology of economic change, sociologists have reduced the family's role and meaning to an exclusively personalistic set of relations under the system of industrial capitalism.

What is missing from this account is a more critical interpretation of the way the family's economic functions have bridged preindustrial and industrializing societies. Historical studies of working-class families, for example, have uncovered a variety of ways in which families tried to resist the incursion of industrial capitalism,[14] but also the ways in which they eased the family's transition to a new kind of economic order, serving as recruitment, training, and welfare agencies in an era that provided few formal support services.[15] If working-class families acted as a resource for its members during the period of industrialization, in what ways did elite families bridge this transition as well? One answer is in the network of kinship relations that bridged and interlaced the discrete economic organizations of an industrializing society.

The kinship network, rather than the family firm, is a key unit of analysis for understanding the role of the family under the impact of economic and social change. Rather than focusing on the discrete business organization as the locus of family control, tracing the web of extended kinship relations and overlapping business ties among the economic elite offers a new perspective on the structure of power. While individuals could wield considerable influence through their interlocking directorship positions, the kinship network offered even more potential for the extensive and cohesive coordination of economic control. As we seek to understand the full range of ways families felt the impact of and reacted to major social structural change, placing the family as a network of interacting kin at the center of this analysis, rather than accepting the premise of the family's inevitable eclipse, offers new interpretive possibilities.

THE FAMILY, POWER, AND SOCIAL CLASS

If the kinship network is a useful concept for tracing webs of interconnection and lines of power and economic influence in any one period, it also holds great potential for tracking the economic continuity of families over time. Such economic persistence, built on the inheritance of property or position across generations of a family, constitutes the foundation for an economic upper class in a system of industrial capitalism. Recognizing that "the family, not the physical person, is the true unit of class and class theory," Joseph Schumpeter noted forty years ago that genealogical research was necessary for "providing a reliable knowledge of the structure and life processes of capitalist society."[16] Yet relatively little such research has been systematically conducted, and the family unit has rarely been used in sociological analyses of social class. The grounds on which the concept of social class has often been equated with social strata, a model of more gradual and permeable layers of economic hierarchy, need investigation. An understanding of power, on which social class is ultimately based, is the starting point for this inquiry.

Interpretations of the nature of power in the United States have generally fallen into the competing camps of pluralism and power-elite studies. The two perspectives differ in terms of accepting the individual or the group as the basis of class analysis, in terms of their respective emphases on achievement and social mobility or ascription and inheritance as the primary mode of gaining access to power, and in terms of the replaceability or the intractability of the power-holding group.[17]

Central to the pluralist view of the wide dispersal of power in the United States is a belief in the decline of the family as the key property-holding institution of advanced capitalism. Accepting the chronology and logic of the managerial revolution in the American economy, a number of sociologists have equated the decline of family power with the "breakup of family capitalism."[18] Following from this premise, it has been argued that "families [who] once controlled through ownership most of the big businesses . . . failed to consolidate their position as the dominant class in the society" from the period of the mid-nineteenth century.[19] With this shift, skill and credentials superseded inheritance as the basis for placement and advancement in society. Power was thus no longer monopolized by the few because "veto groups" were able to act as a countervailing force, providing an equal chance for power among competing segments of the society.[20] In the pluralist view, the decline of the family as the source of inherited privilege and institutionalized power was the key to a more democratic social and political order.

The power-elite argument, as posed by C. Wright Mills, offered a different model of the arrangement of power: as consolidated and coordinated rather than dispersed. While also accepting the Berle and Means hypothesis of the decline of family control with the rise of the corporation, Mills reinterpreted the outcome of this transformation by arguing that a group of top corporate, political, and military leaders had come to dominate the institutional command posts of the American power structure by the second half of the twentieth century.[21] Subsequent power structure research in sociology has focused on the formal and informal networks of interaction that help coordinate this power elite.[22] While concurring that the family has lost its formal economic functions, power-elite theorists nevertheless recognize the centrality of the family in coordinating the social and cultural institutions through which power is mobilized.

Although power-elite theorists reach different conclusions about the outcome of power in the twentieth century than do pluralists, they have made little attempt to construct a detailed historical account of the process through which this consolidated group emerged. Focusing on the mid-twentieth century with the power elite already firmly entrenched, they have not attempted to explain the transition between the alleged decline of family-based power in the nineteenth century and the rise of institutionally-based power a century later. A key criticism of the power-structure research has been its tendency to assume that personal interconnections linking members of a social elite are both necessary and sufficient as conditions of power. How webs of personal relationships become structures of power requires a fuller explanation.

Lacking a detailed historical perspective, the model of power that has predominated in much of political sociology remains static, an analytic concept only. If power is to be seen as a characteristic of groups that emerge in a specific historical context, we need historical studies of how the structure of power has come to be shaped through group strategies to perpetuate their economic, social, and political position over time. We need, in short, to investigate how an elite perpetuates its power and privilege by becoming a more stable and entrenched social class with intergenerational continuity.

The pervasive belief in the decline of the family as an institution with macrostructural political and economic consequences correlates closely with the individualistic orientation to social class that pervades much of American sociology. If the family is no longer the key property-holding institution of an advanced industrial society and if power has been effectively redistributed, then occupational status and income are accurate measures of an individual's achieved position in the stratification order. But if families are seen as extended kinship networks with an interest in building alliances and maintaining economic continuity, then a broader measure of social class as rooted in a set of intermarrying families with similar economic location and shared social-cultural characteristics is needed to understand the ways in which power can be consolidated and intergenerational placement assured.

Tracing more intricate kinship and economic connections than father-to-son occupational patterns is one means of retrieving the family's alliance-building and continuity functions in a modern context. Such a study would bring the family back to a position of centrality in the study of power and class.

PRIVATIZATION OF THE FAMILY: THE SEPARATION OF SPHERES

If the family has not been a central research focus for economists, economic historians, or political sociologists, it has certainly been so for social historians. Their areas of inquiry have directly addressed the family as a social institution that varies by class, race, ethnicity, and gender. Yet there have been two main tendencies in the family history and women's history literature that have limited the macrosociological implications of this research. One is the predominant emphasis on working-class or middle-class family experience, but the exclusion of the upper class—potentially the most powerful family group in mediating the processes of industrialization or in effecting social change. The second has been the tendency to start from, rather than to question and study, the premise of the privatization of family life.

The accumulated literature of the past two decades on family and gender relations in nineteenth-century America has documented one trend in particular: a separation of spheres between public and private, the division of the political economy and the domestic sphere, a split between the worlds of men and women. According to the accepted model of social change in much of this literature, the links between the family and larger community, which closely overlapped in the seventeenth and eighteenth centuries, were progressively pulled apart by the rise of industrial capitalism in the nineteenth. It is in nineteenth-century America that the trajectories of economic history and family history are first seen as diverging. As of this period, economic historians focused exclusively on the rise of a differentiated set of economic institutions dominated by men and a shift in the locus of work, as paid work, outside the home. Family historians turned their attention in this period to the entrenchment of the middle-class domestic sphere as a haven from the world of industrial capitalism and as the primary arena of women and children.

Much of the social historical literature of the past two decades from the fields of family history and women's history has been devoted to identifying and charting the consequences of this separation of spheres.[23] Although there has been a critical response to this literature, focusing on the ways that working-class, poor, and otherwise marginalized families were unable to achieve such a neat division of social spheres, the middle-class bias of this literature is more than an oversight. The notion of distinct public and private spaces was specifically a bourgeois invention and social construction, an ideology molded to the needs of the new economic order and its rising middle and upper classes.

As the architects of industrial capitalism, the middle class had an influence that reached far beyond its own ranks. Part of the social construction of the political economy of early industrial capitalism involved new conceptions of nonmarket relations as well. The bourgeois home was envisioned as a direct counterpart to the competitive individualism of the market, and its primary caretakers, women, were depicted as guardians of sentiment and social responsibility, purveyors of the ties that would bind intensely individualized men to the larger collectivities of family, community, and society.[24] The ideology of separate spheres, then, defined a new set of social relations in nineteenth-century America. The complement to the independent competitive entrepreneur, the male prototype of an industrializing society, was the virtuous, domestic woman, an efficient engineer of the home and, most importantly, a moral mother.[25]

Although the question about what would hold a society dominated by competitive individualism together continued to worry social
critics throughout the nineteenth century, one early answer seemed to
be provided by the kind of personal ties associated with family and
home. Marriage was idealized as the social glue that would bind
together the complementary personalities of men and women and their
mutually reinforcing social roles. The key social function women were
to fulfil was to soothe the excesses of a competitive economic system
and to reinforce that same system. As a dependent wife, a woman kept
her husband committed to his market role as the primary breadwin-
ner for the family, while her own role was defined in terms of maintaining the family as a refuge from the excesses of competitive capitalism. As a mother, she nurtured and socialized her children, the next
generation of industrial workers. Far from being superfluous to this
market economy, then, women fulfilled an important, if relatively
unrecognized, role in the forging of industrial capitalism.

As an ideology, the middle-class conception of domestic privacy
and gender relations was central to the complex system of emerging
industrial capitalism. That most poor and working-class women could
not live up to the ideal of domesticity does not refute its claim to being
part of the dominant value system of the era; it simply makes the dis-
crepancy between accepted ideology and real behavior more pointed.
The functions of this social role, for those women of the middle and
upper classes who did live out this ideology as part of their everyday
life experience, particularly in an era in which the family's general economic functions were being redefined and reshaped, is an important
subject for study.

The ideology of separate spheres had significant ramifications for
many nineteenth-century women and men. For economically privileged
women, whose husbands gained social status as sole breadwinners for
a family of dependents, the domestic sphere was an all-encompassing
world, shaping values as well as activities. The idea that shared experience produced a new basis for gender identity among women has been
important in offering historians a way to think about the strengths, as
well as the limitations, of lives lived within the domestic circle. A shared
identity rooted in gender provided women with a new sense of sisterhood, of cultural as well as political efficacy.[26] As women's lives were
defined by the ideals of domesticity, men were defined by their exclusion from this gendered space.

But for all of its influence in the literature, the doctrine of separate spheres has been overstated and its impact has been misleading. Gender may be one significant differentiator of life experiences and values, but the cleavages produced by race, ethnicity, religion and social class are significant others.[27] Critics of the ideology of separate spheres argue that it has been used too inclusively, defining both the oppression of and the solidarity among women, and conflating too many aspects of the social world and social experience.[28] Accepted as a starting premise in historical study rather than the proper subject of investigation, this concept has become reified as "fact" in women's history, and crucial questions about when, where, under what social conditions, and with what consequences the social spheres of men and women create separate or overlapping public and private domains are rarely asked.

The study of separate spheres in the lives of upper-class Bostonians promises to contribute in a number of important ways to a revision of these assumptions. Undeniably, women of Boston's upper class in the nineteenth century did live in the privileged, private domestic sphere afforded by their husbands' class position. Their experiences, then, were relatively unusual in that they fit the contours of the ideology of domesticity. But it is particularly important to understand upper-class women's domesticity and kin-keeping roles in the larger context of the economic meaning that kinship networks held for their fathers, husbands, brothers, and sons. An ideology of separate spheres may have masked the extent to which the family continued to fulfil important economic functions for the upper class in this era of change. What role did women play in fostering an ideology that served these economic interests?[29] To what extent were the spheres of work and family therefore really separate for the upper class in nineteenth-century America? These are questions that need more detailed study in a broadened inquiry about the interrelationship between the variables of family, economy, and social change.

There are numerous outcomes of accepting the premise that the privatization of the family and separation of spheres were the irrevocable consequences of industrialization. One has been to obscure the ways that women participated in the public world of the political economy through informal channels and associational networks.[30] Another has been to obscure the extent of men's involvement in their family networks as economic actors. In the nineteenth century, the family did become an important sphere of private life and personalistic ties in a world increasingly dominated by a rationalized market and bureaucratic state. But kinship ties may also have provided a bridge between those two spheres, placing the bonds of family loyalty and kin solidarity at the service of collective economic interests.

Expanding the study of the family to include analysis of both men and women in their interconnected public and private lives is another important step in reviving a more macrosociological approach to family studies. At the same time, it may provide a glimpse of the way the family as an institution resides at the intersection of individual experiences and structural consequences. While one goal of my historical sociological inquiry is to revive interest in the family's continued role in the political economy, another is to keep sight of the way in which families were the setting of lived experience, where perceived choices, competing motivations, past successes and failures—rather than purely structural imperatives—helped shape behavior.

The tendency to assume a sharp divergence between the institutions of family and economy under the impact of industrialization has been widespread among economists, historians, and sociologists. The consequences of this assumption have had far-reaching effects in several disciplines. Sociological theory-building and historical study, which, when combined, can be complementary and mutually enriching, have curtailed their common dialogue on questions about family and economy. Economists and business historians have ignored families as viable economic units. A more nuanced understanding of class, power, and the dynamics of social change in American society has been foreclosed by the dominance of one interpretation about the direction of change. In the interest of grounding the broader sociological questions in more concrete historical study, then, it seems appropriate to turn to a specific setting for the investigation of kinship, class, and economic change.

The particular subjects of this study were members of a new economic elite emerging in Boston in the post-Revolutionary era. The setting for this group is more than a backdrop, for Boston was poised on the brink of major social, political, and economic changes by the beginning of the nineteenth century. In this urban setting, a highly defined upper class took shape. It is in the construction of new physical space and through the development of new institutions and networks of social relations that this social class history can be read.

Chapter 2

THE SETTING OF BRAHMIN BOSTON

*Boston is just like other places of its size; only perhaps,
considering its excellent fish-market, paid fire department,
superior monthly publications, and correct habit of spelling
the English language, it has some right to look down upon
the mob of cities.*

—*Oliver Wendell Holmes*

*There is a region, lovelier far than Eden's vales and vistas
are; Serene and sheltered in repose from every stormy wind
that blows; A place than all besides more sweet; At once you
know it, Beacon Street!*

—*"Boston" by A.F.W.*

Visiting Boston for the first time in the 1830s, Harriet Martineau
noted that it was "perhaps as aristocratic, vain, and vulgar a city, as
described by its own 'first people,' as any in the world."[1] What particularly distressed Martineau was the evidence of an aristocracy of wealth
amid a new republic, a group whose cultural pretensions and social
exclusivity she saw as particularly at odds with the democratic ideals of
egalitarianism and inclusive citizenship. Yet the very characteristics of
Boston society that so offended Martineau have long been the identifying cultural markers of the city and its most prominent citizens. Staid
and proper Brahmin Boston, with its austere Puritan past, defines the
popular image of this city.

Despite the claim by one of its most prominent citizens, Oliver
Wendell Holmes, to being "the Hub of the Universe," Boston has generated considerable ambivalence in American cultural and social history. In novels and historical memoirs, Boston and its Brahmin inhab-

itants emerge as the epitome of a staid aristocracy in decline. As New York and Chicago began to represent the cities of new immigrants, urbanism, and dynamic social change in the novels of William Dean Howells and Theodore Dreiser, Boston served as an effective counterpoint. Faced with the encroachment of immigrants and social change, particularly in the second half of the nineteenth century, fictional Brahmins—paralleling many of their real life counterparts—responded with attempts at closure.[2] Yet despite its established reputation for conservatism and staid gentility, Boston was a city of tremendous growth and change in the nineteenth century. Much of that vitality had to do with the shaping of its upper-class settings and institutions.

Like most cities, Boston's pattern of population movement and expansion is one clue to its social history. What is unique, however, is that the particular nature of Boston's physical layout required a series of massive landfill projects to accommodate the city's expansion in the nineteenth century. These projects, often led by members of the Boston elite themselves, reshaped the physical setting of the city and, in the process, sharply demarcated and circumscribed Boston's residential enclaves by class and ethnicity. To no small extent, the social cohesion of the Boston Brahmins as a class was forged by this geographical restructuring between 1790 and 1890.

THE GEOGRAPHY OF BRAHMIN BOSTON

Boston in 1790 had changed relatively little in geography or size of population since colonial days. The physical setting for the town's 18,038 inhabitants was an area of less than one square mile on a peninsula extending into Boston Harbor. Resembling a "tight little island," Boston was surrounded by deep coves to the north, east, and south, by the Charles River to the northwest, and by the Back Bay, an estuary of the Charles, to the southwest. Only a small neck of land connected Boston to the mainland communities of Dorchester, Roxbury, and Brookline to the south. In addition to being surrounded and contained by water, the town of Boston was physically defined by five hills of the peninsula: Copp's Hill in the North End, the area where most of the residents lived before the Revolution, Fort Hill in the southeast (the district known as the Old South End), and three peaks of the Trimountain—Mt. Vernon, Beacon Hill, and

Cotton (or Pemberton) Hill—in the peninsula's center.[3]

Population growth within the city limits of Boston sharply increased during the nineteenth century: from 24,937 (in 1800) to 58,277 (in 1825); 136,881 (in 1850); 362,839 (in 1880); 560,892 (in 1900).[4] A population explosion of this magnitude created the physical need for a more intensive use of urban space. But the fact that much of the increase came from Irish immigration at mid-century and southern and eastern European immigration by the end of the century meant that geographical shifts were shaped by the class politics of inclusion and exclusion. How the elite residential communities of Beacon Hill and the Back Bay came to assume their shape in nineteenth-century Boston is therefore not only of topographical and architectural interest, but a critical piece of Boston's social class history.

A key step in creating a distinctive elite residential enclave in Boston came from the work of Charles Bulfinch, a young architect of wealthy background, who brought a new style of European elegance to Boston building in the late eighteenth century. Bulfinch's imposing public buildings—the Massachusetts State House, the County Court House, commercial banks along State Street, and India Wharf among others—were matched by the residences he designed and built for wealthy Bostonians through the early nineteenth century. Three residential areas, in particular, were characterized as newly fashionable addresses because of Bulfinch's designs: the Tontine Crescent and Franklin Place in the previously undeveloped area of the Old South End, Park Street and Colonnade Row along the northeastern and southeastern boundaries of the Boston Common, and mansions on the first of the Trimountain hills to be developed, Mt. Vernon.[5]

The residential development of Mt. Vernon was the first of the major Boston landfill projects. It was begun in 1795 when the Mt. Vernon Proprietors, a syndicate of wealthy merchants, bought the land of John Singleton Copley and began leveling the peak by sixty feet, using the dirt as fill to create additional property for development along the Charles River. The Bulfinch mansions built for the proprietors themselves were large and stately; subsequent houses were built as connected units to make more efficient use of limited space.

There were two significant consequences of this building project. The first was to set a new standard of architectural grandeur for wealthy Bostonians of the early nineteenth century. In this sense, the social status of Boston's elite families began to keep pace with their economic achievements, as residential areas reflected a new, more sophisticated, taste for European architectural styles.

The second consequence was also a mark of the growing status consciousness of the elite, and it was manifested in their active attempts to draw a more restrictive boundary between their properties to the south and others along the north slope of the hill. The line marked the area where Boston's black population then resided, as well as where a more itinerant group of "drunkards, harlots, spendthrifts, and outcasts" who had contributed to the area's original name of "Mt. Whoredom" were drawn to the local dance halls and bars. This would not be the last time that neighborhood tensions flared over class and status differences among Boston's urban residents. However, it is indicative of the growing hegemony of the elite and their capacity to define new residential boundaries according to their own interests that the Mt. Vernon tensions were resolved when Mayor Josiah Quincy organized a House of Correction specifically to clean up the area in 1823.[6]

The leveling of Mt. Vernon was only the first in a series of land transactions that succeeded in turning the Trimountain into an elite residential area. Beacon Hill was also lowered by some sixty feet in the 1810s and 1820s, with land carted away to fill the Mill Pond along the Charles River. In 1835, the eastern peak, Cotton or Pemberton Hill, was leveled and developed as a newly fashionable area for wealthy Boston families.[7]

By the 1850s Beacon Hill, as the collective Trimountain redevelopment was now called, had been built up and was fully occupied. Forbes and Greene, in a published survey from 1851, reported that all forty-one men in Boston worth between $500,000 and $3 million were living in the vicinity of Beacon Hill, Park Street, Pemberton Square, Colonnade Row, or Franklin Street.[8] The density of this elite enclave— and the closeness of its social ties—is also suggested in a Boston memoir:

> Summer Street was the home of the Sam Gardner family; Lees, Jacksons, and Putnams, all related to each other, congregated about Chauncy Place and Bedford Street; Perkinses in Temple Place; Lawrences and Masons in the part of Tremont Street between West and Boylston, then called Colonnade Row; Eliots in Park and Beacon; Amorys in Franklin Street (then such a pretty place with a little grass park down the middle); the head of the

Sears family lived in the house of the Somerset Club . . . and their married children lived on each side; Curtises and Lorings were in Somerset Street.[9]

The dominance of Beacon Hill and vicinity as the preferred residential area of the Boston elite in the first half of the nineteenth century was therefore determined by a number of structural pull factors: newly created physical space at the center of a growing city; the spread of an architectural style that conferred status on the occupants; the social and cultural benefits of living in close proximity to other members of an increasingly self-conscious elite. At the same time, there were significant push factors that began to draw tighter boundaries around the more circumscribed residential enclave of the elite by mid-century. In particular, the wave of Irish immigration and the subsequent rise of new ethnic enclaves in the North End and Fort Hill region of the Old South End quickly redefined those areas as less desirable addresses for the elite.[10] An encroaching business district also had this effect. In 1857, Bulfinch's once-elegant Tontine Crescent and Franklin Place were demolished for warehouses. The combined effects of population growth, land scarcity, and the impingement of ethnic neighborhoods placed substantial residential pressures on the Boston elite, simultaneously enhancing the prestige of a Beacon Hill address and raising new concerns about preserving the kind of class insularity that had become characteristic of Brahmin experience by the mid-century.

In the 1850s a number of new residential projects were launched in Boston. The new South End was developed in the area where the Boston Neck led into Roxbury, but it never fulfilled its promise of becoming one of the fashionable residential enclaves of the Boston elite. In William Dean Howells's novel, *The Rise of Silas Lapham*, a South End address was the distinct marker of the parvenu, the place where the Laphams had lived "ever since the mistaken movement of society in that direction ceased."[11] By the 1880s and into the early decades of the twentieth century, the South End had become an area of lodging houses of rural migrant and immigrant families.[12] The new residence of choice among the Boston elite was, instead, the Back Bay, new land created by the largest Boston landfill project in the nineteenth century.

In the early nineteenth century, the Back Bay had been seen primarily as an effective source of water power for mills along its southern shore. As a consequence, the Mill Dam was built as a fifty-foot

FIGURE 1A
Back Bay in 1836.

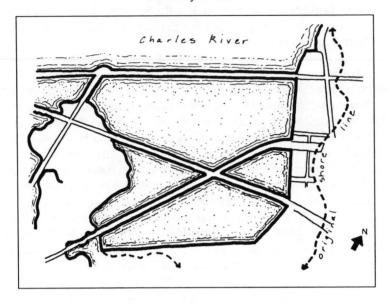

FIGURE 1B
Back Bay in 1861.

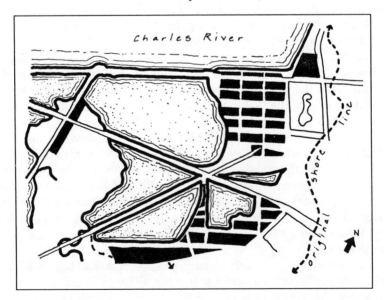

FIGURE 1C
Back Bay in 1871.

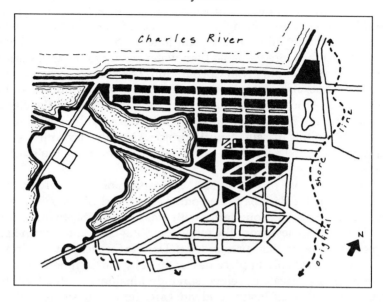

FIGURE 1D
Back Bay in 1888. Fill basically complete.

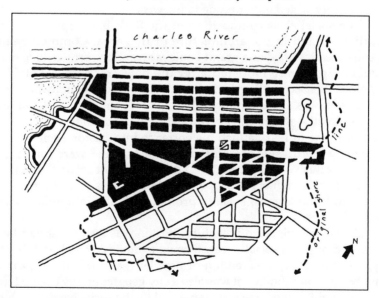

wide, mile-and-a-half long causeway across the Back Bay to regulate the tidal flows, also serving as a toll road connecting Boston with Brookline.[13] But by mid-century, additional land for real estate development was far more valuable than water power to the investors of the Boston and Roxbury Mill Corporation. The unsanitary conditions of the tidal flats also prompted a public demand for the filling in of the Back Bay. In 1856, the Commonwealth of Massachusetts, the city of Boston, and the Boston and Roxbury Mill Corporation were authorized to begin this massive landfill project. Over the next thirty years it added some 450 acres to the original 783 acres of Boston's urban space.[14]

As in the case of Beacon Hill, two aspects of this newly created urban space in the Back Bay stand out: the class exclusivity of its inhabitants and the distinct boundaries with which it was able to maintain a sense of separateness from the ethnic working-class and poor neighborhoods in Boston that surrounded it. Despite the fact that the land of the Back Bay was sold in piecemeal fashion by the Commonwealth at auction and by private developers in individual lots, it was, from the first, defined as an exclusive residential area for elite Bostonians. Some wealthy investors purchased lots in the mud flats before the construction began; many others built and occupied houses as new land was progressively added each decade to the west.

The social class composition of the Back Bay population was clearly reflected in the architecture of this area. Commonwealth Avenue was designed as a grand boulevard, and the brownstone mansions lining it were modeled after the new architectural style of Napoleon III's Second Empire in Paris.[15] The status hierarchy of a Back Bay address was also internally differentiated: both "the water side of Beacon Street"—where the ever-hopeful Silas Lapham was building his new home to help launch his entrance into Boston society—and "the sunny (north) side of Commonwealth Avenue" were considered the most exclusive and prestigious addresses.[16] Not surprisingly then, the names of the owners of property on both streets read as a roster of the wealthiest and most socially prominent Brahmin families of the era.[17]

By the late nineteenth century, Boston was a city that had been geographically and socially transformed from its colonial past. Vastly expanded through the creation of new land and the annexation of neighboring communities, it was also a city geographically divided into distinct neighborhood enclaves separated by the social barriers of both class and ethnicity. Following the urban migration patterns of other American cities in the nineteenth and early twentieth centuries, the North and West Ends of Boston were inhabited by successive waves of new immigrants: first the Irish, followed by Jews, Italians, Poles. Boston's black population lived on the western and northern slopes of Beacon Hill, marking the social barrier between the elite portion of "the Hill" and its bordering racial ethnic neighborhoods. As the immigrant population moved into the reaches of the stable working class and middle class, they escaped the tenements by moving to new suburbs in an expanding radius of Boston, thus leaving the center of the city more sharply divided between rich and poor.[18]

The social homogeneity of the Back Bay was a product of these class and ethnic patterns that shaped Boston in the nineteenth century. Both of the primary historians of Boston's topographical and architectural development allude to the way in which the physical boundaries of the Back Bay helped preserve and enhance its class cohesion:

> Thus confined by the Public Garden on the east, the Charles River on the north, the Muddy River on the west, and railway lines on the south, the Back Bay developed in splendid isolation. While the magnificent breadth of Commonwealth Avenue swept one naturally into the Public Garden and the Common, only Berkeley and Dartmouth Streets and Massachusetts Avenue clumsily bridge the railway barrier to the South End. In consequence, the region bounded by Arlington and Beacon Streets, Massachusetts Avenue and Boylston Streets, developed as a well-defined unit which retained for many decades a reputation for social homogeneity that lived up to the handsome appearance of its buildings.[19]

> Because of its clearly defined and almost unbreachable boundaries, the Back Bay district has been remarkably resistant to the contamination of slum and nondescript commercial activity.[20]

Thus insulated by both natural and built barriers demarcating their enclaves, the Boston elite was remarkably successful in preserving its hold over the neighborhoods of Beacon Hill and the Back Bay until the Depression of the 1930s. In 1894, it was estimated that 45.1% of

Boston's upper-class families lived in the Back Bay; in 1905, 47.8%; in 1914, 42.3%; in 1929, 32.5%; only by 1943 had the numbers dropped more precipitously to 18.8%.[21] Coupled with their country residences in the communities of Brookline, Longwood, and Chestnut Hill to the southwest and summer homes on the North Shore, the urban setting of the Boston Brahmins was a significant factor in shaping their strong internal and external identity. The kinds of cultural institutions that developed in this urban space solidified that identity and ensured that it would be preserved intergenerationally.

DEFINING THE CULTURAL BOUNDARIES OF THE UPPER CLASS

A key sign of the emergence of an upper class is the development of a self-conscious style of life and set of shared values that act as symbolic markers of that class's social and cultural boundaries. Residential density contributed to shaping those characteristics among the Boston elite, but perhaps even more important were the cultural institutions that developed in the nineteenth century to give coherence and cohesion to Boston's emerging upper class. Among the earliest and most important of these cultural institutions was Harvard. Here a pattern of elite organizational control, internal fund-raising strategies, and socialization to a set of well-defined cultural values developed by the 1830s, a model that would be replicated in other significant cultural organizations identified with the Boston upper class in the late nineteenth century. The parallel between the development of Harvard and the development of a Boston upper class is best summarized by a historian of this institution who has argued that "the great families built Harvard, so to speak, while building themselves."[22]

In its administration, faculty, and student body, Harvard was strongly associated with Boston's mercantile and industrial elite by the early nineteenth century. The elite-dominated Corporation—a group of seven men who supervised the finances, personnel, and general institutional activities—had wrested greater control of the governance of the college from the largely nonelite Board of Overseers by the 1830s. The faculty members recruited in the early nineteenth century were most often men of substantial means and graduates of Harvard College themselves. This selection process thus led to a more standardized set of values and outlook among the faculty, even as their numbers increased. Students of this era were also drawn primarily from the families of the Boston elite, and part of Harvard's project was to inculcate in them a more coherent set of values consistent with a consolidating upper class. The undergraduate housing plan drew them together in close proximity, producing a sense of peer identification that was an effective basis for extrafamilial class solidarity.[23]

The most important aspect of Harvard's cultural role in shaping a Boston upper class by mid-century was in its capacity to shape values and promote their persistence across cohorts and generations. Other institutions that developed in the second half of the nineteenth century would help fulfil that class function as well.

The proliferation of cultural institutions in the Back Bay was another testament to the upper-class orientation of that enclave. Along with the new private residences, a number of churches, colleges, and institutes relocated or were newly established in the Back Bay between the 1850s and 1880s. Two of the most significant of the cultural institutions were the Museum of Fine Arts and the Boston Symphony Orchestra, keystones of high culture, which, by the end of the nineteenth century, had become the hallmark of Boston's upper class.

The museum and the symphony were not simply the inevitable products of an expanding urban culture, but organizations specifically planned, directed, staffed, and attended by members of—and those with aspirations to membership among—the upper class.[24] The success of upper-class institutions is ultimately determined by achieving a delicate balance: the ability of the founders to monopolize the status claims to their cultural product, and, at the same time, to establish legitimacy among a broader-based audience. By the 1880s and 1890s, the Museum of Fine Arts and Boston Symphony were highly successful as institutions that served to reinforce the taste culture of Boston's upper class. Like Harvard, they existed for the manifest purpose of promoting the particular cultural products of education, art, and music, but their latent function was in shaping and reproducing the shared tastes and values that gave the upper class its strong sense of identity and solidarity. The active attempt to create high culture was the mark of a defined social class, and by the beginning of the twentieth century Boston's cultural capitalists had fully succeeded in the task of developing a set of class-reinforcing cultural institutions.[25]

In geographical and cultural terms, then, the boundaries of a distinct Boston upper class were clearly drawn by the late nineteenth century. Few observers have disagreed with this picture of a firmly established and well-entrenched social aristocracy. Yet on the question of the political and economic continuity of the Boston upper class, there has been a great deal more debate. The nature of this debate is significant, for it centers on the important issue of whether class and power are fundamentally reshaped in the process of social change.

THE POLITICAL AND ECONOMIC HISTORY OF THE BOSTON BRAHMINS

The erosion of upper-class power in the face of the Irish political ascent is part of the standard lore of Boston's history. This shift more than any other has come to symbolize the fluid nature of American class relations, as new and marginal groups gained the appropriate footholds to climb to positions of power and influence. The political history of the Boston upper class itself must start with such a rise to power, in this case in the new political context of the post-Revolutionary era. Under the political umbrella of the Federalist Party, the Boston mercantile elite dominated state and local politics between 1780 and 1823 in the first phase of elite political consolidation. In granting both the state constitution in 1780 and the city charter in 1821, this group was able to ensure that their own economic interests were politically grounded.[26]

The decline of federalism by the second decade of the nineteenth century was followed by the rise of the Whig Party during the 1830s and 1840s, the new political home of Boston's manufacturing elite who were consolidating economic power in the same era. The great majority of rich Bostonians could be counted among the Whig membership. Between 1834 and 1848 the governorship, state legislature, and majority of U.S. Senate and Congressional seats were consistently filled by Whig politicians.[27]

Through the first four decades of the nineteenth century, wealthy Bostonians achieved a remarkable degree of political hegemony. The policies they supported through the political process at the national, state, and city levels were closely linked to their economic interests.[28] By most political historical accounts, however, this hegemony had unraveled by mid-century. In 1848 the Whig Party split into "Conscience" and "Cotton" factions over the question of the annexation of

Texas and the party's antislavery stance. The breakup of the party in the 1850s marked a dramatic end of an era in Massachusetts politics, with the gradual slide of most Whigs into the Republican Party after the Civil War and the ascendancy of Democratic-ethnic politics in Boston.

While the kind of domination in the political sphere that the Boston elite had achieved by the first half of the nineteenth century was not sustained, there are two qualifications of this historical account that must be included in an assessment of the political decline or continuity of the Boston upper class. In the first case, there continued to be a significant alliance forged between Brahmins in the Democratic Party, the Irish leadership, and an Irish working-class constituency until 1900. Such an alliance mediated the displacement of the upper class from Boston politics and allowed a stronger role in the city's political structure for Brahmin leaders than was the case for other urban upper classes.[29]

As a second measure of the retention of political power, Brahmin Republicans who were excluded from local city politics were able to maintain and solidify control at the state and national levels. In the forty-six years between 1884 and 1930, while the Irish dominated the office of mayor, Brahmin Republicans controlled the statehouse for thirty-seven years, Brahmin Democrats for seven years, with the governorship also remaining in Brahmin control for all but two years.[30]

Many of the political conflicts of the late nineteenth century involved attempts on the part of state politicians to wrest control of key institutions and services from city officials. After many years of debate over the organization of a metropolitan police force, the state legislature in 1885 placed control of the Boston police in the hands of a board appointed by the governor.[31] The tension between local and metropolitan interests was exacerbated with the demographic and residential changes taking place in Boston in the late nineteenth century. But as early as 1863 a committee of the Massachusetts legislature had pinpointed the key class-based concern about the locus of political power: "It is necessary to adopt the metropolitan principle in order to prevent the elements which are destructive of property and laws from keeping practical control of the city."[32]

At least through the early twentieth century, this policy of metropolitan control was successfully pursued. A new charter of 1909 expanded state control over the sphere of local politics, requiring the mayor's appointments to be approved by the state Civil Service Commission and establishing a gubernatorial board to oversee city finances.[33] Although the argument for the political decline of the Boston upper class by mid-century has been based on evidence of a decline in Brahmin leadership positions, it has tended to overlook the more subtle or covert ways that this group managed to wield considerable political clout into the early twentieth century. It is in these strategies of more covert forms of control that class longevity must ultimately be assessed and judged.

The standard historical interpretation of a socially and culturally prominent upper class with an eroding base of political power has also been extended to the economic sphere. Debate has been even more pronounced around the question of economic decline or persistence than around the question of political power. At stake is the question of whether the upper class remained rooted in the structures of power within the political economy of industrial capitalism or became a status group primarily concerned with maintaining its prestige and social honor. Most of the historical accounts of the Boston Brahmins have argued on the side of the economic decline of a social aristocracy.

The primary period of economic ascent for the Boston elite was concurrent with the development of their political power. Among historians who have studied Boston, most agree with Frederic Cople Jaher that between 1790 and 1860 the structural possibilities for gaining economic power were open for enterprising capitalists. During "the golden years" between 1820 and 1860, many Boston families added to the mercantile and manufacturing fortunes they had established with other timely speculative investments. But eventually the demands of family continuity and persistence of wealth turned pioneering entrepreneurs into more conservative family patriarchs.[34]

Once Brahmin entrepreneurs had established their fortunes and family prominence, it is argued, they were forced to turn to conservative financial strategies to consolidate and maintain their position. They established trust funds to restrain spendthrift heirs, but in doing so undermined the possibility of continued innovative economic activities. Their group closure into a social and cultural aristocracy thus coincided with their economic decline. The early economic lead of the Boston upper class was increasingly overshadowed by the rise of new managerial businessmen after 1870.[35]

In comparative studies of the elites of New York and Chicago, the opportunities for economic growth within developing industries in those cities opened wealth, power, and social status to "new men." The economic decline of the Knickerbocker patriciate, New York's upper class, was swifter than that of the Boston Brahmins because of the more rapid pace of economic change there and the relative lack of insularity of the New York elite. The fortunes of New York millionaires were rarely perpetuated over several generations to form the basis of an economic upper class.[36] The Chicago business elite was also more innovative than Boston's and was able to sustain its vitality by recruiting new talent, particularly in the developing meat-packing and railroad industries of the mid-to-late nineteenth century.[37] Historians have argued that the longer persistence of Boston's elite was as an exclusively social aristocracy rather than as a leading economic group. Thus from this perspective it has been claimed that, despite their longevity, Bostonians suffered "irreparable losses of commercial and class position" in contrast with these other regional elites made up of new economic leaders.[38]

In arguments that claim the economic eclipse of the Boston Brahmins, structural opportunities and entrepreneurial motivation have been cited as the key variables of economic vitality. Both are understood to have declined for Boston's upper class by mid-century. The loss of vitality in one group and its replacement by another emergent elite is the theoretical model that undergirds this historical account.[39] Thus, Jaher argues, "inheritance enhances acceptance of traditional practices and blunts desire for material achievement . . . making men less competitive, and it constricts the social mobility necessary for an adequate supply of talent."[40] Elsewhere, he has linked economic success with the entrepreneurial willingness to cut one's roots and break with tradition, an attitude ultimately at odds with the goal of establishing family roots for upper-class continuity.[41]

The growing conservatism of family founders and a constricting of entrepreneurial opportunities with the development of industrial capitalism were thus the conditions that seemed to spell the demise of the Boston Brahmins as an economic upper class by the second half of the nineteenth century. In his memoirs about Boston, Frederic J. Stimpson cited the institution of the trust fund, in particular, as undercutting the economic vitality of Brahmin businessmen:

> Somewhere about 1830, [the Massachusetts courts] decided that a man could tie his children's inheritance up either by deed or will,

so that he could not spend or risk his principal or, indeed, embark in any business. Immense wealth had been accumulated in Boston in the first sixty years of the republic, but instead of trusting their sons and sending them out at their own risks with all their argosies upon life's seas, as they themselves had done, they distrusted their abilities and had them all trusteed. No new enterprise could be undertaken by them for under court decision they had no capital to risk. Perforce they became coupon cutters, not promoters of industry. . . . The result of making Boston's youth mere four-percent men was to choke off their own energies and largely to divorce business and the Brahmins.[42]

Against such a backdrop of economic decline, the social and cultural prominence of the Boston upper class could have only a hollow ring. It should come as no surprise then, least of all to twentieth-century Americans for whom the conditions of mobility are paramount, that William Dean Howells would characterize Boston in 1889 as "no life, but death-in-life" and choose to move to New York.[43]

This depiction of the rise and fall of the Boston Brahmins has widespread currency as a more general model of social class experience in America. While the questions of familial-based business acumen and the structural basis for continued economic success are ones to which I will return in later chapters, it is appropriate here to suggest an alternative interpretation of Boston's social class history. Critical questions about economic upper-class continuity might well arise from the theoretical insight that social status is more likely to be supported by a strong economic foundation than to be severed from its material base.[44] An investigation that seeks to uncover the new and perhaps hidden means by which wealth, economic control, and social status remained interconnected for Boston Brahmin families in the second half of the nineteenth century would start from such a theoretical premise.[45]

A more differentiated and complex bureaucratic system was a fact of nineteenth-century economic life in Boston, as in other American cities. But the impact on the family was not necessarily a simple lessening of its central economic functions. If one looks at the changing relationship between the family and the complex of economic institutions that developed over the nineteenth century, it appears that at least some Boston Brahmin families were not prepared to let the material base of their social and economic position disintegrate. They saw both the dangers and the opportunities inherent in this period of social and economic transformation. They thus set about building economic alliances that would preserve and, if possible, enhance their wealth and social placement.

Chapter 3

KINSHIP NETWORKS AND
ECONOMIC ALLIANCES

There is little dispute about the rise of a new economic elite in Boston in the first half of the nineteenth century. Even among the historians who disagree about the timing of the Brahmins' eventual economic decline, the facts of ascendancy are uncontested. The group of families who had achieved renown as a consolidated upper class by the late nineteenth century were primarily products of post-Revolutionary ascent, rather than descendants of Boston's colonial elite. According to Cleveland Amory, the popular chronicler of the Boston upper class, the prerequisites for inclusion among the Brahmin "old families" were an eighteenth-century mercantile ancestor and a nineteenth-century fortune.[1] Ultimately about forty families were included in this group, the core of whom were the entrepreneurial founders of the New England textile industry.

THE BOSTON ASSOCIATES AND THE TEXTILE INDUSTRY*

In the early nineteenth century, a small group of Boston entrepreneurs began to turn from mercantile trade to the manufacturing of domestic textiles. These key entrepreneurs, known as the Boston Associates, included Francis Cabot Lowell, Patrick Tracy Jackson, Nathan Appleton, and Amos and Abbott Lawrence.[2] As individuals, each of these men had an impressive career in business, and each played an equally important role in shaping the political and cultural life of nineteenth-century Boston. In economic and social terms, they were the true "family founders" whose wealth and position established a place for their descendants in the Brahmin establishment. But it is the nature of their interconnections that is particularly significant, for it was as a group that they directed the economic development of the textile industry in New England.

Brief biographical accounts provide a starting place for the collective history of this group. Two of the Boston Associates shared a similar background as sons of well-established mercantile families from Salem, Massachusetts. Francis Cabot Lowell (1775-1817) and Patrick Tracy Jackson (1780-1847) were brothers-in-law as well as close friends and business associates. Their fathers were both influential men in Newburyport in the second half of the eighteenth century who were linked by ties of friendship and shared interests in business and politics.

The marriage of Francis Cabot Lowell, son of Judge John Lowell and Susanna (Cabot) Lowell, to Hannah Jackson, daughter of Jonathan Jackson and Hannah (Tracy) Jackson, formally linked these two families in the late eighteenth century.[3] But unlike the more formal family partnership marriages of an earlier era, this connection simply solidified an ongoing relationship between two brothers-in-law rather than establishing a family-partnership business relationship. Francis Cabot Lowell and Patrick Tracy Jackson were primarily significant as innovative entrepreneurs of their generation whose own business histories, rather than family backgrounds, established their positions as the inner core group of the Boston Associates.

Francis Cabot Lowell, like the other Boston Associate manufacturers, started his career as a merchant. The extensive property holdings he acquired and commercial ventures he followed are evidence of his early success in that field.[4] In 1810, failing health sent Francis Cabot Lowell and Hannah (Jackson) Lowell abroad with their children, leaving his business in the hands of his agent and brother-in-law, Patrick Tracy Jackson. During this trip, Francis Cabot Lowell made extensive visits with Nathan Appleton to textile factories in Manchester and Birmingham to observe the industrial operations and machinery. In spite of the strict prohibition on the export of patents or machinery from Britain,

Lowell was able to reproduce the designs of the cotton spinning machines and weaving looms on his return to the United States. With the help of a mechanical engineer, Paul Moody, he added important technical alterations that improved the machine, and he organized the first consolidation of the spinning and weaving processes under one roof.[5] By 1813 Francis Cabot Lowell had made a complete transition from merchant to textile manufacturer through his organization of the Boston Manufacturing Co. in Waltham. His personal impact on the development of the textile industry in New England, while great in these first years, was cut short by his death in 1817.

Patrick Tracy (P.T.) Jackson, descendant of a long line of Newburyport merchants, also began his career in mercantile trade. Through the first decade of the nineteenth century, he worked in Boston as a sedentary merchant. When Francis Cabot Lowell returned from Europe with plans to engage in cotton manufacturing, he included Jackson, who was his brother-in-law, as a partner in the development of the company. Like Lowell, Jackson shifted his business concerns from mercantile commerce to manufacturing after 1812. With the incorporation of the Boston Manufacturing Company in Waltham in 1813, Patrick Tracy Jackson took over the active management positions of treasurer and agent until 1827 when he relinquished control to his successor, John Amory Lowell, the nephew and son-in-law of Francis Cabot Lowell.[6]

Between the years 1820 and 1830, Jackson was one of the undisputed leaders of the Boston Associates in his role as organizer and manager of various textile mills. In a biographical letter to the children of P.T. Jackson at the time of their father's death, James Jackson noted the important direction that had been provided by his brother, even when he was not holding an official position as agent of the companies.[7]

Two other Boston Associate entrepreneurs, Nathan Appleton (1779-1861) and Abbott Lawrence (1792-1855), also came to the group with mercantile experience, but from rural New England families.

Nathan Appleton's business history reflects the important patterns of careful financial and managerial policies underlying his success. First as a merchant and later in textile manufacturing, he was known for his astute administrative skills. Appleton's early mercantile ventures were conducted in partnerships with his brothers, Samuel and Eben. When the War of 1812 and the depression of 1819 curtailed his mercantile operations, Appleton turned to new domestic investments. His switch to manufacturing interests occurred as a result of increasing governmental intervention in trade, political changes, the economic incentive of a new market for investment of his surplus capital, and the personal solicitation of friends such as Francis Cabot Lowell and Patrick Tracy Jackson who had received permission to incorporate the Boston Manufacturing Co. in 1813. As one of the original investors along with a small group of closely tied Boston businessmen, Nathan Appleton's role in the formation of the Boston Manufacturing Co., the Merrimack Manufacturing Co., and the Locks and Canals Co. in 1822, and eleven other companies founded between 1825 and 1845, was primarily one of financial and managerial advisor.[8]

The business policies that had been the foundation of Appleton's mercantile trade were brought into use in manufacturing as well: high capitalization, careful accounting techniques, and a considerable authority invested in the board of directors in overseeing and directing company policy. Known as the Waltham system, this administrative structure formalized in its board of directors the highly personal, individualized control that had been exercised by merchants in their partnerships.[9]

In addition to his role as a developer and director of manufacturing concerns in the first three decades of the nineteenth century, Nathan Appleton formed two partnerships, which acted as the sales agents for the Boston Manufacturing Co. and other textile mills in the Merrimack River valley: B.C. Ward and Co. and, later, James W. Paige and Co. His role as an investor in and director of business corporations, banks, and insurance companies contributed substantially to the new institutional framework that was established in Boston between 1820 and 1840.

Abbott Lawrence, with his older brother Amos (1786-1852), was also a merchant in Boston in the early part of the nineteenth century. Unlike the early shift to manufacturing that characterized the business histories of the other Associates, the Lawrence brothers continued their partnership in the A. and A. Lawrence Co., initially as importers and eventually as retailers of domestic cotton and woolen goods.[10] Abbott Lawrence's career as a textile magnate was established later than that of the other Associates, but his inclusion in the group was no less secure.

Chosen by Nathan Appleton and P.T. Jackson to head a new cotton mill (incorporated as the Lawrence Co. in 1831), the Lawrence brothers consolidated the Suffolk and Tremont mills under this new company and, in addition, became the permanent selling agents for its textile products. In 1844-45 Abbott Lawrence, along with his brothers William and Samuel Lawrence and other Boston Associates including Francis Cabot Lowell II, John Amory Lowell, Nathan Appleton, and

P.T. Jackson, became an incorporator of the Essex Co. Abbott Lawrence was the largest subscriber to stock in this company and was named as its first president. The town of Lawrence was incorporated at the site of the Essex Co. in 1847. During this period, Abbott Lawrence also served as president and one of the largest stockholders of the Atlantic Cotton Mills and the Pacific Mills.[11]

In addition to his career as a businessman, Abbott Lawrence was a central figure in the Massachusetts Whig Party during the first half of the nineteenth century. His national political ambitions were largely unfulfilled in the course of a long political career, although he served as the American minister to the Court of St. James between 1849 and 1852. In his role as a cultural benefactor, Abbott Lawrence was a generous philanthropist, establishing the Lawrence Scientific School at Harvard as well as various charities and public buildings in Boston.[12]

All of these men formed an inner core of the Boston Associate group in their capacity as innovative textile entrepreneurs. Their individual successes, however, are overshadowed by the importance of their collective efforts. As a group, they wielded a powerful control over the development of the textile industry in New England.[13] As men of wealth, they relied on their own mercantile fortunes to finance the textile industry in its initial stages.

The growth of the textile industry was concurrent with but not dependent on the development of early commercial banking in Boston. The primary source of investment capital in the domestic textile industry before 1840 was the equity of the original stockholders. Only after 1840 did textile firms begin to get long-term loan capital from new financial intermediary institutions. Over time, retained earnings and external loans became increasingly important sources of capital funds as equity declined in importance.[14] The evidence provided by financial records of nine of the textile firms in New England between 1829 and 1840 shows that merchant-manufacturers made up the largest group of textile stockholders in this period. The promise of high capital returns provided a strong incentive to invest in the domestic economy.[15] But there were collective incentives to turn to textile manufacturing as well, and the tight control over textile stock ownership that the Associates held throughout the nineteenth century must be understood in this context. It was the Boston Associates' growing power as an economic group, rather than as independently successful individuals, that was most striking in the early stages of industrialization.

The kind of internal financing and exclusively held control characteristic of all the Boston Associates' textile enterprises may be seen in the organization of the first factory to integrate the production processes of spinning and weaving under one roof: the Boston Manufacturing Co. (BMC), incorporated in Waltham in 1813.

The organization of the BMC resembled a family partnership in the closeness of its kin interconnections, even though it had the distinctively modern features of an integrated system of production and a systematic administrative organization.[16] As a model of internal financing for subsequent companies, the organizational structure of the BMC established the kind of tight control that was later extended over the whole textile industry in New England. The original shareholders and the directors of the company were closely linked by ties of kinship to one another. Francis Cabot Lowell (15 initial shares) was related to five other subscribers through marriage: to Patrick Tracy Jackson, Charles Jackson, and James Jackson (total shares, 35) through his marriage to their sister, Hannah (Jackson) Lowell. He was also brother-in-law to Benjamin Gorham (3 shares), who married his half-sister Elizabeth Cutts (Lowell) Gorham, and to Warren Dutton (2 shares), who married another half-sister, Susan Cabot (Lowell) Dutton. In addition to the shares held by Nathan Appleton (initially 5), forty shares were held by other economically prominent merchants in Boston.[17] By 1820 there were thirteen additional subscribers to the stock of the Boston Manufacturing Co., but the kinship connections of several of these individuals to the Lowells and Jacksons ensured that the original subscribers retained majority control in the company.[18]

The original subscribers to stock in the BMC were not only important as investors, but as the directors and managers who made the strategic decisions about company policy. The initial board of directors included Francis Cabot Lowell, Patrick Tracy Jackson, and Nathan Appleton among its five members. Jackson was elected to the position of treasurer, the most important managerial position in the company. The treasurer was chief executive and financial manager who, in addition, was in charge of purchasing raw materials and selling the finished product. The treasurer was the nineteenth-century equivalent of the modern corporation president. By contrast, the president of a textile firm was largely an honorary position.[19] It is significant that the two directors who were not members of the Lowell kin network fulfilled this more symbolic role in the company.

It is clear that the inner core group of the Boston Associates maintained tight control over stock ownership and decision-making within the BMC. When P.T. Jackson relinquished his position as treasurer in 1827, it was to John Amory Lowell, nephew and son-in-law of Francis Cabot Lowell. The exclusive selling agents for the BMC, B.C. Ward and Co. and later J.W. Paige and Co., were both owned in partnership with Nathan Appleton. Over the course of the nineteenth century, the BMC continued to be staffed and directed by those related or personally close to the key Boston Associate families of Lowell, Jackson, and Appleton. Economic control in this and in subsequent mills was tightly maintained, as stock continued to be held by the original investors and their families.[20]

As a result of the success of the Boston Manufacturing Co., a new site was located for the expansion of the textile industry. In 1822 the Merrimack Manufacturing Co. was incorporated in East Chelmsford (later renamed Lowell) on the Merrimack River, with a list of subscribers who overlapped considerably with that of the Boston Manufacturing Co.[21] Kirk Boott, mill agent of the BMC and a close associate of the founding group, took over management of the Merrimack Manufacturing Co. in 1823 through an agreement that released the patents of the BMC and effectively merged the stockholder interests of the two companies. In 1825 Appleton and Jackson organized a machine shop to build textile machinery and the Locks and Canals Co. (owned by the stockholders of the Merrimack Manufacturing Co.) to secure land and water rights along the Merrimack River for all future development. Subsequent development of the Hamilton Co. in 1825, the Appleton and Lowell companies in 1828, the Lawrence, Suffolk, and Tremont companies in 1831, the Boott Co. in 1835, and the Massachusetts Co. in 1839 secured the Associates' control over the textile industry through the mid-nineteenth century.[22] All these companies were organized as a coordinated set of interests rather than as competing firms. In their patterns of stock ownership, as in their administrative control, they continued to represent Boston Associate interests and economic hegemony.

The close circle of kinship and personal ties that characterized the textile industry allowed the kind of internal accumulation and mobilization of capital necessary to spur initial economic growth in this industry. As an example of a modern corporate organizational form, but one still making use of the personalistic ties of kinship, the textile industry of the early nineteenth century seemed poised between a preindustrial and an industrialized economic world.

In this context, it is appropriate to ask what kind of economic actors the Boston Associates were. According to one recent study of this group, they were motivated by a very limited set of economic interests in building the textile industry, at the expense of promoting broader and more innovative economic change. Historian Robert Dalzell has claimed that the Boston Associates invented modern corporate organizational forms for traditional purposes. I would argue, by contrast, that they used a traditional structure—the family—for very modern economic ends.[23]

To what extent was kinship an effective means of retaining economic control in an era of early industrialization? This question implies the proactive, rather than the reactive, orientation of the Boston Associates. In order to answer it, I turn first to the broader complex of ancillary organizations they built in Boston in this era: commercial banks, savings banks, insurance and trust companies.[24]

THE INSTITUTIONAL BASIS OF AN ECONOMIC ELITE

Three institutional developments occupied the Boston Associates in the first four decades of the nineteenth century. The development of the textile industry in New England established them as key economic innovators in an industrializing economy. The development of a stable banking system provided the basis for the coordination between finance and industry necessary to support large-scale industrial growth. And the development of an additional set of financial intermediary institutions, which initially appeared to usurp some of the economic functions of the family, ultimately provided an even broader economic and social base for family power and control.

These developments were the coordinated strategies of a new economic elite, those individuals who formed, through their multiple and interlocking institutional positions, a consolidated economic group with shared economic interests and long-term goals. It was as part of this coordinated economic strategy that, between 1816 and 1824, three new financial institutions, representing a broad range of economic functions, were organized and led by the Boston Associates. The Suffolk Bank, the Provident Institution for Savings, and the Massachusetts Hospital Life Insurance Co. were the key institutions that revealed, in organizational structure and policies, the expansive economic strategies of this newly coalesced group.

The Suffolk System

The earliest banks in Boston were organized by and for prominent merchants as extensions of their family partnership enterprises.[25] The development of the textile industry was not initially linked to commercial banking, since the Boston Associates used their own wealth to begin their operations. Nevertheless, they developed an interest in revising banking policy, which would provide an increasing overlap between financial and industrial interests throughout the nineteenth century.

The key development that signaled a shift in the purpose and direction of banking in New England was the creation of the "Suffolk system" with the chartering of the Suffolk Bank in 1818. Among the grantees of the charter and among the largest subscribers to the stock of this new bank were four Boston Associates: Nathan Appleton, Patrick Tracy Jackson, and Amos Lawrence and Abbott Lawrence. John Amory Lowell, nephew and son-in-law of the original Boston Associate, Francis Cabot Lowell, was, in addition, one of the most influential officers and directors of the Suffolk Bank from 1822 until the time of his death in 1881.[26]

The Suffolk system was developed as a clearinghouse service for the proliferating number of country bank notes that were circulating in Boston by the early nineteenth century. Under this system, the new clearinghouse bank agreed to redeem country notes at par if the country bank would keep a permanent deposit of $5,000 in the Suffolk, in addition to a sufficient sum to cover all notes received.[27] The benefits to the Suffolk Bank in increasing its deposits and to the public in providing a more coordinated and stable banking system for the New England region were clear. The immediate advantages to country banks were less so. It is a significant indication of the Suffolk's power that, despite controversy and complaints about this proposed system, most country banks did join, persuaded in part by the threat that notes of all nonparticipating country banks would be gathered and returned for immediate redemption by Suffolk Bank officers. As most banks had a high proportion of circulating notes to reserve at any one time, this constituted a powerful threat to the solvency of small country banks and forced them into participation in the Suffolk system.

In 1824, the Suffolk Bank, looking for increased deposits, agreed with similar conditions to act as a central clearinghouse agent for other Boston banks in handling their out-of-town notes. Formerly rival banks (the Boston, State, Merchants, New England, and Shoe and Leather Dealers banks) joined the Suffolk's clearinghouse system. While saving these individual banks the expense and inconvenience of redeeming their own country bank notes, the Suffolk system also set strict regulatory standards for the extension of credit. Its conservative policies allowed many local and regional banks to withstand the Panic of 1837 and the ensuing depression, a period that many other financial institutions did not survive.[28]

By the mid-1850s the Suffolk Bank was clearing notes for five hundred financially sound banks in New England, at approximately ten times the average circulation of other participating banks. It was recognized as a powerful financial institution in the New England region, with its great success in the first half of the nineteenth century based on its ability to provide relative regional banking stability and much needed financial regulation. Although the Suffolk Bank did not remain at the center of Boston's commercial banking system into the second half of the nineteenth century, it was one of the important models for the national system of financial regulation eventually established by the National Banking Act. Its larger significance is in terms of the expanded institutional basis for economic control its founders envisioned and established in its structure and organization.

The Suffolk system was a significant institutional development in New England in the early nineteenth century because it created a more stable system of controlled banking practices. It allowed for continued economic growth in New England, even as cyclical patterns of economic recession hit the region. Most importantly, it represented an early example of a financial institution whose credit policies and board of directors overlapped with those of the textile industry. The Suffolk system had far-reaching implications for the Boston Associates who organized and directed it. First, it provided a coordinated system of banking in Boston rather than a set of rival independent banks through the first four decades of the nineteenth century. As a coordinated system, banks could more easily meet the high capitalization requirements of turnpike, canal, and railroad expansion and other large-scale economic enterprises.[29] The dependence of the textile industry on an improved transportation network was clearly one of the reasons for the flow of Boston capital into western railroads in the 1850s and 1860s.[30]

The officers and directors of the Suffolk Bank exerted considerable pressure in Boston and New England to establish their coordinated system, not only for the advantages of the extensive deposit fund they generated in this bank, but because they recognized the potential of the commercial bank for capital accumulation and mobilization in an era of early industrial growth. The power of financial institutions and bankers to direct industrial growth would not be generally recognized until the late nineteenth century, when financial capitalism reached its zenith.

But members of Boston's economic elite in the early nineteenth century were in a unique position to see the importance of links between finance and industry. With their overlapping institutional positions on boards of finance and boards of industry, they were able to coordinate the flow of capital when and where it was needed.

Specific information about the loans made by banks is difficult to obtain in this early period, but business records of individual companies have shown substantial loans from even the most conservative commercial banks. The Massachusetts Bank, for example, supplied the Lawrence Manufacturing Co. with $17,000 in gold and $3,000 in silver for the purchase of cotton in 1842.[31] Others have argued in this context that the loan contributions of commercial banks have been seriously underestimated in the development of the textile industry.[32]

The claim for the financial astuteness of the Boston Associates in developing the Suffolk system rests not only on their role in developing this single institution, but on the other financial intermediary institutions that they were also instrumental in creating in the same period. The key institutions of the savings bank and trust company added both to the coordination of capital in nineteenth-century Boston and to the broadening base of social and economic power of the new economic elite.

The Provident Institution for Savings

Not all financial institutions were explicitly organized as sources of investment capital for the dominant group of merchant-manufacturers in early nineteenth-century Boston, although they often had this consequence. Savings banks are an important case in point for they reflect the way in which the social concerns of the Boston elite often masked their economic interests. Savings banks were expressly organized by the economic elite for the benefit of the working class.[33] The Provident Institution for Savings, established in 1816, was the oldest and most influential of these institutions. A policy of not paying dividends on balances over $500 was enacted as a way to encourage small investments by the working class. In 1834, Massachusetts passed a law limiting deposits in one bank to $1,000 per person.[34] Nevertheless, a study of the occupations of mutual bank depositors in New York has suggested that the working-class image of savings bank customers was the policy but not the fact of nineteenth-century banking practices. Of all the customers of the Bank for Savings in New York in 1819, for example, half were drawn from the middle and upper classes, while only one-quarter were unskilled laborers. The greatest proportion of all depositors (37% in 1819) were children of middle- and upper-class families, thus disguising the extent of family holdings in savings banks through individual accounts.[35]

Intended for the use of the working class, savings banks had the manifest function of meeting the community and social responsibilities of the new economic elite. But the economic advantages of capital accumulation through savings bank deposits were quickly recognized, and the unspoken use of the savings bank was in adding to the capital reserves of the economic elite.

Despite the policies restricting their deposits, men of substantial means were apparently drawn to savings banks for the advantages of the ready liquidity and accessibility of their capital funds and the security of the banks' investments. Fears that wealthy depositors, if unrestricted, would use the bank to their advantage by depositing their funds during slack periods and withdrawing them in favor of more profitable investment, thus disrupting the sound investment strategies of the bank, were probably not unfounded.[36] Initially, the investment strategies of savings banks were limited to federal and state bonds, real estate and mortgage loans, and small private loans. But by the mid-nineteenth century, "personal security loans," requiring no collateral but only the signature of the chief officer of the firm and two guarantors, were made by the Provident Institution for Savings to Massachusetts textile mills. It has been estimated that fully one-quarter of the Provident's assets was directed to the textile industry in this period.[37] The relative ease with which the Provident turned to new investments in manufacturing by the middle of the nineteenth century, despite its conservative policies and legal restrictions, suggests the importance of the overlapping ties between the officers and directors of the Provident and the textile industry.

The period 1820-1840 is particularly significant in terms of change in the administrative hierarchy of the Provident Institution for Savings. During this time, a powerful subcommittee, called the board of investment, took over making investment decisions, based on their claim that such decisions had become unwieldy for the full board of trustees. The members of this board of investment were merchants, manufacturers, and lawyers whose firsthand knowledge of business helped guide the new investment strategies of the Provident, at the same time as they moved to consolidate their own power. The fifteen men who served on this committee between 1821 and 1856 were all wealthy, with ties to the growing institutional sphere of other financial intermediaries in Boston.[38] By 1840 this committee relinquished most of its power in making investment decisions to the president and treasurer, the most important officers of the bank. Notably, William Appleton, cousin of Nathan Appleton and a member of the new economic elite, served as president of the Provident between 1848 and 1861. In addition to his role as principal officer in Boston's most influential and prestigious savings bank, he held multiple directorships in this period: in the Suffolk Bank, the Boston and Roxbury Mill Corporation, the Columbian Bank, the Commercial Insurance Co., and the U.S. Bank.

The substantial number of interlocking ties established between 1820 and 1840 among the Provident Institution for Savings, other financial intermediaries, and the textile industry is one indication of the new potential for capital mobilization that emerged in this period. Institutional interlocks began to facilitate the flow of capital funds to industry and to the new transportation sector by mid-century.

The concerns of the elite were not only economic, but social as well. The early industrial experiment of the Lowell mills, based on Francis Cabot Lowell's vision of a model industrial community with a trained labor force of young women from surrounding rural areas, was only the first of many social and cultural projects the Boston economic elite initiated as part of their sense of social responsibility, cultural hegemony, and economic interests in the nineteenth century.[39] The spread of savings banks, charities, and various cultural organizations were all signs of their consolidation as a group and of the expansion of their economic power into other spheres.

The new economic elite coalesced economic, social, and political power quickly in the first half of the nineteenth century by developing an economic institutional framework that promoted their group solidarity. The interlocking of their various institutional positions was a significant aspect of this consolidation in the first decades of the nineteenth century. Yet in the process, it has been argued, they may have undermined the capacity of their own sons to inherit their economic positions. The new institutional structure of Boston's economy ensured the existence of an economic elite, but it equally opened the possibility of replacement and new recruitment in every generation. There are indications, however, that there was an active attempt to lay a foundation for *family-based* economic control and influence through that institutional structure. The next case, of the Massachusetts Hospital Life

Insurance Company, is an example of an organization through which the economic elite began to establish the basis for their upper-class continuity.

The Massachusetts Hospital Life Insurance Company

The Massachusetts Hospital Life Insurance Co. (MHLIC), founded in 1818, was the most important example of a modern trust company that served the dual function of a savings bank for families of the economic elite (with minimum deposits of $500) and a source of investment capital for the continued development of the textile industry. Of all the financial intermediary institutions in Boston between 1820 and 1840, the MHLIC was the prototype of the new form of institution that incorporated and rationalized former functions of the family while it aided the development of new kinds of economic activity. Originally chartered as a life insurance company, which would contribute one-third of its annual profits to the Massachusetts General Hospital, the MHLIC moved into the more specialized field of maintaining family trusts and managing investments under the impetus of Nathaniel Bowditch, the principal actuary from 1823 to 1838. By the third decade of the nineteenth century, the MHLIC had become the largest financial intermediary in New England, and by the beginning of the twentieth it still ranked among the largest five institutions in Boston.[40]

The importance of the MHLIC as a financial intermediary institution may be measured by the investments it made in the first half of the nineteenth century, most of which were concentrated in mortgages, collateral loans to officers and stockholders and their families, and to New England manufacturing companies and railroads. It was also significant as part of the institutional foundation of the new economic elite, since, during the first century of the company's history, one-third of its officers and directors were drawn from only eighteen of Boston's wealthiest and most socially prominent families.[41]

The business of accepting money in trust served the dual function of preserving family resources over time and of adding to the availability of the capital pool for investment. In this sense, the MHLIC created a new institutional basis for the close link between family and business concerns that had been more directly and willfully integrated by the marriage and business patterns of elite families up to the end of the first decade of the nineteenth century.

Through trust funds, Boston businessmen could ensure some economic continuity to their families without having to rely on the entrepreneurial skills of their children. Five types of trust funds were offered by the MHLIC: the "G"-type, made in the name of a specific depositor for five years with interest, and four other trust fund types designed to provide an income on the interest while protecting the principal capital from dissipation. The "endowment in trust" was the only one of these four types that turned interest and principal over to the child who had attained majority. The "deferred annuity in trust," which turned the accumulated interest over to the child upon his or her majority but maintained the principal intact, and the "strict female" and "strict male" types, which paid interest but maintained the principal throughout the individual's lifetime, often with an inalienability clause for a woman leaving this income free from her husband's control, offered longer-term investment capital to businessmen. In 1830, "G"-type trusts of individuals and charitable institutions provided the largest source of funds in the MHLIC, while by 1858 the "strict female/male" types had become the most popular and best endowed.[42] As the first generation of the Boston economic elite aged over the first half of the nineteenth century, they apparently saw the need to make use of the stricter type of trust funds in order to maintain family wealth.

The trust funds established by the Boston economic elite have most often been explained as reflecting the growing conservatism of this group.[43] Indeed, the trust fund seemed to promote the gradual transition to a more leisured and socially based family prominence over two generations. It appears that in creating an institutional form to perpetuate the family's economic position, which simultaneously lessened the necessity for a son to follow a business career or for sons and daughters to contract marriages for business partnerships, the Boston elite undercut its own family-based economic power and control. From this perspective, then, other scholars have argued that the trust fund was a strategy of financial conservatism that led to the long-term decline of this economic group.[44]

While the trust fund did tie up family capital in new ways, there are several important qualifications to this interpretation that must be made. It should be noted that family capital first began to be restricted in a period in which the retained earnings of businesses and loans from financial intermediaries were becoming increasingly more important as the sources of new investment capital.[45] Trust funds did limit access of sons and sons-in-law to family capital, but this occurred in a period in which financial intermediaries were assuming the new role of directing the flow of capital from savings to investments. When the new institution of the trust fund is placed in the larger context of other economic institutions that were simultaneously developed in this period of the early nineteenth century, the conclusion may be drawn that the trust fund was not a shortsighted, conservative economic strategy, which undercut entrepreneurship, as much as it was a part of the farsighted strategy of economic institutionalization promoted by the first generation founders of the Boston economic elite.

Trust funds may have limited the business capital of *individual* families, but the collective accumulation of money held in trust substantially added to the investment capital of the economic elite as a group. The trust company was thus another institutional arrangement that gave the new economic elite a broader financial base for their economic activities. It is not surprising, then, that the Massachusetts Hospital Life Insurance Co., like the other key economic institutions of this period, was staffed and directed by those representatives of Boston's new economic elite who stood to gain most from the accumulation and mobilization of capital in this financial intermediary. The Appletons, Lawrences, Lowells, and Jacksons were central figures in the organization of this company.

The presidents, vice-presidents, and directors of the MHLIC were all men drawn from the ranks of the wealthy and most socially prominent families of Boston.[46] In its first forty years, only four men served as president: William Phillips II (1823-1827), president of the Massachusetts Bank and the Provident Institution for Savings, in addition to his involvement in a variety of philanthropic activities; William Prescott (1828-1842), prominent Boston lawyer (whose granddaughter, Elizabeth Prescott, would later establish a kinship link with one of the core Boston Associate families by marrying one of Abbott Lawrence's sons); Peter C. Brooks (1843-1848), the merchant reputed to be one of the two wealthiest men of this era; and Nathan Appleton (1849-1861).[47]

The chief executive office of the MHLIC was the actuary, and, following the term of Nathaniel Bowditch (1823-1838) who led the formation of the MHLIC as a trust company, two men with substantial ties to the textile industry served in this capacity. Francis Cabot Lowell II served as the third actuary of the MHLIC from 1845 to 1854. As the son of the textile entrepreneur, Francis Cabot Lowell, and cousin of John Amory Lowell, his ties to the textile industry were well-established from an early age. He was a clerk in the Hamilton Co. (Lowell, Mass.) from 1825 to 1829, treasurer of the Merrimack Manufacturing Co. from

1836 to 1838, and incorporator and investor in the Stark Mills and Manchester Mills (Manchester, N.H.) and the Essex Co. (Lawrence, Mass.). In addition he was a director of the Columbian Bank and the New England Mutual Life Insurance Co.[48] Other actuaries throughout the nineteenth century were also men from wealthy families with many important institutional affiliations, but the particularly dense web of interconnections linking the MHLIC and the textile industry in this period of the early nineteenth century lends support to the argument that this institution was an important financial intermediary and a cornerstone of the newly consolidated economic elite.

The organizational structure of the MHLIC, like that of the Provident Institution for Savings, directed power not only to the officers of the company, but to the members of the committee of finance who were advisors on policy and investments in the company. This influential committee, composed of three directors of the MHLIC, included at least one and often two members of the Appleton, Lawrence, and Jackson families at any one time in its history through the mid-nineteenth century.

The preponderance of these key representatives of the emergent economic elite among the officers and directors of this company and on this important committee is particularly significant in light of the financial links between the MHLIC and the textile industry. Beginning with its first significant loan of $20,000 to the Boston Manufacturing Co. in 1826, endorsed by P.T. Jackson and Nathan Appleton with the collateral of only five shares of stock in the Suffolk Bank, the MHLIC became the largest supplier of loans to the New England textile industry and remained so throughout the nineteenth century. According to the Massachusetts census of 1855, the MHLIC was supplying half of the capital invested in the cotton textile industry and an even greater percentage of the capital in the woolen textile industry. Every one of the textile mills or related companies with outstanding loans from the MHLIC in 1855 had a director linking both boards, suggesting that personal connections were channels of economic influence.[49]

The MHLIC never directly purchased textile stock, but through its loan policy by which it made loans to individuals who signed over their textile shares as collateral, the company eventually acquired much of the stock of eleven Massachusetts textile mills whose company records have been studied for the years 1829 through 1859. The MHLIC held a minimum of $80,000 of stock in these textile companies during this 30-year period and, in 1854, it held as much as $390,500.[50]

TABLE 1

Membership of the Committee of Finance in the Period 1823-1855

Year	Committeeman	Committeeman	Committeeman
1823	Amos Lawrence	Ebenezer Francis[a]	P.T. Jackson
1825	Amos Lawrence	E. Francis	Samuel Hubbard[b]
1828	Amos Lawrence	E. Francis	John Bryant[c]
1831	Amos Lawrence	Daniel P. Parker[d]	John Bryant
1838	Abbott Lawrence	Daniel P. Parker	Nathan Appleton
1842	Abbott Lawrence	William Sturgis[e]	Nathan Appleton
1850	Ebenezer Chadwick[f]	William Sturgis	Nathan Appleton

adapted from: White, *History of the MHLIC*, pp. 11, 25, 69, 71

a. Ebenezer Francis: merchant and financier; director of Boston Bank; first president of Suffolk Bank; investor in textile industry; president of Cocheco Manufacturing Co. (N.H.)
b. Samuel Hubbard: attorney; first solicitor of the MHLIC
c. John Bryant: merchant, with firm of Bryant and Sturgis
d. Daniel P. Parker: mercantile partner of Nathan Appleton; founder of Appleton Co. (Lowell); Boston Associate textile investor
e. William Sturgis: merchant in firm of Bryant and Sturgis; investor in Hamilton, Appleton, Lowell, Prescott companies (Lowell); Perkins Mills and Dwight Manufacturing Co. (Chicopee); incorporator of Essex Co. (Lawrence); director of railroads
f. Ebenezer Chadwick: treasurer of the Merrimack Manufacturing Co. from 1839 to 1854; investor in Hamilton and Middlesex companies and the Atlantic Cotton Mills; director of Boston and Lowell Railroad, Merchants Insurance Co., and Suffolk Bank

Trust funds deposited in the Massachusetts Hospital Life Insurance Co. by economically prominent Bostonians, then, had the dual function of conserving family fortunes and adding to the investment capital that drove the continued economic growth of industrialization. That the original Boston Associate core group would create an institution such as the MHLIC, which tied up their own capital during their lifetimes and restricted access to family capital by their sons, suggests not their shortsightedness but the strength and effectiveness of the institutional framework they had forged. The Boston Associates, now more solidly entrenched as an economic elite than as a group of businessmen, recognized in this new institutional structure that they developed and then directed a potential for collective economic success which far surpassed the individual resources available in the old family partnership.

The Massachusetts Hospital Life Insurance Co., like the other financial intermediaries organized and directed by the economic elite, combined the important functions of the accumulation and the mobilization of capital. In itself, this was a crucial economic breakthrough in the development of industrial capitalism.[51] But the MHLIC is also an important example of an economic institution that had far-reaching consequences for its founding members. Through this institution and others created in this period of the early nineteenth century, the economic elite fundamentally transformed the economic role of the family.

The case of the MHLIC, more than any other single institution organized in this period, supports the argument that the Boston Associates promoted economic institutionalization as a way to expand their economic and social-cultural power. Through the organization of this company, the family founders of the Boston economic elite created the basis for family continuity by institutionalizing the preservation of wealth. Boston's older vintage wealth has often been noted as evidence of its financial conservatism, especially as contrasted with the economic dynamism of New York.[52] But preserved wealth is also the basis for an economic upper class, and the development of the family trust fund by the first generation of the economic elite might alternatively be read as their earliest attempt to transform their status as a single-generational elite into that of a multi-generational upper class.

While providing a means for the continuity of fortunes to make this transition from economic elite to economic upper class possible, the institution of the trust fund simultaneously broadened the occupational and marital opportunities of sons and daughters of the Boston Associates. A wider range of occupational choices for sons and sons-in-law, including no occupation at all and the pursuit of a variety of aesthetic and cultural interests, is noticeable among birth cohorts after the original Boston Associate entrepreneur. Marital choices also became more independent of family-business concerns among these families throughout the nineteenth century, a phenomenon that had characterized the marriage patterns of the middle class even earlier. New institutional sources of investment capital meant that the immediate economic considerations in contracting marriages were lessened. In addition, trust funds established for daughters meant that they would be provided for regardless of the business success or family wealth of their husband. The development of the trust fund thus helped sever the family from the traditional economic function of direct occupational inheritance. But in the process, it helped to broaden the economic power of elite families beyond the narrow economic function of succession.

The first generation of the Boston economic elite created an institution in the Massachusetts Hospital Life Insurance Co. that ultimately gave greater occupational and marital choice to their sons and daughters. This institutional development signaled not the irrevocable loss of the family's economic functions, but a new, carefully circumscribed framework in which occupations could be pursued and marriages contracted without the explicit intervention of the family. Sons moved into the professions of law and medicine or pursued cultural interests in addition to business, areas that expanded the sphere of influence of a narrow economic elite.[53] Sons and daughters, given greater individual choice of marriage partners, nevertheless continued to marry into recognized families of Boston's social and economic elite. Through much of the nineteenth century these marriage patterns continued to be remarkably regionally endogamous as well as class endogamous. One of the important consequences of the new institutional framework of the Boston economic elite was that it gave a broader latitude to the occupational and marital choices of sons and daughters, which had previously been constrained by family obligations, yet it safely circumscribed these choices within an institutional structure that provided for the continuity of the family's economic and social position over time.

The organization of the Massachusetts Hospital Life Insurance Co., like the other central institutions discussed here, was part of the broad institutional strategy of a newly consolidated economic elite in Boston. Their efforts were clearly directed toward expanding their economic and social power. The processes of differentiation and rationalization, which have long been recognized as the consequences of economic development, need to be investigated and reassessed in light of their active promotion of new institutional development and in recognition of the important family and personal interconnections that lay hidden in such an economic strategy.

Ultimately, of course, it was not only the development of the new institutional structure that defined the power of the emergent economic elite, but their continued economic control over the set of discrete institutions they helped to create. It is on this issue that the case for the family's loss of economic functions under the process of industrialization finally turns. The personal bonds of loyalty and trust that operated the family business could not be expected to withstand the development of highly rationalized organizations with their more impersonal forms of social ties.

In building a case for the coordinated control of an economic elite, theorists have pointed to the significance of interlocking directorates, where a single individual sits on several boards of directors, thus serving as the personal conduit through which information can flow among companies and through which policies can be coordinated. However, in early nineteenth-century Boston, another model of active and highly personalized economic coordination may be posited, one with an increased potential for power by the new economic elite. Coordination through the kinship network offered the potential of a highly dense set of interconnecting ties, which much less visibly, yet very significantly, overlay the newly developed institutional structure. The use of the kinship network as a new unit of class analysis allows an alternative investigation of the family's economic role in a period of economic change. Investigation of the kin networks of the Boston Associate leaders in the period between 1820 and 1840, when the original members were actively building the new institutional framework of an economic elite, reveals more economic influence centered in the family unit than the study of individual histories or discrete institutions alone would suggest.

KIN NETWORKS OF THE APPLETONS, LAWRENCES, AND LOWELLS: 1820-1840*

In the period of early economic development in Boston, between 1820 and 1840, members of the elite held multiple directorships in the new financial intermediaries and textile firms. These interlocking directorates were important channels through which the investment capital for continued economic growth could flow. Interlocking directorates, however, were only one type of channel of influence and economic control.

A much more dense web of significant interconnections between the new institutions of finance and industry was created by the multiple institutional affiliations of members of the same family unit. Since the significant kinship relationships of members of the economic elite extended well beyond the immediate nuclear family to secondary and even tertiary relationships, the kin network is an important structure through which to assess the extent of interlocking between economic institutions. The personalistic ties of kinship laced together the discrete, rationalized economic organizations that had developed in the early nineteenth century, allowing the family to retain a measure of economic control under conditions of major social structural transformation. A reconstruction of these kinship networks of the Boston Associates, then, provides a clue to the way the family's economic interests were met in this new era.

Brothers and Cousins: Horizontal Extension of the Kinship Network

Two of the core Boston Associates, Nathan Appleton and Abbott Lawrence, were embedded in larger kin networks of brothers and collateral kin.[54] Nathan Appleton had established mercantile partnerships with his brothers, Samuel (1766-1853) and Eben (1784-1862), and he maintained close business ties with his first cousin, William Appleton (1786-1862), throughout his career. Amos and Abbott Lawrence also had brothers: Luther (1778-1839), William (1783-1848), and Samuel (1801-1880), with extended business and political affiliations of their own. In addition, the Lawrence kin network of the 1820 to 1840 period included Amos Adams Lawrence (1814-1886), son of Amos Lawrence. In both of these cases, the original Boston Associate entrepreneur was embedded in extensive family networks primarily within the same generation. With the growth of the textile industry and new set of ancillary institutions in the period between 1820 and 1840, the economic significance of the family lay less in the traditional organization of the family firm and increasingly in its capacity to coordinate the multiple, diverse institutional affiliations of its individual members.

Nathan Appleton's importance as a powerful individual businessman is indicated by the extent of his interlocking directorships. Between 1813 and 1861 he was a director of nineteen textile companies and president of nine. His ties to financial intermediary institutions included his important role in organizing and leading the Provident Institution for Savings and the Massachusetts Hospital Life Insurance Co. In addition, he was a director of the Boston Bank throughout the period from 1820 to 1840 and a director of the American Insurance Co. between 1825 and 1836.[55] While Nathan Appleton held a considerable amount of power and influence through his own multiple directorships, the scope of his economic power was even greater when measured through the additional business and financial ties of his close kin.

Banks and other financial affiliations were especially extensive in the Appleton kin network. Brother Samuel Appleton was director of the Bank of the U.S. between 1820 and 1831, the Columbian Bank between 1836 and 1840, and the American Insurance Co. continuously from 1820 to 1840. Brother Eben Appleton was a director in the Columbian Bank between 1822 and 1829, and the Columbian Insurance Co. between 1823 and 1829, in addition to being a prominent stockholder in the State Bank. Cousin William Appleton held directorships in the Suffolk Bank from 1820 to 1821, the Columbian Bank between 1822 and 1838, the Bank of the U.S. between 1823 and 1826, the Boston Marine Insurance Co. between 1828 and 1840, and the National Insurance Co. between 1832 and 1840.[56]

Nathan Appleton's important roles as trustee (1818-35) and vice-president (1832-34) of the Provident Institution for Savings, and as director (1823-34) and president (1849-61) of the Massachusetts Hospital Life Insurance Co., were only part of the Appleton kin network involvement in those institutions.[57] William Appleton served as a trustee (1837-45; 1848-61) and vice-president (1840-44) of the Provident and as the president of the Massachusetts General Hospital between 1844 and 1851. The Massachusetts Hospital Life Insurance Co. had Appletons on its board of directors and in executive positions continuously. In addition to Nathan Appleton's extensive influence in the company, Samuel Appleton served as vice-president between 1825 and 1847, and William Appleton as vice-president between 1845 and 1862.

Strong evidence for the influence wielded by the kin network over significant financial decisions and policies is in the record of loans made by the MHLIC to individual borrowers. In the period before 1840, William Appleton was the company's most frequent borrower, receiving a total of thirty loans. The second most frequent borrower with twenty-two loans was David Sears, a frequent business partner of William Appleton. Other loans made to institutions, such as the $200,000 granted to the Dover Manufacturing Co. of New Hampshire in 1827 and 1828, disguised the extent of investment capital loaned to William Appleton who ran this company.[58] Although William Appleton was a well-known Bostonian and a successful businessman in his own right, the influence of and close connection to his cousins as officers and directors of the MHLIC undoubtedly played a significant role in allowing him to secure these substantial loans with only minimal collateral.

The multiple directorships of individual Appletons were well established by the fourth decade of the nineteenth century. But even more complex were the overlapping institutional affiliations of several members of the same family. Through these channels of the kin network, lubricated as they were by the bonds of family loyalty, investment funds and influence over economic decisions could readily flow.

The case of the Lawrence family in the period between 1820 and 1840 bears a striking similarity to that of the Appletons in terms of the overlapping and interconnected positions of the original Boston Associates and their siblings. Both Amos and Abbott Lawrence, as key Boston Associates, had extensive institutional ties as directors of Boston banks and insurance companies. Abbott Lawrence was a director of the New England Bank between 1820 and 1825, and of the Bank of the U.S. between 1821 and 1840. Amos Lawrence was a director of the Massachusetts Bank in 1821, the Columbian Bank between 1822 and 1833, the Suffolk Bank in 1840; a director of the Manufacturers Insurance Co. in 1823, the Commercial Insurance Co. between 1823 and 1826, and a trustee and vice-president of the Provident Institution for Savings between 1825 and 1838. The consecutive terms of Amos and Abbott Lawrence as directors in the MHLIC extended over the first half of the nineteenth century from 1823 to 1855.[59] Three other Lawrence brothers, as merchants, politicians, and businessmen in New England, also developed extensive ties to the textile industry, commercial banks, and insurance companies in this era.[60]

Amos Adams Lawrence (1814-1886), who was to follow the path of his father and uncles as a successful textile manufacturer, director, and investor over the course of the nineteenth century, began his career as a director in the Suffolk Bank in the period 1820 to 1840. Over the next several decades, he served as a director and trustee of the Provident Institution for Savings and the Massachusetts Hospital Life Insurance Co., director of the American Insurance Co., and first president of the New England Trust Co. In addition he held and managed family property and trusts, including his own substantial property investments in the upper midwest.[61]

In both the Appleton and Lawrence cases, institutional affiliations were considerably broader within the kin network than those held by any individual alone. The channels through which personal influence might have operated for the purposes of securing a loan or influencing company policy decisions were multiplied in the kin network by the diverse institutional affiliations of different family members. The potential for economic influence of the individual Boston Associates was therefore even greater than their own multiple positions would suggest. The family provided the structural basis for the coordination of these multiple ties. In an era when the personal influence of any wealthy and socially connected individual was already considerable, the potential for economic influence and control by a consolidated group was even greater. The kinship network offered a basis for coordinating economic control under conditions of major social and economic change.

The case for the economic importance of the larger kin network is supported not only in the way the family laced together institutions, but in the way wealth accumulated the basis for family economic power. Nathan Appleton's investments made him a wealthy man, but the impact of this wealth was felt by a number of other members of his family who were also the beneficiaries of his shrewd business investments. At the time of his death in 1861, for example, Nathan Appleton held about $800,000 of stock in twenty-four textile companies.[62] In addition to his own holdings, however, Appleton family wealth would also include the stock he had distributed to his children during his lifetime.

There were fourteen Appletons listed as stockholders in the Hamilton Manufacturing Co. in 1836. During the decade of the 1850s, Nathan Appleton bought bank stock as a safe investment, including stock in the new Tremont Bank for his daughter, Fanny, in 1852 and stock in the Merchants Bank for his son, Thomas Gold Appleton, in 1857. His children, Mary (Appleton) Mackintosh, Fanny (Appleton) Longfellow, and Thomas Gold Appleton, were frequently listed as stockholders in the Boston Manufacturing Co., and Appleton stock in several companies was transferred to son-in-law Henry W. Longfellow as part of Fanny Appleton's dowry at the time of her marriage.[63]

Buying and transferring stock in the names of his children, even as they reached adulthood and married, suggests one strategy Nathan Appleton pursued to ensure the economic position of his children. Few second-generation Appletons held the kind of institutional affiliations that had characterized Nathan Appleton's own career, but their economic position was secured nonetheless. Throughout the nineteenth century, the Boston Associates continued to hold tight control over ownership of the textile stock. The shares they bought for their children never caused the threat of a loss of this control. The willingness of the Boston Associates to transfer their stock holdings to their children suggests that the kin network was held together by a corporate family control over its individual members.

Another important clue to the way individuals were bound

together in a corporate family enterprise can be seen in the disposition of Boston Associate wills. The will of Abbott Lawrence is particularly revealing as evidence of the wide extent of his kin relationships and familial obligations. Trust funds for his wife, Katharine (Bigelow) Lawrence and two daughters, Anna (Lawrence) Rotch and Katharine (Lawrence) Lowell, were established in the MHLIC. In addition, each of his daughters was to receive $150,000, while his wife was to receive an immediate settlement of $25,000, the mansion house, household goods, and the profits on his property investments. His sons, one son-in-law, Benjamin Rotch, and a friend, Charles H. Parker, received $75,000 each; his sons also received an additional $125,000 for themselves or their heirs.[64]

Beyond the members of his immediate family and their spouses, Abbott Lawrence also named siblings, nieces, nephews, sisters-in-law, and brothers-in-law as beneficiaries in his will. This will also reflects subtle differences in his extended family relationships and perceived obligations. To his married sisters he left $10,000 each, while to his only surviving brother, Samuel, he left "no pecuniary bequest—such is not rendered necessary by his circumstances." Nevertheless, he provided $3,000 for trust funds in the MHLIC for each of Samuel's children, but only $240 to each of the children of his brothers, William and Amos, since presumably they were already well provided for.[65] This carefully drawn will reflects the closeness of kin relationships that tied one highly successful Boston businessman to his family network both before and after his death in 1855. It may also reflect Abbott Lawrence's foresight in providing for those descendants in the kin network who had neither married within the wealthiest families of the Boston elite nor had established business careers of their own through which to maintain their economic position.

The multiple institutional affiliations among the siblings and collateral kin of Nathan Appleton and Abbott Lawrence gave them broad access to the reins of economic power consolidated within the new, differentiated economic framework of Boston in the early nineteenth century. The combined family wealth in the kinship network was also the basis for more extensive economic power and control. The collective wealth of Nathan, Samuel, and William Appleton was estimated in 1846 to be $3 million; that of Amos, Abbott, and William Lawrence was estimated at $5 million.[66] The family provided a basis for collective economic power that was far more extensive than the power of any single individual, however successful he may have been. It also provided the basis for some continuity of economic power beyond the life span of the original Boston Associate entrepreneur, as the case of the Lowell family best demonstrates.

Sons, Nephews, and In-Laws: Vertical Extension of the Kin Network

Although Boston Associate entrepreneur Francis Cabot Lowell died in 1817 as industrial growth was just beginning to take off in New England, other members of the Lowell kin network were economically important in the period between 1820 and 1840. Unlike the cases of the Appletons and Lawrences, the economically significant kin network of the Lowells was not primarily composed of relatives of the same generation, but of sons, nephews, and sons-in-law born in the late eighteenth and early nineteenth centuries.[67]

Neither of F.C. Lowell's half-brothers, John Lowell (1769-1840) nor Charles Lowell (1782-1861), followed his lead into business, although each headed a line of Lowell descendants who achieved economic or social and cultural prominence of their own. John Lowell was a lawyer and well-known Federalist, called "The Rebel" after a pen name he used in writing political tracts, who took an active role in the organization of the Massachusetts Bank, the Provident Institution for Savings, and the MHLIC. Charles Lowell was a minister with no active affiliation with the economic institutions of Boston. The Lowell brothers-in-law of this generation were also relatively underrepresented in institutional connections between 1820 and 1840, outside the shares they held in the Boston Manufacturing Co. Only brother-in-law Warren Dutton was affiliated with any of the financial intermediaries, as a director of the Columbian Bank between 1822 and 1824, and the Boston Marine Insurance Co. between 1822 and 1825.[68] Nevertheless, the Lowells became firmly grounded in the economic elite in early nineteenth-century Boston through the institutional affiliations of the sons and nephews of Francis Cabot Lowell and his brothers.

The most important and influential businessman among the Lowells was John Amory Lowell (1798-1881), son of John Lowell and nephew, as well as son-in-law, of Francis Cabot Lowell. John Amory Lowell graduated from Harvard in 1815 and entered the firm of Kirk Boott and Sons, Importers. Kirk Boott, Sr., who had been one of the original subscribers in the Boston Manufacturing Co., died in 1817 shortly after Francis Cabot Lowell. One son, Kirk Boott, Jr., retired from his father's business to become an agent of the BMC and Merrimack Manufacturing Co. Another son, John Wright Boott, established a partnership with John Amory Lowell between 1822 and 1824. In 1822, John Amory Lowell also became a director in the Suffolk Bank in Boston. He remained in this position for the next fifty-nine years until his death in 1881. In this capacity he exerted the greatest influence over the organization of the Suffolk banking system of any individual of this era.[69]

Throughout the first half of the nineteenth century, John Amory Lowell played a major role in developing the textile industry that had been initiated by his uncle. As one of the chief owners of the stock of the Boston Manufacturing Co. in 1820, along with his cousins, John Amory Lowell, Jr., and Francis C. Lowell II, John Amory Lowell was also part of the closely related group who organized the Merrimack Manufacturing Co. in the town of Lowell in 1821. He served as a director in the Boston Manufacturing Co. between 1827 and 1877. In addition he was the treasurer between 1827 and 1844, and the president at various times throughout this period (1844-49, 1852-54, 1865-66, 1868-71, and 1874-77).[70] His directorships in many other mills and companies—for example, in the Boott Mill (director, treasurer, and president), in the Massachusetts Mill (director and treasurer), in the Essex Co. and Pacific Mill (director and large shareholder), in the Locks and Canals Co., and in the Boston and Lowell Railroad—made him one of the most influential textile manufacturers of this period.[71]

In addition to his important positions in the textile industry, John Amory Lowell held several directorships in the financial intermediary institutions that firmly grounded him in the Boston economic elite. He was a trustee of the Provident Institution for Savings between 1824 and 1850, and 1856 and 1876; a member of its board of investment between 1835 and 1850 and in 1857; vice-president between 1857 and 1863; and president between 1864 and 1876.[72] Following his father's lead, he was a director in the MHLIC between 1834 and 1878, and in addition was a director in the Massachusetts Mutual Fire Insurance Co. between 1829 and 1837 and the National Insurance Co. between 1832 and 1840.[73] His central position in Boston's economic elite was complemented by his involvement in prominent social and cultural organizations associated with the elite. He was the first trustee of the Lowell Institute, trustee and president of the Boston Athenaeum, educational benefactor, and a "dominating member" of the Harvard Corporation for over forty years.[74]

John Amory Lowell was not the only member of his generation of

Lowells to establish a top place in the economic and social hierarchy. His cousins, John Lowell, Jr.(1799-1836), Francis Cabot Lowell II (1803-1874), and Edward Jackson Lowell (1807-1830), sons of the original entrepreneur Francis Cabot Lowell, also established important institutional affiliations in the 1820-1840 period. John Lowell, Jr., and Edward Jackson Lowell died as young men, but even by the age of thirty-seven John Lowell, Jr., had served as a director of the New England Bank (1826-1829) and had acquired a sizeable fortune in the textile industry, which he designated for the founding of the Lowell Institute after his death.

Francis Cabot Lowell II, although less noted as an economic leader and innovative entrepreneur than his cousin, John Amory Lowell, nonetheless established important institutional connections during his career. He was a director of the Columbian Bank from 1830 to 1831; director of the Merchants Insurance Co. between 1830 and 1835; trustee of the Provident between 1841 and 1842, 1862 to 1864, and its president between 1862 and 1864; and director of the MHLIC between 1846 and 1873, as well as the actuary of that company between 1845 and 1854.[75]

In the third line of Lowell descendants, another cousin, Charles Russell Lowell (1807-1870), son of Charles Lowell and Harriet Traill (Spence) Lowell, solidified the already strong ties between the Lowell and Jackson families by marrying Anna Cabot Jackson, daughter of Patrick Tracy Jackson, in 1832. A merchant whose business failed in the Panic of 1837, Charles Russell Lowell devoted the remainder of his career to cataloguing the books of the Boston Athenaeum, while his wife opened and conducted a successful school for girls in Boston.[76] Other children of Charles and Harriet (Spence) Lowell, most notably Mary Traill Spence (Lowell) Putnam, a novelist and linguist, Robert Traill Spence Lowell (1816-1891), ordained deacon and later professor of Latin, and James Russell Lowell (1819-1891), poet, essayist, editor, and scholar, expanded the traditional Lowell professions of law and commerce to the arts and education.[77]

The limitations of looking only at the male Lowell genealogy for placement in the economic elite are clearest when the descendants of another half-sibling of Francis Cabot Lowell are included in the Lowell kin network. Rebecca Russell Lowell (1779-1853), sister of Charles Lowell and half-sister of John Lowell and Francis Cabot Lowell, married Samuel P. Gardner (1767-1843). Gardner children and in-laws were therefore the cousins of John Amory Lowell, Francis Cabot Lowell II, and Charles Russell Lowell.[78]

Mary L. Gardner doubly ensured her inclusion in the Lowell kin network by marrying her cousin, Francis Cabot Lowell II. Her sister, Elizabeth Pickering Gardner, married John C. Gray, who had multiple institutional affiliations as a director of the MHLIC between 1823 and 1832, and vice-president between 1851 and 1862; trustee of the Provident between 1827 and 1853, vice-president between 1841 and 1852, and member of the board of investment between 1831 and 1841; director of the Massachusetts Mutual Fire Insurance Co. between 1830 and 1833; and director of the National Insurance Co. from 1832 to 1833. Another sister, Sarah Russell Gardner, married Horace Gray, a director in the Bank of the U.S. between 1823 and 1835, and the American Insurance Co. between 1822 and 1834. Their brother, John L. Gardner, was a director of the Massachusetts Bank between 1828 and 1840, the Shawmut Bank between 1838 and 1840, the Boston Marine Insurance Co. between 1826 and 1838, trustee of the Provident between 1837 and 1849, and later the president of the MHLIC between 1879 and 1884.[79] All the Gardner and Gardner in-law ties considerably broadened the scope of the institutional affiliations of the Lowell kin network in the period from 1820 to 1840.

The kin networks of the Appletons, Lawrences, and Lowells, whether constructed horizontally to include brothers and collateral kin or vertically to include sons, nephews, and in-law descendants, show considerable spread throughout the new economic institutional structure of Boston in the first half of the nineteenth century. The extended family, or kinship network, thus had a new role but a continued economic function in a period of economic institutionalization and rationalization. Through the multiple institutional ties of its members, the kinship network laced together the separate economic organizations of early nineteenth-century Boston. Differentiation produced separate organizational structures within industry and finance, but shared class interests, coordinated through the family, helped to mitigate the impact of this differentiation process. The development of an institutionally defined economic elite in Boston was thus well-established by mid-century.

Reconstruction of the kin networks of the Boston Associates in this early industrial period helps re-create the social and familial context of elite economic activity. Although the very process of institutional growth initially appeared to undermine the economic functions of the family, kinship ties in fact played an important coordinating function by lacing together these new and distinct economic organizations.

The structural pattern of elite family networks, which linked the new industrial and financial organizations of Boston and New England, suggests but does not reveal the kinds of economic decisions, influence, or capital that flowed through these channels. Direct evidence of the flow of power through kinship networks in this era is as limited or as inaccessible as evidence of power and economic control flowing through interlocking directorates has proved to be in more contemporary studies. The existence of structural channels between organizations allows only a speculative rather than a definitive interpretation of the uses to which those channels were put. Nevertheless, the active role of the first generation of the economic elite in organizing and directing the new economic organizations in the first four decades of the nineteenth century would strongly suggest that they took advantage of those personal ties of kinship to maintain control over this expanding institutional sphere.

Important as the kin network may have been in this particular period of early industrialization, there is other evidence that indicates its importance over the long run. The Boston Associates, Nathan Appleton, Francis Cabot Lowell, and Amos and Abbott Lawrence, established their places in the economic elite of the early nineteenth century with the solid support of a strong kin network. In each case, the kin network provided a broader economic base than any one individual, however well-connected, could have achieved alone. The counter case of another Boston Associate, Patrick Tracy Jackson, whose economic success was independently achieved without broader-based family support but was also relatively short-lived, suggests that the lack of a strong kinship network in this initial period may have had serious consequences for family continuity in the economic elite over time. The case of the Jacksons therefore points to one significant yet hidden contribution that strong kinship networks may have made to the shaping of a Boston upper class.

THE KINSHIP NETWORK AND ECONOMIC CONTINUITY: THE COUNTER CASE OF THE JACKSONS*

As one of the original Boston Associates, Patrick Tracy Jackson (1780-1847) shared many characteristics with the Lowell, Appleton, and Lawrence entrepreneurs. As with the Lowells, the Jackson family had been long established in the mercantile circles of Essex County, Massachusetts, during the eighteenth century.[80] With his brother-in-law, Francis Cabot Lowell, P.T. Jackson made the transition from merchant to manufacturer with the founding of the Boston Manufacturing Co., thus establishing himself in a family with a long tradition of business success. As with Appleton and the Lawrences, P.T. Jackson had the basis for a close kin network with his two brothers, Charles Jackson (1775-1855), a friend and classmate of F.C. Lowell at Harvard, and James Jackson (1777-1867).[81]

Yet despite these similarities of background and family structure, Patrick Tracy Jackson forged his career as an individual without establishing a solid kin network of business and financial support. While his success as a Boston Associate was equal to that of Lowell, Appleton, and the Lawrences, he did not establish the same basis of family continuity as the others did. Thus his case history presents an interesting counter example to that of the other Boston Associates. The singular difference seems to have been the lack of a Jackson kin network with extensive institutional affiliations that would have rooted not only the original entrepreneur but his family in the ranks of the economic elite. Instead, P.T. Jackson was a leading member of the economic elite of his generation, but the Jacksons and their kin were greatly underrepresented in economic positions in Boston after 1840. The Jackson history thus makes a case for the importance of establishing a solid kin network in the 1820 to 1840 period of early institutional growth.

The career and family patterns of P.T. Jackson and his brothers reveal some crucial differences with other Boston Associate families. Of the three brothers, P.T. Jackson was the sole businessman; his brothers Charles and James established themselves prominently in the fields of law and medicine, respectively. Between 1803 and 1813, Charles Jackson practiced law in Boston, and from 1813 to 1823 he was a justice of the Supreme Judicial Court of Massachusetts. James Jackson practiced family medicine in Boston throughout his career from 1800 to 1866. In addition, he helped establish the Harvard Medical School in 1810, where he was a professor from 1812 to 1836 and professor emeritus from 1836 to 1867, and the Massachusetts General Hospital, where he was a visiting physician from 1821 to 1837 and a consulting physician until his death in 1867.[82]

All three Jackson brothers thus established prominent places in the professions in Boston in the first half of the nineteenth century. It is particularly surprising, then, that there were so few Jackson affiliations with the boards of Boston's financial and industrial institutions in this period. Patrick Tracy Jackson served as a director of the Suffolk Bank from 1820 to 1821, the Columbian Bank between 1823 and 1840, and the MHLIC between 1823 and 1847. But during the period from 1820 to 1840 there were no listed directorships held by either Charles or James Jackson.

Jackson marriage patterns, even more strongly than business or career patterns, show some crucial differences between this family and others of the Boston Associates. Charles Jackson married, first, Amelia Lee, and one year after her death in 1808, he married her cousin Frances (Fanny) Cabot (1780-1868), daughter of John Cabot. Brother James Jackson married, first, Elizabeth Cabot (1776-1817), the daughter of Andrew and Lydia (Dodge) Cabot and niece of George Cabot, the Essex County Federalist. One year after her death, James Jackson married her sister, Sally Cabot (1779-1861). Another sister, Lydia Cabot (1787-1869), married Patrick Tracy Jackson several years later.[83]

The significance of the Jackson marriages within such a tight network of Lees and Cabots is that they replicated a traditional pattern of multiple sibling exchange marriages, which had been economically important for capital accumulation and business recruitment in the seventeenth and eighteenth centuries.[84] By the early nineteenth century, however, such a close pattern of intermarriage may have had another, unintended effect: the restriction of multiple connections within the growing circle of the economic elite and the subsequent curtailment of diverse and extensive institutional affiliations created by a wide kin network.

Patrick Tracy Jackson and his brothers forged a strong connection with the Cabot family through their marriages, a pattern that would be repeated by their descendants through the nineteenth century. Nevertheless, it appears to have been significant for the family's economic continuity over the long run that the Jackson brothers neither built on P.T. Jackson's position in the economic elite themselves nor expanded their ties to a wider segment of the economic elite through marriage. Unlike the Appleton and the Lawrence networks of strong sibling and collateral kin support, the position of the Jackson clan in the Boston economic elite thus rested on the economic connections of the original Boston Associate only.

The lack of a strong kin network with established ties to new institutions of finance and industry was evident among the second generation as well. Charles Jackson had one son and three sons-in-law, Charles Jackson, Jr. (1815-1871), Charles Cushing Paine (1808-1874), John Torrey

Morse, and Dr. Oliver Wendell Holmes (1808-1894); none of these men, despite the achievement of great distinction within their professions, had institutional affiliations with the new financial intermediaries in the period between 1820 and 1840. One son of James Jackson, Francis Jackson (b. 1815), was a director of the Washington Bank between 1832 and 1839. Two other sons-in-law, Charles Storer Storrow and George R. Minot, held directorships in the MHLIC in the second half of the nineteenth century, yet had no other affiliations in Boston financial institutions in this period.[85]

Patrick Tracy Jackson, Jr. (1818-1891), son of the Boston Associate, served as a director of the Provident between 1848 and 1857. However, neither of P.T. Jackson's sons-in-law, Charles Russell Lowell nor William Russell, were officers or directors in those institutional positions that would have identified them as members of the new economic elite in this period. Thus, although members of the Jackson kin network were represented in the MHLIC and the Provident Institution for Savings along with other families of the Boston Associates, Jackson channels to the developing economic institutional structure in Boston were severely limited in contrast to those of other Boston Associate kin networks. One effect of this limited access to positions in the economic elite may have been the inability of the Jackson family to build on the fortune of the Boston Associate entrepreneur for long-term continuity in the economic upper class.

Over the course of his career, P.T. Jackson's investments and positions brought him wealth that matched the fortunes of other Boston Associates. During the period 1813-1835, for example, Patrick Tracy Jackson invested in ten manufacturing companies: the Boston Manufacturing, Merrimack Manufacturing, Hamilton, Dover, Cocheco, Lowell, Suffolk, Lawrence, Appleton, and Concord companies. During this period he also held stock in other miscellaneous companies: 200 shares in the Susquehanna Canal, 50 shares in the MHLIC, in addition to smaller amounts in lesser-known companies.[86] Between the years 1831 and 1835 he also bought substantial stock in railroads: 75 shares in the Providence Railroad, 100 shares in the Worcester Railroad, 199 shares in the Boston and Lowell Railroad, and an unspecified number of shares in the Quincy Granite Railroad.

Besides linking him to the other major investors in manufacturing enterprises in this period, Jackson's investments had produced a considerable return by 1835. Starting with approximately $13,000 in 1810, P.T. Jackson had acquired nearly $400,000 by 1835. The subsequent financial difficulties associated with his Pemberton Hill real estate investment in 1836 cost him $60,000, and he also suffered heavy losses in investment in coal lands in Lycoming County, Pennsylvania (estimated to be between $120,000-130,000), thus reducing his wealth to approximately $60,000-80,000 by 1840.[87] After 1836, no doubt because of his financial losses, Jackson took on several new managerial jobs: first as president of the Concord Railroad Corporation, between 1838 and 1845 as an agent of the Merrimack Locks and Canals Co., and in 1840 as an agent of the Great Falls Manufacturing Co.[88] His financial condition improved again after 1840, and just before his death in 1847 he was listed as having a fortune of $100,000. The combined wealth of Patrick Tracy Jackson, Charles Jackson, and James Jackson was listed as $350,000, thus substantially below that of the Appleton, Lawrence, and Lowell kin networks, estimated to be in the range of several million dollars each.[89]

Although a full financial accounting of the family's wealth is difficult to reconstruct from available historical records, substantial evidence of the economic decline, rather than the economic continuity, of the Jacksons may be found in the Suffolk County probate records covering forty-two years over the second half of the nineteenth century. P.T. Jackson's will, at the time of his death in 1847, designated that his full estate be turned over to his wife, Lydia Jackson, for her use and for her disposition to their children, "in such a manner and such proportions as she shall think best." Unlike the wills of other Boston Associate members that indicated a substantial kin network in their intricate dispositions, P.T. Jackson's will was a model of simplicity, designating only nuclear family members as beneficiaries and mentioning only his wife by name, except to include his son, P.T. Jackson II, along with his wife, as executor of the will. The "first executors' account" of Patrick Tracy Jackson's estate was recorded in the probate records as $177,445.23.[90]

Twenty-two years later, at the time of Lydia Jackson's death in 1869, the Jackson estate was appraised at $82,072.65. This will also listed only members of the immediate family as beneficiaries, but with considerably more restrictions than had been specified in her husband's will. While all the children were to receive equal shares of her estate, the four surviving daughters, three of whom were married, received their shares in trusts overseen by both brothers, "the income thereof for [their] separate use during [their] life." One unmarried daughter received her share herself, but with the stipulation that, if she were to marry, the share would also be placed in trust. P.T. Jackson II, the eldest son who was again named as one of the executors of the will, also received a special stricture. His share of the estate was similarly to be placed in trust (under the direction of a younger brother) during his lifetime, but to be used for "the maintenance and support of his wife and children," with the stipulation that "if . . . said son Patrick T. shall at any time in writing represent to the trustees for the time being that he is in solvent circumstances and free from the embarrassments under which he now labors . . . the trust fund may be conveyed and trans-ferred to him."[91] The specificity of this note in the will of Lydia Jackson, and the parental censure it imparted to an eldest, adult son, was per-haps not unjustified. By the time the will of Patrick Tracy Jackson II was filed in probate court, only twelve years later in 1881, the total inventory of his estate was worth only $3,126.36.[92]

While these estate appraisals may underestimate total family wealth, the pattern reflected in the probate records would suggest that the substantial fortune established by the original Boston Associate by the mid-nineteenth century was not maintained through the next gen-eration. In a list of American millionaires in 1892, there were no Jackson descendants identified, another indication of the decline in family for-tune.[93] When coupled with the lack of a wider network of institutional affiliations that could have kept the Jacksons in the economic elite over several generations, the lack of a family fortune significantly lessened the potential of the Jackson influence in Boston's economic upper class.

As the Jackson case suggests, family continuity in the economic elite required more than the position and fortune of the original Boston Associate entrepreneur alone. This case suggests that family continuity may have required a wider circle of kin with multiple institutional affil-iations, or additional input into the original entrepreneurial fortune by other family members, or both. While the cases of the other Boston Associates show that there were a variety of ways a kin network could be structured and could function, it was this common pattern among the Lowells, Appletons, and Lawrences, but lacking in the case of Patrick Tracy Jackson, that appears to have had an impact on family continuity.

The kin network that provided individual members of the eco-nomic elite with the structural basis for becoming an economic upper class was established during the period of early industrialization in Boston. The Jackson lack of a strong kin network of economic alliances in this period between 1820 and 1840, then, was a crucial difference from other Boston Associate families. Although the Jacksons and their descendants continued to have professional and social prominence in Boston society through the second half of the nineteenth century, they were not central members of an economic upper class.[94]

A case for the economic importance of the kin network as the lacing together of institutional affiliations through family ties or as the basis for the accumulation of family wealth is suggested by this family history. In the process of organizing and directing a new economic institutional structure in Boston, the Boston Associates had to develop a new economic organization for the family as well. While all the Boston Associates established individual places in the economic elite, those who had the support of a broader kin network were better able to transform that elite membership into economic upper-class continuity for the family.

Chapter 4

KIN-KEEPING AND MARRIAGE TIES: THE DOMESTIC SIDE OF KINSHIP NETWORKS

In the early nineteenth century, Boston Brahmin men made innovative use of the traditional economic form of the family. Surpassing the capacity of the family business, the kinship network provided a new way to mobilize capital and broaden institutional affiliations in the rapidly changing economic context of early industrialization. Yet kinship networks were never purely instrumental means to the economic ends of capital mobilization and coordinated economic control. To see them only in this light is to overlook their significance as *family* systems, with all the densely personal kinds of attachments, loyalties, obligations, and reciprocities through which family interaction is normally carried out. Brahmin families were not simply bound by genealogical connections with instrumental functions, but by interactions that carried social meaning and emotional resonance as well as economic consequences.

Family "work" involved both the building and the sustenance of kinship networks. In a particularly apt metaphor, Pierre Bourdieu has argued that functioning kinship networks, like functioning roads and paths, require maintenance and care if they are to remain viable:

> The network of relationships between contemporaneous relatives is a system of relationships that may or may not be used and represents only one part of the entire network. The kinship relations that are actually and presently known, recognized, practiced and, as the saying goes, "kept up," are to the genealogical construct what the network of roads that are presently built, traveled, kept up and therefore easy to use . . . is to the geometric space of a map furnishing an imaginary representation of all the theoretically possible paths and itineraries. To carry this metaphor even further, all genealogical relationships would soon disappear, just as abandoned paths disappear, if they were not constantly kept up, even if they were used only intermittently.[1]

In addition to an analysis of their structure, then, kinship networks must be analyzed in terms of the process through which they were built and sustained. It is in this process that women's activities appear to be particularly central, for it was through the social and personal interactions of daily life, not simply the economic transactions, that the paths of the kinship network were kept up.

The question of where women and men were positioned in the social spaces newly created by industrial capitalism has been posed most starkly in terms of the doctrine of separate spheres. For the middle class in this era of early industrial capitalism, the notion of a distinct separation between the public world of work and politics and the private world of the family served the ideological function of explaining and legitimizing a gender dichotomy between male and female roles. Even among the middle class, however, for whom the values of privacy and domesticity were primary, behavioral reality did not fit the prescriptive contours of completely separate spheres. Middle-class women could be found in many facets of public life, their reform activities and social activism stretching nineteenth-century ideas about female caretaking and nurturing capacities well beyond the domestic sphere.[2] More recently, scholarly attention has also been directed to reconstructing middle-class men's participation in the private sphere by studying their emotional ties to family and friends. The gendered nature of public and private spheres operated as an ideology, but in fact men and women of the middle class could be found in both social spaces.

The public and private lives of men and women of the upper class have been far less central in this debate. While men of the Boston elite were actively engaged in economic institution-building, Brahmin women rarely appear in the kinds of economic documents that so clearly recorded the accumulation of wealth and position of their fathers, husbands, and sons, except as occasional individual stockholders. Their experience has thus been portrayed as exclusively domestic and private; it was economic only to the extent that they were the leisured status appendages of their wealthy husbands—or, in the words of the late nineteenth-century social critic Thorstein Veblen, the objects of conspicuous consumption.

Yet this characterization of the lives of privileged Brahmin women is certainly incomplete. As in the case of their middle-class counterparts, many nineteenth-century elite women could be found in the public world of political reform, cultural institution-building, and charitable volunteer work. A Boston directory published in 1886 listed 177 charitable and benevolent societies in the city, more per capita than in either New York or Philadelphia, and many of them drew on the volunteerism of women. The influential New England Women's Club, founded in 1868 by Julia Ward Howe, included many women of Boston's upper class among its officers and members.[3] Although a detailed analysis of the charitable and political activities of the women of the Boston elite has yet to be done, historical and contemporary studies from other cities suggest that both club membership and participation on the boards of the major cultural, educational, and charitable institutions were significant ways in which elite women entered the public arena while helping to preserve their family's class power.[4]

But these elite women in public life were not the only ones for whom the division of social spheres into public and private has misrepresented experience. Even those women whose lives were primarily defined by domesticity and family relations deserve new consideration for their hidden contributions to the economic continuity of their families. For, unlike the relative domestic insularity of middle-class women in nuclear families, upper-class women experienced domesticity in the context of extended family systems and a milieu that emphasized intense sociability. It was primarily through women's social activities within and across elite families that the paths of the kinship network were smoothed and kept open.

While marriage and family caretaking defined the contours of women's domestic lives in nineteenth-century Boston, the round of activities that made up elite women's daily experiences is also worth scrutinizing in light of how kin networks functioned. Certainly, from the comparative perspective of women's experience along the continuum of social class, elite women were remarkably leisured and privileged. Released from the economic burden of finding paid work for subsistence, which characterized the lives of poor and working-class women, released even from the full-time tasks of childcare and household maintenance, which defined the domesticity of the middle class in the nineteenth century, upper-class women had both the resources and the leisure time to shape their social activities according to their own class-based norms. It is the collective outcome of these individual social activities—in particular, the continual traversing of the network paths that linked the families of the upper class—that suggests a larger economic significance to women's domestic lives.

Diaries and engagement calendars from all decades of the nineteenth century reveal remarkable consistency in the round of social activities that made up elite women's daily lives. Both before and after their marriages, social visiting patterns—within the extended family and among other families of the Boston-based upper class—constituted their primary activity. It is often the most mundane journal entries that are the most telling about the intensity of women's familial and class-based sociability. Mary L. Gardner Lowell (1802-1874), wife of F.C. Lowell II, kept a "line-a-day journal" in which she typically recorded her daily calls, her visitors, dinner engagements, and the weather for twenty of the years between 1825 and 1849. "George called in morning. Mr. L. went to theatre. . . . Day rather dull, sun overcast," she noted in a typical day's summary.[5] The extraordinary events in the life of this elite woman included parties, rather than political involvements, as recorded in the following entry:

> *January 1, 1845:* At home all day preparing for a party in the evening which went off very pleasantly. One hundred three people here, although the strictest attention was paid to keeping the numbers down in invitations. Mrs. G. Peabody and five children here. Ellen and Augustus danced the polka. On my feet from morning to night. Aunt Sally and her girl here.
>
> *January 2, 1845:* Very tired. Called in the morning to see Aunt Harriet, Mrs. Bigelow, and Eliza Brooks. Dined at Gorham Brooks's

5 o'clock with Mr. and Mrs. Peabody, John and Katy and [?]
Peabody. We stopped afterwards as Aunt Dutton's for an
hour. . . .[6]

The extensive sociability of Mrs. Lowell's life was reflected even more
broadly in another notebook—her "Invitation List" of 1840—which
reads like an early version of the *Social Register* with some 350-400
names of individuals drawn from the families of the Boston elite.

Over half a century later, from 1901 to 1919, Mary Gardner Lowell's daughter, Georgina Lowell (1836-1922), also recorded her social
round of visiting patterns in seventeen small daily journals. The remarkable consistency in the daily activities of mother and daughter over
nearly a century speaks not only to the continuity in the Lowell family's
economic position, which afforded such leisure to women, but to the
central ways in which their lives were shaped by an ethic of sociability.

Yet another diary entry by a young Brahmin woman from the
1870s provides a more detailed account of the dense flow of social interaction that characterized the lives of the Boston elite:

The house seems like a hotel, people coming and going all the
time. M. Fosdick came last Monday, Helen Loring went, C. Lover-
ing, F.C. [fiancé] and F. Dexter called. Wed. I went to Medford. Fri.
night Aunt Hetty, Nora and Lottie Gordon spent the night. I
returned Saturday. Sunday Mr. Norton dined here. Roger and
Edith called. Today H. [sister] returns from Swampscott, and Julia
L. [sister-in-law] comes from Rye for the night and expects to meet
Wm. [brother] here tomorrow from Mt. Desert. Amory, Frank L.,
Lucius and Mamie S. happened out to dinner; Jenny and F. came
in the morning.[8]

With friends as well as family part of this continuous social whirl, the
ties of social interaction clearly extended across kinship networks as
well as within them. And while men as well as women engaged in the
activity of visiting, it was an accepted part of women's role to sustain
this round of social interaction.

The "separate sphere" that many women of the Boston upper class
occupied in the nineteenth century was a world dominated by the social
relations of family and friends, but it was not privatized and cut off
from the economic world of men. Although their direct involvement in
formal political and economic institutions may have been limited,

women were centrally involved in the task of maintaining the kinship network as an ongoing social entity. Visiting and corresponding with relatives and friends were female activities allowed by the conditions of economic privilege that defined the families of Boston's upper class. But these activities had consequences beyond the simple expenditure of leisure time. Women's central role in their families was one of "kin-keeping," of keeping up the most meaningful social connections in the kinship network. They did this as part of their expected roles of domesticity, out of a sense of family loyalty rather than through shrewd economic calculation.

In many ways, women's lives do appear remarkably separate from those of their fathers, husbands, and brothers. Nevertheless, their interests in maintaining family ties for personal and sentimental reasons paralleled the kinds of economic interests that male members had in sustaining their kinship networks. Keeping the extended family together by reinforcing bonds of attachment and loyalty was a central task of women's "work" in this social class. The outcome was a functioning, "kept up" kinship network with multiple uses and meanings—one of which was providing its members with the close personal ties that could be turned to the significant task of building and maintaining economic alliances. The female ritual of sociability, which characterized the most traditional domestic routine of elite women, was one of the significant yet less visible means by which the family networks of the nineteenth-century Boston Brahmins were built up and sustained.

If maintaining the paths of the kinship network in a particular era is central to an understanding of the process through which kinship networks operated, so was the means by which they were extended over time. That was one of the consequences of marriage, an individual act by which collective family continuity was promoted. Over the course of the nineteenth century, successful kinship networks were built on the connections produced through marriage. Intermarriage has always been one of the key means through which families created alliances,[9] but it also served as a means of promoting longer-term economic continuity in the upper class. Parents could provide trust funds for their children's economic security, but marriage within the ranks of the upper class was a way doubly to ensure class continuity over several generations.

How did Boston Brahmin families ensure their class continuity through the marriages of their sons and daughters? To what extent was the system of courtship and marriage regulated and constrained by the dictates of social class? These questions take on a special significance in the nineteenth century, an era in which the norms of the middle class were redefining family life as privatized, individualistic, and domestic. As marriage became more and more subject to the individualistic norms of romantic love and family privacy, the extended and corporate family structure on which the elite rested faced a new challenge. In an era of individualism, how could continuity in the elite be preserved?

One answer to this puzzle may be seen in the set of institutional controls over the marriage market that Brahmin families collectively organized and used over the course of the nineteenth century. From the middle of the century onward, a set of ancillary institutions—men's social clubs, country clubs, educational and cultural institutions, and social activities such as debutante balls—reinforced residential concentration as the means of enhancing Brahmin social position and defining an upper-class marriage market. From the mid-nineteenth century on, the very insularity of the Brahmin social circles made it unnecessary for parents to intervene directly in order to ensure that their children's marriages would be both socially and economically endogamous, "appropriate" to the task of maintaining long-term class continuity. Instead, the circumscribed nature of family and friendship circles, social activities, and residence made the process of meeting eligible spouses and contracting engagements a more "natural" event and hence a more personal decision in the lives of young women and men of the Boston upper class.

At no time since the late eighteenth century was there evidence of substantial parental involvement in the marriages of the Boston elite. Yet as chapter five will demonstrate, there was considerable evidence of patterned marriages over the course of the nineteenth century, which transformed the elite into an economically-based social upper class. How marriages were contracted is every bit as crucial to our understanding of class formation and consolidation as the structural analysis of their outcomes. Nevertheless, the process by which decisions of such a personal nature were made by individuals in the context of families, peer groups, and socially bounded yet permeable communities is highly elusive. It is, at best, possible to capture some sense of how the sons and daughters, grandchildren, and great-grandchildren of the early economic elite in Boston contracted the marriages that laid the foundation of an established upper class through an investigation of individual case histories.

Four such cases, based on the correspondence and diaries of young Brahmin women, chart the process of change in courtship and marriages in nineteenth-century Boston. While these cases reveal some striking similarities in the lives of these young women, they also highlight significant historical changes in the norms and institutions that defined family life over the nineteenth century. Greater individualism in marital choice and more emphasis on the nature of romantic love as a basis for marriage became more pronounced among members of this class by mid-century. Those shifts signaled not the general decline in Brahmin family control over young adults, however, but new and more subtle ways in which individual choice could be shaped by the institutions of social class, rather than by direct family pressure or parental intervention.

Diary accounts also illuminate the *meaning* that marriage had for young upper-class women in nineteenth-century Boston. While marriage was a key social event that created the nodes of the larger kin network, it was also, fundamentally, an intensely personal life decision. Of all the kinds of life decisions people make, marriage lies most directly at the intersection of individual choice and normative social control. An examination of four young Brahmin women's often conflicted experiences of becoming engaged and getting married in the 1830s, the 1850s, the 1870s, and at the turn of the twentieth century offers a glimpse into the meanings of marriage and the way they forged a renewed sense of family commitment among successive cohorts of nineteenth-century Bostonians. These case studies may thus begin to suggest some of the complex ways individual choices and family interests frequently overlapped within the institution of marriage.

THE COMPETING LOYALTIES OF FAMILY AND MARRIAGE: ELLEN SEARS D'HAUTEVILLE

In the 1830s, a particularly full correspondence between Anna Sears Amory and her mother, Miriam Mason Sears, opens a window onto some of the boundaries of the courtship and marriage norms of the Boston elite. The following discussion is based on a detailed set of Boston Brahmin family letters from the 1830s and 1840s concerning the misalliance of a younger daughter in the Sears family.[10]

Anna Powell Grant Sears (1813-1895) was the oldest daughter of

David and Miriam Mason Sears, prominent and wealthy Bostonians of the early nineteenth century. In a memoir written at the time of his death, David Sears (1787-1871) was noted as having received "an inheritance which, at the time, was considered the largest fortune by descent ever received in Boston." Over the course of the nineteenth century, Sears's property investments increased this fortune, allowing him to support a large family and a social life that included many years spent in Paris as well as Boston.[11]

In 1834, at the age of twenty-one, Anna Sears Amory began a correspondence with her mother who was preparing to leave for Europe. Over the next four years, many of the letters in this collection concerned Anna's sister, Ellen, whose engagement and marriage to a Swiss aristocrat, Paul David Gonzalve Grand d'Hauteville, precipitated a crisis in the family over her impending separation from the family of origin. These letters, sent between Mrs. Sears and Anna Sears Amory, reflect great concern about this marriage. The worry was not that this was an inappropriate match in terms of social class, but that it would sever Ellen from her family of origin by the geographical and cultural distance between Boston and Switzerland. Mrs. Sears spoke of the "disagreeable hurry of preparation for Ellen's wedding."[12] It is also clear from this correspondence that she had tried to prevent the engagement, without success. The final decision about the engagement was left to Ellen, although Mrs. Sears was convinced that her daughter had made the wrong choice, as she expressed in this letter to her oldest daughter:

> I feel very low spirited. I can hardly say I ever felt so much so before, but if Ellen is happy, for the trial that I must inevitably endure for the remaining part of my life, I shall not repine, or put myself in competition. You know I am a Predestinarian and believe that Heaven arranges all things for us, and I never was more thoroughly convinced of the truth of it than I am now. Had it been at a time when her health was less feeble, I should still have persisted in the refusal she *twice* gave him, but I feared the effect upon her, and left it to herself to decide. She, poor thing, always believing it was a sacrifice she never could and never would make, persisted in seeing him, against my advice, and then seeing what he had suffered, and softened by his earnest entreaties, in a moment of agony abandoned herself to her Fate. Thus it is. For himself, he is one of the most interesting characters I ever knew, and I am much attached to him on every account, but

that is not sufficient for me. I can never believe E. [Ellen] will be happy without myself and her family, neither could she ever be reconciled to giving him up. I am however in my own mind *decided* the latter would in the end be the most for her happiness, tho' she might never meet with an attachment like his, or his equal in many other respects. *For fortune* he has nothing extraordinary, that is not *tied down* to the death of both his Parents. . . . I have just written to Dr. Warren to England, and faithfully promised Gonzalve I would write him today how Ellen was, after he left, as I was obliged to take him myself down to the Malle Post, or I would never have succeeded in getting him off and he has written me 5 notes since, so you see how things go.[13]

By September, Mrs. Sears had written to Anna with even greater apprehension, not so much about Gonzalve d'Hauteville himself ("you may put your heart entirely at rest with regard to Gonzalve, he is a very serious, excellent person and with him I am entirely satisfied. . . . I am entirely satisfied that he has for Ellen the most doting affection"),[14] as about the effect on Ellen of the inevitable separation from her family that marriage to a foreigner would involve.

In a particularly telling response to Anna's concerns about her sister's marriage, Miriam Sears revealed not only her apprehensions, but the extent of her direct intervention in the engagement process:

I entirely agree with you in all your apprehensions and have thought from the first, the sacrifice of quitting country and friends much too great to be undertaken by a person like Ellen. . . . All I can say is, *I never thought*, or had the least idea, of its (the engagement) taking place, and the moment I had, I broke it off twice, and tried hard to the last day, *all I could* to prevent it. . . . I do not mean to speak lightly when I assure you, for myself I shall never be happy or anything like it again, if I could possibly think she would, it would lighten it, but I know her too well, never for an instant has she wavered in the strong feeling for myself and her Father and brothers and sisters, and it is vain to expect it; it is a *perfect sacrifice*.[15]

Ellen's account of her own engagement and marriage in a letter to her sister, Anna, was also steeped in terms of fate, sacrifice, mistakes, and the bitter consequences of her separation from her family of origin in Boston:

I would give worlds to look upon you once more, and I sometimes think I would fain rest my weary eyes for the sacrifice is
more than I can support. Circumstances led me on, one by one,
until I found myself bound; I try to comfort myself in thinking it
was God's work, and not in my power or any one's else to avert
my fate. I submit myself to his guidance and endeavor not to mur-
mur, but it is, at times, a hard task. A great want of character was
my only fault, and I have bitterly paid for it, but I could not see
things in their true light, nor foreseen consequences; but it goes to
my soul, sometimes, to think that I might have done differently
and saved both him and me, for when he knows the truth, he will
feel it, I know, *most* deeply. I discovered my mistake too late; Gonzalve, I am *very* certain knew *nothing* of the circumstances, but
was deceived by his injudicious friends, for he is too honorable,
too high minded, too religious and too much devoted to me to
have considered *for an instant* his own feelings of distress, in competition with mine, he would have sacrificed his life, pride and
every thing before risking my happiness. He is very kind and ami-
able, and if he were in America, away from his friends, I should be
happy and contented, but I cannot look back, my dear Anna, on
my own bright life there, it was happiness to live and to breathe,
and I was gay and light hearted as the day was long. I recall my
walks with you and Harriet, and how fond you both were of me,
but oh with such an aching heart, excuse me, dearest Anna, for I
am but adding to your trouble without alleviating mine, but he
assured me that other ties and other feelings would never take
the place of my own brothers and sisters, and where ever my lot is
cast, and what ever my destiny, my attachment for them rests true
and devoted, and I can never cease to regret my happy home,
where we all have been brought up together, but we shall meet
again, dearest Anna, and I try to console myself with that idea. I
entreat you to write to me very often, and that will be a great comfort and sometimes look at my picture and do think of me as you
have always done. I know you will miss me, but you will be *at
home.* . . . Do not let any one see my letter, I am almost resolved to
tear it up, for why should I trouble you? Time I hope will make me
better.[16]

Ellen's marriage continued to be the subject of many of the letters exchanged between Anna and her mother. Even after David Sears

and the younger Sears children returned to Boston, it was to her mother, Miriam Mason Sears, who had stayed in France with Ellen, that Anna turned for information:

> For the first few days after Father's arrival, he was much occupied with paying and receiving visits, but one afternoon I took courage and invited him to walk with me, that if possible, I might gain some new view of the subject now occupying my thoughts so entirely. He gave me the general outline which I had previously gathered from your letters, but as it is a topic painful for both of us to allude to, it is hence forward, on my side at least, forbidden ground. It cannot be undone, and there is nothing to be said. . . . There are some points in Ellen's story which I would give worlds to ascertain from you. They are questions which I cannot write, which of Father I have no right to ask, and which perhaps only she can answer. I must wait till I have three or four long hours with you, for you, if you choose to answer what perhaps only my love for her will sanction my asking, are the best judge.[17]

This letter, like others written by Anna Sears Amory, reveals the special tie between mother and daughter that neither generational nor geographical distance could efface. That they should continue to have such a strong attachment to each other at a time when their respective nuclear family responsibilities were expanding seems to have fit the social expectations of mother-daughter relationships for women of their class and era. It was the portent of Ellen's married life, by contrast, that was the distressing anomaly: a marriage that would involve geographical and emotional separation from her family of origin and the severing of social connections to family and friends in the closely knit circle of the Boston upper class. This marriage therefore stands as an example of a misalliance that was approved within the dictates of social class, but which nevertheless stretched the paths of the kinship network far beyond normative expectations. It suggests that not only status, but proximity—particularly among female kin—was an important consideration for an appropriate marriage in this period.

The Sears family concern over losing Ellen to a life in Europe was deepened in the course of the next year by a greater concern about the very nature of her marriage and the subsequent decline in her physical and mental health. The letters that reveal this story most fully after her marriage in August 1837 were not those of her mother and sister, but those of her father, David Sears. They reflect this father's intense emotional involvement in his daughter's life and his continued caretaking role over her property interests into her adult years.

Early letters from David Sears to Gonzalve d'Hauteville and to his London bankers concern the details of Ellen's marriage settlement: a total of 100,000 francs, with an additional 5,000 francs per year (for twelve years) provided to the couple to support a six-month residence in Paris.[18] In a separate explanatory letter to Ellen, attached to her copy of the marriage contract, David Sears stated that she also brought an additional 360,000 francs to the marriage, the income of her trust fund and stockholdings, which was explicitly noted as "exclusively your own, your Husband is never to have control over it."[19] To his son-in-law, David Sears offered advice to "delicately and faithfully fulfill your new duties of Husband and Son," particularly through attention to preserving the continuity of Sears family ties:

> I know your feelings for Ellen, I know that you will ever be ready to sacrifice yourself for her happiness and that no effort will be wanting on your part to soothe and gratify her—and you must have also seen before this, that the surest way to gain her heart was thro' the heart of her mother. Here she is sensitive, and here her affectionate feelings will respond tenfold, to the smallest act of civility or friendship. Be assured also, my friend, that whoever pursues a different course can never gain her—to them she will be as cold as marble.[20]

Despite the advice, the marriage did not proceed smoothly. In the spring of 1838, the Sears family was forced to send Ellen's doctor—the renowned Boston physician, Dr. John C. Warren, David Sears's brother-in-law—to Europe to provide legal testimony on the state of her health. Dr. Warren reported that he had seen Ellen repeatedly, and that she was feeble in body and in an anxious state of mind: "produce[d] principally by the desire to return to America with her mother, and from the fear of not being allowed to accompany her. The state of mind was such that I thought she would become deranged, or probably fall into apathy or fatuity if not allowed to return to Boston with her mother."[21]

As her family physician, he reported that she had always been in fine health and good spirits while she lived in Boston, and that her current condition was particularly alarming since she was pregnant and in danger of miscarriage in such a state of mind. A return to Boston was effected, for on September 27, 1838, a son, Frederick Sears d'Hauteville, was born there. But by this time Ellen had also retreated to the protection of her father's household, never to return to her marriage or to the d'Hauteville estate.

This intriguing case of a misalliance in one of Brahmin Boston's wealthiest and most socially entrenched families was described in full detail in her father's letters to the Swiss curator in charge of her marital property. The charges leveled against Gonzalve d'Hauteville included both his authoritarian manner and his acquiescence to a domineering family. In particular, the d'Hauteville family's early attempts to sever the connection between Ellen and her mother, Miriam Sears, "to dissolve or break down every filial tie, to force her to change, in a single day, her habits and her feelings, to forget that she had a mother, and to cast from her every thought of friends, parents, and country,"[22] were seen as harsh in the extreme. That d'Hauteville had reneged on the plan to live in Paris for half the year, despite the provisions of the marriage contract, was an equally grave offense in David Sears's opinion, since it severed Ellen from the European circles of family and friends who provided her with an ongoing link to Boston.

A different interpretation of the case was presented by one of d'Hauteville's compatriots in a letter of 1840. He referred to Ellen's "attack of a horrible homesickness . . . which threatened her life," yet concluded:

> One cannot reason with the sick, and undoubtedly hers was an affection of the mind, but after having yielded to that caprice it is right that the voice of duty should be heard and that her father, her mother, her friends should recall to her the obligations which she has contracted, the profound grief that she causes, the state to which she has reduced her father and mother-in-law whose health is seriously injured, the unpardonable injustice of which she is guilty towards a man who has confided so much in her love.[23]

Two such different accounts of this marital dispute reflect a fundamental difference of belief in where a young married woman's familial loyalties should ultimately lie. To Ellen, the pronouncement made by her parents to another married daughter that "you will always be one of us," no doubt had great resonance. After only one year of marriage, it was to both her extended family and her Boston social circle that Ellen Sears d'Hauteville returned to spend the rest of her life.

The repercussions of this marital dispute lasted for the next eight years, as an American child custody suit, a European divorce and child custody suit, and claims for the full restitution of Ellen's property from the marriage settlement were negotiated. Through all of this, David Sears continued to be centrally involved in his daughter's affairs, pursuing her individual claims and sponsoring legislation about minor children and women's property protection in divorce cases. The child custody case was finally settled in Philadelphia in 1840 in favor of Ellen Sears d'Hauteville. In reaching this decision, the state supreme court established an important legal precedent favoring maternal custody following divorce. Legislation sponsored by the Sears family was subsequently passed in Rhode Island in 1841 curtailing the custody rights of foreign husbands.[24] Somewhat paradoxically, perhaps, this case added a precedent to nineteenth-century law that promoted a more individualistic and less paternalistic model of the family, at the same time as it demonstrated the power and reach of a family such as the Boston Searses, organized effectively along corporate kinship lines.

A full seven years after Ellen Sears d'Hauteville had returned to Boston and her family of origin, David Sears—one of the wealthiest men in Boston who could casually note in his journal that "the trust fund of the Massachusetts Hospital Life Insurance Company gives a capital to each of my [seven surviving] children of $78,961.43, interest quarterly"[25]—was still pursuing the return of the last 2,174 francs owed to Ellen, from the 100,000 francs of her original dowry. When this last notarial notice was served, he could claim: "The struggle is over, the parties are free, and when the above disagreeable duty is performed, and the debt recovered, I shall endeavor as quickly as possible to forget [all.]"[26]

Such letters as these exchanged between Anna Sears Amory, Ellen Sears d'Hauteville, and their mother, as well as the letters of David Sears written in his capacity as the head of household, illustrate the intensely emotional side of family relationships in the larger kinship network. The letters cited here sound a repeated refrain—reflecting a strong concern—about women not being cut off from their families of origin after marriage. Indeed, continuity with the family of origin was clearly seen as crucial to women's emotional well-being. Such ties to the family gave a resiliency to the structure of the kinship network that economic interest alone could not have produced.

This case is most revealing, however, in terms of the norms about marriage it makes visible and the extent of family involvement it elicited. By the 1830s an elite young woman's decision to marry was ultimately her own, but family approval or censure still hovered around the edges of that decision. Although considered "appropriate" in class and status terms, this marital alliance was strained both by cultural differences and geographical distance between the two families, indication that the emergent Boston economic elite was still more locally based than it was cosmopolitan. The process by which elite families would become less immediately involved in the courtship and marriage decisions of their children involved more institution-building in nineteenth-century Boston, replicating in the social sphere the process by which families had retreated from family partnerships yet still retained extensive control in the economic sphere. This process took place over the second half of the century, and it is reflected in the very different kinds of concerns that separate the case of Ellen Sears d'Hauteville from those that follow. Twenty-three years after the d'Hauteville marital misalliance, the courtship experiences of a younger cousin suggest a much more socially bounded world among the Boston elite, with very different kinds of concerns surrounding the process of getting married.

INDIVIDUAL CHOICE AND THE NORMATIVE PRESSURE TO MARRY: ELIZABETH ROGERS MASON CABOT

Elizabeth R. Mason was the daughter of William Powell Mason (1791-1867) and Hannah Rogers (1806-1872), and the niece of Miriam Mason Sears and David Sears. Born in 1834, she was therefore the contemporary of the youngest son in the David Sears family, Knyvet Winthrop Sears (b. 1832), and of the children of her older cousins, Ellen Sears d'Hauteville and Anna Sears Amory.

The closeness of Boston family and friendship networks at mid-century is illustrated by the fact that Anna's daughter, Harriet Sears Amory (1836-1865), was one of Elizabeth's closest friends and later married one of Elizabeth's suitors, Joseph P. Gardner (1828-1875). Relationships this interconnected were typical of the bounded social world that defined the experience of the young men and women of the Boston elite by the middle of the nineteenth century.

Elizabeth Mason's most pertinent diaries span the period from 1854 to 1860 when she ranged in age from twenty to twenty-six years old.[27] They offer a detailed account of her courtship years, during which she received and refused several offers of engagement, observed the engagements and marriages of friends and acquaintances, and recorded her thoughts on marriage and family relations. As such, these diaries provide an intriguing insight into the meaning of marriage and the process of engagement for a young Brahmin woman in an era in which marital and family norms were undergoing change. What seems new in the twenty years that separate the courtship experiences of Ellen Sears d'Hauteville and her younger cousin, Elizabeth R. Mason, is the lesser involvement of Elizabeth's family in her courtship and marriage choices, yet her expression of even greater individual anguish about the process of getting married.

Several themes appear in Elizabeth ("Lillie") Mason's diaries, amid the notes on friends, family, and the round of her social activities. Despite her youth, she had developed strong opinions about the importance of love in marriage and about the kind of man she would consider marrying. At the age of fifteen she remarked in her diary, "how many persons marry merely for the sake of marrying or for money or some such low object, and sacrifice their comfort and happiness for life!"[28] Nearly eight years late, she wrote:

> My husband! He must embody or suggest to me all that is beautiful, his faults seen through my love must have lost their edge, he must be my complement, which shall give me what I have not, and elevate and draw forth what I have. For him no sacrifice must seem great, circumstances must be nothing, my trust must be entire, my rest in his love perfect, he must be my refuge in grief, my partner in joy, for whom I can forget the universe.[29]

But for all her idealization of this future husband, the diaries also made careful observations of the difficulties of marriage for women. Engagement and marriage threatened to sever the ties among female friends, and many of the diary entries in these years reflected her fear of a potential loss of connection to and sociability with other women.[30] Elizabeth Mason also frequently noted the problematic nature of relationships between husbands and wives, ranging from the "wretched lot" of her cousin, Ellen d'Hauteville, to the "trials from married life, even with the best assorted couple," which she saw at first hand in the new marriages among her circle of friends.[31] An ambivalence about marriage pervaded these observations, as reflected in the following comments on the marriage of a close friend:

She is certainly devoted to Daniel [her husband], and absorbed in him. It is funny to see all the energy of impulse and feeling, which has before led her in a gay dance, from flower to flower, now all settled on this one object. Daniel is certainly wrapt up in her, as kind thoughtful and attentive as man can be; and yet she confessed that she doubted whether a girl would ever marry, if she could see the future plainly before her. It is hard to sustain a wife's part to any man, for whom you have given up all, and involves many bitter experiences, though more sweet ones. If one loses much one is saved much.[32]

Elizabeth Mason herself fluctuated between the idea that women lost much in marriage, but that their adult status also crucially depended on it. In the several years of diary entries that deal most fully with courtship, she received and rejected four engagement proposals. The fifth, received when she was twenty-five years old in 1859, was from Walter Cabot, the man she eventually married.[33] What is particularly striking in her diary accounts is the progression in her ideas about marrying: from a youthful disdain to the growing despair that she might never marry, a deep concern that was nevertheless juxtaposed to her ideals about marrying only for love and never, as she announced to her father, "for wealth or position or eligibility in any way."[34]

Because the shift in perspective on marriage represents not only one young woman's experience, but the weight of social expectations impinging on this personal decision, it is worth looking at the sequence of the diary entries in greater detail. An entry in 1854, when Elizabeth had just turned twenty years old, reflected her early, carefree approach to engagement and marriage:

I have promised to send her [Lizzie Ticknor, a friend] the receipt to catch a beau, the moment I have discovered it, and myself proved its efficacy. . . . Lizzie says that Mary Lowell's engagement was not altogether a surprise, altho' they never imagined it would be arranged so soon. Telle est la vie, what will six months achieve in one's destiny. The idea of being an "old maid" seems hard to bear and yet harder still would it be methinks, to choose from the small number of eligibles, offered to one's notice.[35]

Two years later, she made more extended observations on the prospects of remaining unmarried, still—at age twenty-two—capable of a sense of humor about her own status:

We often fail to improve our opportunities, by not foreseeing and preparing for them. I often think that women who remain unmarried, gradually succumb to what there is of pernicious in their mode of existence, because they grow up and continue to live on in expectation of marriage, until it is too late to make a stand against their habits. Nothing can be more useful than the life of a single woman of cultivated mind, resources, cheerful disposition, and active disinterested benevolence, nothing can be more beautiful or lovable, yet how often instead of this do we see discontent, narrowness of mind, selfish uselessness, or sour or busy interference and dependence. If I am to be a spinster, which I shrewdly suspect, I will be a pattern, won't I![36]

By the next year, however, this prospect did not appear so comforting. As Elizabeth approached the ages of twenty-three, twenty-four, and twenty-five, her diary entries were progressively dotted with foreboding concerns about remaining unmarried. "The world now seems very lonely, the future very hopeless," she wrote in 1857. Seven months later, she added: "Sorrows do not cease, for I have felt during the last fortnight as if a life such as I must look forward to, was hardly bearable, but this is at times only, I do not look forward, every day life is more to me, I can bear better than I could the thoughts of a life of loneliness, obscurity, monotony."[37] These concerns only increased as she observed the engagements and marriages of friends and acquaintances within her social circle. By the spring of 1859, they were common enough to be recognized as a pattern:

> Every year my experience brings up the same problem, never solved—where the fault lies in the intercourse now carried on in civilized society between young men and women? And it is not of theoretical interest alone. Each spring I pass thro' the same trial of disappointment, bitterness and struggle, each summer I recover, each autumn feel strong and self dependent, each winter gradually lose my equilibrium, to suffer for it again in the spring.[38]

Yet against this backdrop of Elizabeth's growing concern about getting married, her rejection of one eminently eligible suitor, Josiah Quincy, from a family line of Boston mayors and a Harvard president, is noteworthy. "Turned to stone" and "cold as ice" were Elizabeth's diary descriptions of her responses to his several marriage proposals, first in October 1856 and then nearly a year and a half later in April 1858. "Henceforth Joe Quincy will be a stranger, whom I shall care to know about very much, and shall be interested in his fate, but whom I never hope to meet again on any but the most outside and formal footing," Elizabeth proclaimed.[39] Two weeks later, she had extended second thoughts:

> I have at times a feeling of presentiment that Joe Quincy is my fate, and it is less impossible to me than it once was. I never felt it to be a thing to dislike, or dread, but simply a thing impossible. Now again and again rises the question, why? Has he not what I most prize, intellectually and morally, may I not be throwing away my life's happiness from mere fear and indecision? If I settle into an old maid—and is not the probability on that side—I know from my character and tastes that it is settling to a life of endurance, of struggle with myself. I may become peaceful through discipline, blessed by rising above the world, but not happy or satisfied. . . . I think I never should fall in love quickly or easily, nor any one else fall in love with me; it must be the growth of time. I cannot help feeling that it accords with my character and experience, to take a great step as this, after much delay, and doubt. And yet, oh my God, the other side rises before me, and I feel as if on the very brink of a precipice. Is this the way in which one should marry? Is it noble or worthy? Am I not driven to it by fear and policy and weakness, rather than by feeling, and nobleness? I would marry, my chance is fading. I will grasp ere it is too late. It may turn out well. . . . If I could only know him! . . . And how can I ever know more?[40]

Elizabeth R. Mason's problem was resolved in December 1859, when—at the age of twenty-five—she accepted the marriage proposal of Walter Cabot. "A man saved from drowning could not give description of his feelings in being snatched back to life—neither can I,"[41] she wrote in her diary. On January 1, 1860, she could safely add: "A New Year indeed has begun for me. Ten days more of happiness since I last wrote. . . . No doubts, fears, disappointments, no anything but joy and peace." Her engagement had been preceded by seven months of anxiety, as her attraction to Walter deepened without clear signs that he returned the sentiment. In this period, as the prospect of losing a man she believed she loved increasingly dominated her journal entries, Elizabeth's ambivalence about marriage was resolved.

Plans for a June wedding progressed quickly after that, once the Mason and Cabot families had agreed to provide the new couple with an income of $3,000 per year, including a house and furnishings, "so that we are started without any necessary dependence on Walter's business."[42] Due consideration was also given to setting up the new residence close to Elizabeth's mother, who had become reconciled to the marriage of her daughter when their continued proximity made it "a step . . . hardly like leaving home." The prospect of this shift to a new status evoked Elizabeth's final extended reflection on marriage in this same diary entry:

> The reality, that in two months I shall have left home forever, that I shall no longer be Lillie Mason, that Walter will be mine—that I shall have started beyond possibility of return on a new and untried road, which looks now all sunlight, but which I know must be checkered with many a black cloud—all this is words to me only, and I laugh as freely, and walk on as little anxious, as if I could see no change. It is wonderful how gently we are led up to these great things, and what in speculating upon seems sufficient to overwhelm one with its momentous importance, in experience steals softly upon us like the yearly recurring seasons, or daily duties. But yet the change is not less great—I feel as if I had gained new senses, new perceptions, new powers—a new life—what was barren, seems filled up—empty—satisfied.

Following such a detailed account of courtship and marriage in the life of one young Boston Brahmin woman in the mid-nineteenth century offers a rare opportunity to understand the meaning that these activities and life events held. Although there is no evidence to suggest that Elizabeth Mason was ever explicitly pressured to marry by her family and every indication that she made her own marital decisions independently, the larger social pressures that promoted marriage as the most fulfilling event in a young woman's life were clear, if unarticulated, factors in the choices she made.

Faced with the choice between marriage defined as providing love, comfortable domesticity, and social respectability or singleness defined as producing "loneliness, obscurity, monotony," it is hardly surprising that she actively chose marriage. Her commitment both to maintaining the ties to her own family of origin and forging new attachments to her husband's family—who, she noted, "treat me like one of themselves"[43]—must have been enhanced by the perception that marriage was a choice she had independently made.

Twenty years later, many of the same issues appeared in the marital decision of another young Boston Brahmin woman, Hetty Sullivan Lawrence. This additional detailed journal account of the dilemmas involved in the decision to marry reflects many of the continuities in women's marital expectations and family experience made against a backdrop of sweeping normative changes about love and personal choice in the courtship market.

INDIVIDUAL CHOICE AND THE QUANDARY OF ROMANTIC LOVE: HETTY S. LAWRENCE CUNNINGHAM

Hetty Sullivan Lawrence was the seventh of eight children born to Amos Adams Lawrence (1814-1886) and Sarah Elizabeth Appleton Lawrence (1822-1891). As the granddaughter of two of the original Boston Associates—Amos Lawrence and William Appleton—and as the daughter of the key Lawrence businessman of his generation, she was born into the Boston upper class and firmly established in its circles during the second half of the nineteenth century. Typical of many young women of her social class and era, she married a man whose family was also well established in Boston. After marriage, they continued to live, work, and raise their children in the same social milieu in which they had both been raised. Hetty Sullivan Lawrence's life would thus be relatively unremarkable in the history of upper-class Boston women if it were not for the detailed journal she kept between the years 1876 and 1881, the period encompassing her engagement and marriage to Frederick Cunningham. Both personally and socially revealing, this private journal is another important document that reveals the way in which marriage was anticipated and experienced by elite women in late-nineteenth-century Boston.[44]

The journal began in July 1876, when Hetty Lawrence was twenty years old. From the start, interspersed with her accounts of the social occasions and family activities that defined her social world, there were increasingly frequent references to Frederick Cunningham ("F.C."), a young man who sent bouquets, made social calls, and requested her photograph: "F.C. came out in the afternoon—asked for my photo. I haven't one, and do not think I should give it if I had. There was a sort of pleasure in refusing, for he wanted it—and in such a case one feels their own power, a petty tyrant."[45]

Hers was a limited power, nevertheless, as Hetty revealed in the first year and a half of her journal entries. For immersed as she was in a world in which engagements and marriage were the key events in the lives of her female friends, that "pleasure in refusing" extended only to the mildest of flirtations, never to the idea of marriage itself. Marriage was clearly a status she desired. Yet even as she recorded "a jealousy which tries to have possession of me when I hear of a nice engagement [of a friend],"[46] she experienced tremendous ambivalence about her own engagement to Frederick Cunningham, an ambivalence that lasted up to the time of her marriage in December 1877 when she was twenty-two.

This ambivalence was expressed in journal entries that varied between private, introspective ruminations and more self-conscious passages, which she anticipated would be read by her fiancé after their engagement. The reasons for her anxiety were always personal rather than social, cast in terms of whether or not she really loved him, as the following extended passage from her journal suggests:

> I had a most grateful letter from F.C. Tues. thanking me for a Bible I gave him last Sunday as a Xmas present. He said his heart was full of thankfulness to God more so than for a long time. How glorious to feel I may have done his soul some good. But O Lord may I not be puffed up; it was Thou who didst use me as an instrument. . . . I will write how I feel to him and he to me and if we are never more to each other than now I can tear this out. He loves me with all his heart, he told me so one Sunday and asked if I thought I c'd ever be more to him than now, as I told him I took an uncommon interest in him; but whether it would ever be more I could not say though I thought there was more likelihood that way. Though I felt quite hopeful myself I did not tell him so for fear I sh'd raise hope which perhaps I never c'd fulfill. He hardly thought it right to speak to me till he felt able to be married but he was in such uncertainty and restless state he could not study. I am glad we understand each other; I think it is better. I told him he might come and see me once in a week or ten days perhaps was better. At times I think I shall never be greatly in love with him as it is called. I feel as if I never sh'd be with anyone, but I think I may love him very dearly and yet not realize it—perhaps even now I

love him, though sometimes I think it is only a deep interest. I wonder if a long separation could break up my feelings for him; that is quite a test. I think it might did I not know he loves me; but that *is* a power and shall I not yield to it? I am glad when the day comes when I shall see him and yet when I know I shall not see him for some days after a little while I am content; what strange creatures we are! But some days it seems as if something will be struck which will make things fall into their right places and there will be a grand harmony, perhaps yes grander for the confusion at first, but it will not be fully so in our lives, though we may catch feeble glimpses of it. It is more than two years since I told Julia Ap.[Appleton] at the Farm one night as we looked at the moon that the two men I liked the most were F.C. and Frank Peabody whom I scarcely know. I think I mentioned him rather to cover the other; it seems as if I were going to love him I sh'd have been nearer to it during this length of time than I am now. There are the two sides of it. I told him I wished I c'd say to him as sincerely as he said to me "I love you with all my heart."[47]

A profound ambivalence about contracting this specific engagement recurred repeatedly during the first year this journal was kept, a period in which entries were made several times a week. Following this initial private conversation about their relationship, Hetty referred to rumors about their engagement, which had surfaced among their acquaintances only a month later. Despite the more public nature of their relationship, she continued to express an ambivalence about her attachment to Frederick Cunningham:

Hauled Aunt Susan over the coals for writing and believing I was engaged; how people make something out of nothing. It was rather amusing. . . . F.C. said he did not come out Sunday as his Mother told him it made me conspicuous. I don't see why he does not come here and see me; it is a long time since he came. He left me some songs to learn and sing with the flute and he might have asked to see me. I must try and occupy myself with other things and my faith will be shown me in this way. I think I shall be less apt to deceive myself.[48]

By March the same rumors of an engagement had spread widely enough for Hetty Lawrence to feel compelled to explain to her mother "exactly how matters were," although this seemed more a response to her family's concern about observing social proprieties than to their disapproval of the match. "The family joke me about him," she noted in an entry made only five days after she had remarked on "a stormy week . . . for a report about my engagement with F.C. was coming out."[49] By April, the couple had had a "very plain talk," covering not only the general possibility of their marriage, but the economics of whether or not partially living on her inheritance, which was estimated at $108,000 on her twenty-first birthday five months earlier, would cause him to lose his self-respect. "Plain talk" appears not to have resolved Hetty Lawrence's ambivalence about this engagement, however, since several weeks later she recorded:

> Met F.C. while walking with Emily Meyer; he joined us and made me a little call. After he left I felt quite blue, a sort of sick feeling at my heart, for fear I really do not love him and am deceiving myself and him. May God help me and make me desire to do that which is right in His sight. Oh! Oh! Oh! It is so confusing and oppressing to think. Do I love him or do I not. May I not mistake the desire to do so for the act itself? What a mistake it would be.[50]

The desire to be in love and to marry—and thus to live up to the social expectations of her family and social circle—was clear, despite the provocative question she posed to herself. Instead, Hetty Lawrence's ambivalence was focused on the meaning of romantic love in marriage, and whether or not this particular suitor, who was clearly drawn from the appropriate ranks of the Brahmin upper class, met her personal expectations.

By the end of May, both Hetty Lawrence and Frederick Cunningham had "written out what we thought right about a man marrying before he could support a wife by his own exertions," exchanged with each other what they had written, and agreed to postpone the engagement decision until the following September "when I [Hetty] am to say a decided yes or no to him."[51] That this decision was primarily Hetty's alone was confirmed by a talk she had with her mother a month later:

> When Mother came to bed at 10 1/2, he [F.C.] had just left which was rather late; she asked when I was going to have it settled with him. I told her September. She seemed to think it was hard to keep him waiting so long. I fear I did not explain it to her very

well as I was very much disturbed and of course it made me cry like a goose, but I see that I was wrong in not saying no and then he could ask me again in the autumn if he still remained of the same mind. Altogether the different kind of excitement and the dentist were too much for me and I stayed in bed till 2 with a headache.[52]

By late August 1877 Hetty was again encouraging Frederick Cunningham's social visits ("We talked upon commonplace subjects most of the time, but I know he feels just the same to me"[53]). After a gap of a month, however, she officially resumed writing in her journal with a significant entry that captured much of the dilemma behind her decision to marry "Fred"—now so named in her subsequent journal entries:

> I begin my journal again. Since I last wrote I have been through such varied feelings I dare not write them on paper: sometime when it is further in the past I should like to put them down, but now I do not feel like examining them and so bro't face to face with them again, but I did fear that my reason was not sound or that it would become so if the strain upon it lasted long. Thank God since Sunday I have felt much more like myself; I began to feel so in church in the morning and since then I have had hardly any of what I called to Fred "my fits." But he was very sweet to me. So patient and gentle. I wish I might love him much more. He does love me so very very much, but I am beginning to have a more natural feeling for him, I think, and it seems as if I liked him more and more. This is not complimentary to you my dear Boy, but you know what I have been thro' and sometime I hope to love you as truly as you do me. God bless you. I will try to make you a true and loving wife. . . . Good night Freddie; I know you will read this sometime: at least I suppose so.[54]

Over the next two months, there were only occasional entries alluding to the ambivalence about love and marriage that Hetty Lawrence had recorded in her journal for over a year. These "fits" or "misgivings," as she variously referred to them, were increasingly submerged in the practical details of the engagement: arranging the wedding list, receiving and cataloguing gifts, choosing and furnishing a residence for after their marriage. The wedding took place on December

11, 1877, and, despite all Hetty Lawrence's anticipation of this event for a year and a half preceding it, the journal entry was short and noticeably matter-of-fact:

> Our wedding day: a very light fall of snow during the night, sun not out bright but otherwise a good day. I was the well one of the family. Father having had a very poor night—indigestion—too much thinking probably; he seems to feel my leaving home very much; he did not come down to breakfast. Mother seems to have taken cold and does not feel perfectly well. H.[Harriet, a sister] not feeling well and Sue [a sister] had to have her wound opened again yesterday which was very painful. Everything went smoothly dressing, did not feel as frightened as last eve'g, but my knees did shake when I got up to the rail but I was all right again as soon as I spoke. The church was full and everything seemed to go off well, about 200 people came to the house afterwards and it seemed to me not a stiff reception. I had Mother's wedding veil pinned on behind; it is lovely. At a little before 3 we went upstairs and had something to eat and at 1/2 past we drove off in a hack with my trunk; the family and cousins threw rice after us and after taking a drive thru Brighton and about Jamaica Pond we bro't up at the St. James in Boston which we found very comfortable.[55]

After this significant and definitive event in Hetty Lawrence Cunningham's life, the journal never again recorded the kind of emotionally wrenching ambivalence about the complicated relationships of love and marriage that had concerned her so repeatedly both before and after her engagement. Rather, within a month after marriage, she had wholeheartedly embraced her new social status as a married woman, coolly claiming—in response to a theater performance much discussed in her Boston circles, which portrayed a woman not in love with her husband and contemplating eloping with a cousin—"I dare say I should have been more shocked before being married."[56] Except for a brief line in the journal, which conveys more insight into the relatively circumscribed nature of women's lives in nineteenth-century America than its author surely intended, our window on the kind of personal ambivalence involved in one upper-class woman's courtship experience closes here: "A week today since we were married. I think this eve'g much pleasanter than that; things are so much more agreeable when one is used to them."[57]

The kind of personal ambivalence about the meaning and experience of love reflected in the journal of Hetty Lawrence is most striking
when seen in contrast to the clear social approval that surrounded her
engagement and marriage. Except for two instances of advice from her
mother—one expressing concern with her daughter's long delay in
making a decision about accepting the engagement, the other about the
impropriety of a young woman visiting her fiancé at his sickbed in his
family home[58]—there is remarkably little evidence of any family intervention in Hetty Lawrence's choice of a spouse or decision about if and
when to marry. Given the structural importance of marriage in building
the kinship networks of members of this social class, an orientation
toward individualism over a more corporate family role in decision-
making seems surprising, at least until the "individual" choices of Hetty
Lawrence's seven other siblings are juxtaposed beside her own.

Broad intermarriage patterns were characteristic of the Lawrence
family, with two brothers marrying relatively widely outside the immediate circle of the Boston upper class (the first to a Silsbee, followed by a
Rice, then a Dugan; the second to a Cleaveland). The third brother,
William Lawrence, an Episcopal bishop, married into the same Cunningham family as his sister Hetty. But most notably, Hetty Lawrence's
four sisters married into families—the Amorys, the Brookses, the
Hemenways, and the Lorings—whose wealth, directorships, and social
standing located them centrally in the Boston upper class of the late
nineteenth century. That such a class-specific set of marriages was individually contracted by the members of one family strongly suggests
that powerful social norms and a social process designed to filter out
"inappropriate" marriage choices were at work in framing the larger
context in which these individual choices were made. Social class acted
as an external barrier and internal screen in shaping the tastes, choices,
and range of behavioral options open to women like Hetty Lawrence
Cunningham. Although consciousness of her class position dots her
private journal in the form of comments about the appropriate street
clothes of "first-class" people, concerns about making charitable contributions to the deserving poor, or a speech she rehearsed at the age of
twenty-one to a future son admonishing him to "remember you were
born a gentleman's son and do nothing unworthy of him,"[59] most of
the ways in which social class had shaped her attitudes and behavior
were hidden from her view and from ours, part of the taken-for-granted
world in which she lived that even her most introspective journal
entries never articulated.

If Hetty Sullivan Lawrence chose her husband against the back-drop of parental and peer approval, her choice sanctioned and eased by her social class similarities to her fiancé, why then her great ambivalence in making this decision? It is worth noting that none of her anxiety or ambivalence concerned the legitimacy of the institution of marriage itself or of the rituals of courtship. In the year and a half of writing in her journal prior to her own marriage, she recorded nearly a dozen engage-ments and at least five weddings of friends from her immediate social circle. Engagements and marriages were an occasion for celebration, even for jealousy; they were clearly an expected part of most women's lives. For all of Hetty Lawrence's private ambivalence, she never con-templated the choice of not marrying at all, although her inheritance placed her in the select company of women in nineteenth-century America who could claim economic independence. On her eighth anniversary, her commitment to marriage secured, she noted simply, "8 years married today—happy years, especially the last. I cannot be too thankful."[60]

Rather than ambivalence about marriage itself, these detailed jour-nal entries express concern about the nature and experience of romantic love, reflecting the normative spread of a middle-class ideology among the upper class, as well as throughout the broad middle-levels of Amer-ican society as other scholars have documented. In keeping with the experience of women since the colonial era, Hetty Lawrence recognized that her choice of a spouse, despite the general social approval that sur-rounded it, was the weightiest decision of her life.[61] Given the impor-tance of the domestic sphere in her life and of the family relationships she saw everywhere around her, it is no wonder that this important personal choice was the source of both intense longing and anxiety.

In one further way, the journal of Hetty Lawrence Cunningham helps provide a more general insight into the significance of courtship and marriage for upper-class Bostonians in this era. Although the his-torical and anthropological literature is replete with examples of the way in which explicitly arranged marriages have functioned for the task of alliance-building, sociologists have been far less interested in examining the social and economic consequences of marriages con-tracted under an ideology of romantic love. As we seek to understand the process through which kinship networks were built and maintained as a means of promoting class continuity, it is worth noting that marital ties and family attachments were even more emotionally binding when based on personal choice and forged by romantic love than they were when arranged by family heads for explicitly instrumental ends. The freedom to choose one's marital partner based on love, against the backdrop of the strong social approval of this choice by family, peers, and a class-based community, must have been a potent combination for producing resilient family ties and the kind of cohesive kinship networks on which families like the Boston Searses, Masons, and Lawrences depended for their social and economic continuity.

THE INSTITUTIONALIZATION OF AN UPPER-CLASS COURTSHIP MARKET: MARIAN LAWRENCE PEABODY

Marian Lawrence, the daughter of William Lawrence and Julia Cunningham Lawrence and the niece of Hetty Lawrence Cunningham, is an intriguing fourth case to look at in terms of the courtship and marriage patterns of elite Boston women. Born in 1875, she was not only part of a family firmly entrenched in the Boston upper class by this period, but a member of the generation whose lives were most distinctly shaped by the set of institutional structures that promoted class solidarity.

The Boston world into which she was born was a world of elite social and cultural institutions. Her father and paternal grandfather were members of the Somerset Club, the most prestigious men's club in Boston. Her extended family became members of the Country Club when it was founded in 1882 in Brookline. Family residences included Beacon Hill, Back Bay, Cambridge, and Brookline, with the summer homes of kin and Boston friends in Nahant, on Boston's North Shore. She attended the Cambridge School, located on the present grounds of Radcliffe College and, at age 16, Miss Folsom's School on Beacon Hill where she received instruction from, among others, Professor Kittredge of Harvard and Professor Dewey of M.I.T. Intermittently, from age eighteen until she was married at the age of thirty-one, she attended the Art School associated with the old Art Museum in Copley Square. Harvard played an important role in her life, through her father's official connection to it for over fifty years and through the family's regular attendance at games, boat races, the Hasty Pudding shows, and Class Day. From the age of thirteen she attended dancing school, took music lessons, and later riding lessons. Her charitable work included (at age seventeen) a girls' benefit for the Vincent Hospital, the North Bennet Street Boys' Club (at age twenty-three), and, later, raising money for the Sailors' Haven in Charlestown, where she worked with her future husband, Harold Peabody.[62]

Marian Lawrence was enmeshed in that broader institutional web of educational, charitable, cultural institutions that had developed in Boston over the second half of the nineteenth century. Her published memoir, drawing on excerpts from the diaries she had kept since the age of twelve, offers insights into the ways in which a young woman's life continued to be shaped by family, peer, and social class norms and institutions at the end of the nineteenth and beginning of the twentieth centuries.

The key institution that defined an elite young woman's coming of age by the last quarter of the nineteenth century was the debutante year. Generally occurring by ages seventeen or eighteen, this transition year signaled a young woman's entrance into adulthood and the courtship market. For Marian Lawrence, the preface to this debutante year was her move, at the age of sixteen, with her sister Julia from their Cambridge home to the Boston residence of their aunt, Susan Lawrence Loring, where they could receive "a little polishing up, and more social contacts, which the big city could give."[63] The daily routine of such "polishing up" included attending school on Beacon Hill, riding lessons at the New Riding School on the Fenway two afternoons a week, music lessons, and dancing class; attending theater performances and art exhibits; and maintaining an active social visiting schedule of relatives and family friends. As an institution that inculcated both social values and peer group sociability, Papanti's Dancing Class was especially noteworthy: "Every girl of fifteen or sixteen went to the Friday Evening [dancing class] if she could get in, and danced with freshmen from Harvard and some sub-freshmen. When they were seventeen they went to the Saturday evening, and danced with sophomores."[64]

Detailed descriptions of these dances are included in Marian Lawrence's account:

> The German (or Cotillion) usually began about one o'clock. Everyone took seats around the hall. The leader was apt to be one of a few gentlemen who were used to doing it, and he and his partner would ask the first eight or twelve couples (depending on the size of the party) to go out and dance, giving each person a favor. After dancing a short time they would break off and each would take a new partner by giving their favor to anyone they liked in the hall, making sixteen or twenty-four couples. Shortly, they

would return to their seats, and the leading couple would then ask another eight or twelve couples to do the same thing, and so on until everyone had had the chance to go out and give a favor to someone. Of course the more favors you got the more pleased you were.[65]

The institution of the dancing class soon extended to chaperoned parties among the same set of friends. Harvard provided another setting for such family-approved sociability among young upper-class Bostonians. In her diary account of the Harvard Class Day on June 24, 1892, for example, Marian's description of the round of activities points to some of the ways in which family and peer groups were bounded by a culture of shared values:

> My dress was organdy muslin with blue in it and blue bodice and sash. Very stylish. Even Papa approved. Mamma had not seen it till today—it was all my own idea. It had a train and elbow sleeves, trimmed with deep lace. My hat was trimmed in front with white ostrich plumes and was immense, which did not make dancing any easier. Papa and I went to the Gymnasium spread. This was the best ever, a prettily decorated hall, plenty of room to dance and splendid music. The snappiest band I ever heard. Even Papa thought it was great when they played "Ta-ra-ra boom-de-ay." I started off at once with Arthur, then Rodman, Frank White and never stopped a second as people came up and wanted the next and next. Even law students would say, "May I have the last half of the next?" etc. Finally I had to cool off and went out on the lawn and had an ice with R. Walcott. . . . The seniors had a terrific struggle to get the flowers which circled the big tree far above their heads. They climbed on each other's backs and finally the wreath was bare and all the flowers gone. Hal de Wolfe gave me some he got, which I wore with great pride.[66]

These annual festivities paled by comparison, however, to the social whirl of the "bud year," Marian Lawrence's offical entrance into Boston society in 1893.

During this year, young women of the Boston upper class were presented in a series of evening dances and afternoon teas. The height of the season was the two months from early December through early February, during which one or even two dances were scheduled

nightly. A round of daily social activities—including lunches, teas, mat-
inées, and concerts—dominated the calendars of the new group of
"buds" (debutantes), in addition to the dinners and dances that
occurred nightly. Marian Lawrence's schedule was restricted to only
three dances a week and to a curfew of 1:00 A.M. by her father, who
thought the bud year a waste of time. But most parents and extended
family members fully supported and sustained this institution, as both
the sponsors of and guests in attendance at these events.

As a carefully prescribed social ritual, the debutante ball started
with dinner at 8:00 P.M.; a dance commencing between 10:30 and
11:00 P.M.; a sit-down, four-course supper at midnight; followed by a
cotillion from 1:00 to 3:00 A.M. In addition, the families of debutantes
hosted more informal house parties at which "one knew everyone else."
The following extended account of Marian Lawrence's first coming out
parties gives the flavor of these events as social occasions celebrating the
sociability of family, friends, and peers as much as they announced a
young woman's experience of entering adulthood:

> *June 15:* My "come out" reception, and to our great joy a lovely
> day. Mamma has been working hard on the list for this tea for a
> long time, and I think we asked about two thousand people but
> did not expect more than five hundred to come as so many have
> gone away for the summer. All my girl friends and most of the
> College boys have gone, but [Mabel Davis, a friend] came back
> from York Harbor and most of those I knew from the North Shore.
> The place looked lovely. The long French windows were open
> and red-carpeted steps led down from them to the lawn where
> benches and chairs had been arranged in shady corners. The
> house was full of roses which friends had sent. The first hour was
> hard work! Besides the ushers and pourers, who were outside
> enjoying themselves, there were in the parlor two ministers (one
> deaf), two theologs, two old ladies who wouldn't speak to each
> other, a most unhappy-looking Harvard student, Emily Proctor
> and her brother, and Uncle Jeff Coolidge and Cousin Mamie Sar-
> gent looking very swell! They left before the stream of guests
> began to arrive. The ushers worked valiantly. Two girls poured tea
> in the dining room, and iced things were in the oval room. The
> lawn with people going in and out of the house all in their gay
> Class Day dresses made a very pretty picture. Many people spoke
> of it so I finally went out with Harry to enjoy it. Old George Becker

was at the front door and said there were 720. Mrs. Sturgis and Maizie and Mr. Jim Scott happened to be on their way to Bar Harbor so they came and Mr. Sigourney Butler came, and a lot of people I had not known before. It was almost eight o'clock before they had all left and, as I had had a headache all day, I went right to bed.[67]

The next week, Marian's official coming out party was held at the home of her aunt, Minnie Sargent:

There were only twenty girls and about twenty seniors and a dozen older men. I seemed to be the only Bud there, the rest were all older. After supper Freddy Dabney came up right away for a dance and then Starling Childs (a Yale man in Winthrop Hall and very attractive) then Bert, Harley and Gordon Bell and the latter asked me to sit out on the porch and was very entertaining. Some of the girls sat out there amongst the palms and flowers all the evening. Just as I was beginning to think Bell might be getting bored, Lawrence Haughton [an older cousin whom I had not known before] came up and introduced himself, and then someone introduced a married man. While I was with him Aunt Minnie went by and in a moment came back and seeing me still with the married man introduced the man she was with—Mr. Kidder, who was rather patronizing and I suppose they both thought I was a pill. Soon Aunt Minnie came back and introduced Alfred Weld—to relieve Kidder I suppose. I hated to have her think she had to look after me and as soon as she was out of sight both Bob Bowler and Ned Weld came up so I had three then for awhile. Except for this incident I had a pleasant evening and got along very well. It was a perfect house for a dance with the tiled terrace overlooking a pond and rolling fields like an English place and in the house four large rooms for dancing and adjoining conservatories. It was really like a ball in a novel by the Duchess.[68]

Nearly a full year of parties followed from these opening events, most of which included several generations of kin from Marian's extended family:

Jan. 30: The night of Aunt Harriet's party for me at 273 Clarendon Street. It was awfully nice of her to give it and it was a lovely party. The house was beautifully decorated with smilax and vines and lovely roses and lilies. It was done by a decorator. The rooms were all cleared for dancing and at the back of the third room was a long counter with waiters behind it, serving sherbet and champagne all evening. The big library upstairs was fixed for sitting out and they also sat on the stairs all the way up to it. There were chairs around the dancing rooms for the chaperones and older people to sit and watch. Aunt H. and I received in the hall. I wore a dress that Ma got in Paris when she came out. It was muslin, all shired and ruffled with lace edging and insertion over pink taffeta so it was a very pretty light shade of pink. I had an aigrette in my hair, which had been done by a hairdresser, and I wore my new necklace of twenty-three little diamonds hanging on a chain, and my diamond star. We asked two hundred and twenty people, many older ones and lots of Collegians, but not as many of the buds as I would have liked. I received with Aunt H. till suppertime, and then danced as hard as I could till one thirty when Aunt H. had them play "Home Sweet Home" until they took the hint. I was awfully tired, but had a fine time, and think everyone thought it a great success. They were all swept out anyway.[69]

In Marian Lawrence's recollection, few engagements resulted directly from the debutante experience, and during the years immediately following, her female friends were more often devoted to cultural pursuits and charitable work than to preparing for marriage. But the debutante experience was surely a powerful institution in shaping a shared culture and in defining a circle of friends who were members of a potential marriage pool of the Boston upper class. Along with closely knit residential enclaves; social, cultural, and political networks of associations and shared activities; and the common set of values that evolved from this structural base, the "bud year" gave shape to patterns of sociability and interaction that carried over to engagement and marriage.

On Christmas 1905, at the age of thirty, Marian Lawrence announced her engagement to Harold Peabody. While her published autobiography offers more limited insight into how she reached this decision than do the unedited journals and letters of earlier cohorts of Brahmin women, there is some suggestion that she resisted getting married and "used to be cross with friends sometimes when a rumor would get about that I was engaged to some one."[70] Her diary account of the engagement, read against the backdrop of the social institutions that guided her choice of an appropriate spouse, is revealing in terms of how tightly bounded the social world of Boston continued to be even at the turn of the twentieth century:

> *December 25, 1905:* Grandpa Peabody had five children, Jack, Cotty, Frank, Martha and George. Jack, Frank, and Martha [Peabody] all married Lawrences, and Cotty married his first cousin, Fanny Peabody. George was the only one who married out of the family, but his marriage did not last long. When the second generation began to marry, Marian [a cousin] married her first cousin, Jim Lawrence, and so we [Marian Lawrence and Harold Peabody] were the fifth such combination without any break, and what then was the use of fighting fate?[71]

The next half year was spent in a full round of social events with family and friends celebrating the engagement. Marian noted, "as soon as we were engaged, everything became easy and delightful. I was amazed at how nice everybody was. I couldn't see why they were all so interested. Grandma Cunningham, who was always very nice to Harold, said we were 'perfectly suited.'"[72] No wonder, then, that on her wedding day of May 8, 1906, Marian Lawrence Peabody could announce in her diary: "I felt very pleased with everything and comfortable and safe and settled. . . . [After the wedding] there was a big reception at 122. We were sent off in a shower of rice and the next day sailed for England, which we both loved. I felt happy and contented and had given up fighting fate."[73]

Four individual cases can help illuminate the meaning of marriage among upper-class women and men in nineteenth-century Boston. In the interstices between each separate story of a courtship experience over twenty-year intervals, normative shifts and institutional changes can also be seen reshaping the marriage market according to the broad dictates of social class rather than along the narrower lines of family interests.

A more comprehensive and systematic picture of marriage patterns and career choices among Boston families will help provide an understanding of how economic continuity was maintained. Against the backdrop of these detailed individual accounts of how the decision to marry was made, a broader cohort analysis of marriages of the Boston upper class reveals an even more patterned response.

Chapter 5

PATTERNS OF
ECONOMIC CONTINUITY

*Boston is the one place in America where wealth and the
knowledge of how to use it are apt to coincide.*
—*E.L. Godkin, 1871*

By the second half of the nineteenth century, it is possible to speak
of the transformation of the Boston economic elite into an economic
and social upper class. The social world of Brahmin Boston, in which
young women such as Elizabeth Mason Cabot and Hetty Lawrence
Cunningham could make their own marital choices, and their brothers, husbands, and sons could pursue a variety of career opportunities,
was one that was at once more individualized and more subject to institutional controls than earlier eras.

Families were the foundation of this Boston upper class, and it
was through their active efforts at economic and social institution-building, which I have traced in previous chapters, that a class structure was
forged. The new industrial and financial infrastructure and the more
institutionalized courtship market, which were in place in Boston in
the second half of the nineteenth century, did not supplant the family as
a functioning economic or social institution. Rather, I would argue, this
new social class foundation refashioned and broadened the system in
which wealthy and powerful families operated. One consequence of

the process of institutionalization was that families could relinquish their concerns about getting sons into business or positioning daughters for strategic marriages. In place of the relatively narrow interests of individual families, the broader class interests of a group of interacting and intermarrying families could be promoted and preserved efficiently and effortlessly through the set of economic, civic, and social-cultural institutions they built and directed.

But class position, once established, was neither permanent nor automatically renewed. A key question is whether or not the wealthy Bostonians of the first half of the nineteenth century were able to exert enough control over the economic succession of their sons, nephews, and grandsons to ensure the economic continuity, in addition to the social prestige, of their families. As important as wealthy and well-connected families may have been in any one historical period in terms of the scope of their economic power and influence, it is *continuity* that is the final measure of the economic significance of the family unit. The central question, then, is the extent to which economic continuity, based on the career choices and intermarriage patterns of successive generations of family descendants, was possible in a society undergoing the shift to advanced industrial capitalism.

There is some empirical evidence to suggest the loss of economic placement in elite institutions among those Boston families who held important business and board positions in the first half of the nineteenth century. Listed in the 1905 edition of the *Directory of Directors in the City of Boston and Vicinity* are only eighteen individuals with the surnames of Lowell, Jackson, Appleton, or Lawrence.[1] For families who had been so well-placed in the economic elite during the first half of the nineteenth century, this limited representation in key Boston directorships by the early twentieth century is particularly striking. The absence of the most readily identifiable elite names from this list implies that the accumulated wealth of Boston families at mid-century was an insufficient basis for launching sons and grandsons into those positions of economic power and influence through which a family's place in the economic upper class would have been secured.

While father-to-son occupational mobility has been the standard way of judging family economic continuity in much of the literature on social stratification, the complexity of surnames within most kinship networks should suggest the limitations of this measure. In the case of Boston's early nineteenth-century economic elite, limiting the analysis of the family to descendants of a single surname would almost certainly underestimate the capacity of the kin network to provide for both the extension and continuity of families. Investigating more complex kin interconnections and their overlapping economic significance is as necessary for understanding social class relations in the early twentieth century, after a hundred years of industrialization, as it was in the early nineteenth century in the initial period of transition to a new economy.

The analysis presented in this chapter focuses on the collective patterns of kinship networks rather than on discrete individuals, and it is based on the longitudinal marriage and career patterns of successive cohorts of the Lowells, Lawrences, and Appletons. The original Boston Associates and their sons and sons-in-law whose kinship interconnections were so significant to Boston's economic development in the second through fourth decades of the nineteenth century were members of the cohorts born in the years from 1780 to 1799, and from 1800 to 1819. The histories of the subsequent birth cohorts of 1820 to 1839, 1840 to 1859, and 1860 to 1879 thus span the whole nineteenth century and the beginning of the twentieth. Genealogical reconstruction of extended families and cohort analysis of careers and intermarriages are the means by which family patterns—as the foundation of social class—can be retrieved from the historical record.

As kinship networks stretch over several generations, their boundaries become less clearly demarcated. In the structure of American kinship, with descent measured equally from both parents, it is difficult to be precise about inclusion in one network and exclusion from another. For the purposes of this analysis, kinship networks have been determined not only on the basis of genealogy, but through evidence of an ongoing social relationship that gave meaning to the family connection. Members of a kinship network were often neighbors, social visitors, or the beneficiaries in each others' wills, as well as lineal or collateral kin. A marriage linking a son and a daughter of two Boston Associate families might have resonance in both kinship networks, or in one, or in neither. Over the course of the nineteenth century, then, kinship networks were not always precisely bounded, but their interconnections did not result in a general merging into one collective Brahmin family either. Different family traditions, rituals, and histories have ensured that the shared values and opportunities of social class did not efface more nuanced family differences.

Under the markedly changed economic conditions of the second half of the nineteenth century, families needed to take active measures to transpose their status as an economic elite into that of an economic upper class. Continuity was necessarily an achieved rather than an inherited characteristic of Boston upper-class family life. But multiple ways of preserving the family's economic position through the structural organization of the kin network were available to the members of the early economic elite and their families at mid-century and beyond.

A strong kin network structure established in the early nineteenth century seemed to provide the opportunity for economic continuity in at least two ways. First, it often provided a solid foundation of collective family wealth, which in itself was a basis for power that could be used as economic or social influence.[2] Second, the kin network could provide the coordination between elite institutional positions, thus maintaining in the structure of family relationships a web of personal connections through which decision-making, influence, and economic control could flow. There is evidence of both of these patterns among the Boston families who established themselves in the economic elite in the early part of the nineteenth century.

At least two kinds of intermarriage patterns by members of the kin network allowed economic continuity into the early twentieth century. One involved marriages with first cousins and among relatively few core families of the Boston elite. This produced a tight network structure, although not one so tight as to produce the kind of insular and constricted network characteristic of the Jacksons and Cabots in the early nineteenth century. In that case, as was noted in chapter three, the multiple marriages of Jackson sons to Cabot daughters, in addition to the lack of broad institutional affiliations among the cohort of Boston Associate P.T. Jackson, created a pattern of family insularity not well-adapted to the new economic conditions and opportunities of early industrial capitalism.

The other pattern involved a much broader set of marriages, often outside the core of elite families. Just as there was a danger in marrying too closely in an era when broader connections were economically useful, so could too wide a set of marriages threaten to disperse the kinship network altogether. The expanded network pattern of some Boston families was therefore one that required maintaining a balance between adding "new blood" and preserving an identity rooted in "old families."

There is no evidence to support the argument that these two patterns were the result of very different rates of fertility across families. Indeed, in both cases presented here in detail, the data from those fam-

TABLE 2
Two Boston Family Marriage Patterns, Cohorts 1780 to 1880

	Percent First-Cousin Marriages	Percent Core Brahmin Family Marriages	Percent Other Marriages	Total
Tight Network Structure (Lowell-Gardner Family)	7.8 (4)	51 (26)	41.2 (21)	(51)
Expanded Network Structure (Lawrence Family)	2 (1)	38 (19)	60 (30)	(50)

ilies whose completed fertility could be traced show remarkable consistency, with an average of three to four children per family across both cohort and network type.

It is important to note that the class continuity of many Brahmin families was achieved in an era that also produced considerable opportunity for social mobility. While some families of the early economic elite successfully made the transition into an economic upper class, this did not preclude the rise of other economically successful individuals and new elites in nineteenth-century Boston. It does, however, suggest the need to reassess the importance of the family as a key variable in the American class structure of the late-nineteenth and early-twentieth centuries.

THE TIGHT NETWORK STRUCTURE: THE LOWELL/GARDNER CASE*

In the structural organization of the kin network, new members could be included either by birth or by marriage. But the significant members of a kin network were those connected to each other by social bonds of interaction and personal influence in addition to their genealogical link. Analysis of the networks of Boston families in this chapter is based on a dual investigation of marriages, through which significant sons-in-law and well-connected daughters-in-law were added to the kin network, and of career patterns, through which wealth was enhanced and key industrial and financial positions were secured. Although in the nineteenth century marital and occupational choice was far more individualized and less subject to family control than it had been previously, the patterns of the kin network as a whole suggest that marriages and careers were also broadly shaped by the collective economic strategy of the extended family group.

A Close Circle of Marriages

Over the course of the nineteenth century, Lowell descendants and in-laws played an active role in promoting the economic continuity of the Lowell kin network. As described in chapter three, the key economic actors who established the Lowell position in the new economic elite of the early nineteenth century were the sons and nephews of Francis Cabot Lowell born in the cohorts 1780-1799 and 1800-1819. Not only were these men important in the early period of economic institutional growth between 1820 and 1840, but they continued to exert an economic influence throughout the first three-quarters of the nineteenth century. The three key Lowells were John Amory Lowell (1798-1881), Francis Cabot Lowell II (1803-1874), and John Lowell Gardner (1809-1884), all cousins. They expanded the Lowell economic influence and wealth through their connections to industry, finance, and mercantile business between the 1820s and the 1870s.

John Amory Lowell and Francis Cabot Lowell II established the Lowell position in the early Boston industrial and financial elite. Both were primary stockholders as well as officers and directors in the Boston Manufacturing Co. and in the textile firms located in the towns of Lowell and Lawrence. John Amory Lowell played a leading role in the organization and operation of the Suffolk Bank system, which had allowed Boston banks and the Lowell textile industry to survive the financial panics of 1837 and 1857. Francis C. Lowell II was the actuary of the Massachusetts Hospital Life Insurance Co. between 1845 and 1854, a position in which he had considerable influence over directing the flow of capital to the textile industry. Both men were, therefore, key representatives of the economic elite at mid-century who had overlapping interests in industry and finance.

In the broad scope of activities and affiliations that extended into the areas of education and culture in nineteenth-century Boston, the case of John Amory Lowell also typified the impact that one individual could have on shaping the spheres of influence of the Lowell kin network. In 1837 he was elected to the Harvard Corporation where, for the next forty years, he played a key role in the selection of six presidents, especially of Charles W. Eliot, who transformed Harvard's role as a leader in professional education.[3] Between 1837 and 1881, John Amory Lowell served as the first trustee of the Lowell Institute, a foundation endowed by his late cousin and brother-in-law, John Lowell (1799-1830), for the purpose of sponsoring public lectures on religion, philosophy, history, and the arts and sciences by leading authorities in these fields. The single Lowell trustee of the Institute was accorded great discretionary power in his selection of lecturers; for over forty years, John Amory Lowell utilized this power to help shape intellectual life in Boston.[4]

In 1862 John Amory Lowell was appointed a vice-president of the newly founded Massachusetts Institute of Technology, thus fully securing his central position in the Boston-Cambridge educational establishment.[5] Between 1860 and 1876 he was president of the Boston Athenaeum where, as further indication of his leadership in Boston's cultural institutions, he was active in the endowment of the Museum of Fine Arts, which was dedicated in 1876.[6]

The scope of John Amory Lowell's interests and activities over the first three-quarters of the nineteenth century suggests how readily economic power overlapped with social and cultural influence in this period. The density of these overlapping connections had even broader ramifications in a social context in which the individual was embedded in important family relationships in the larger kin network. Given his centrality in Boston's social structure, it is understandable that John Amory Lowell was recognized as "the pillar of his family's prosperity for three generations."[7]

John Lowell Gardner was the another key member of this kin network in the 1800-1819 cohort to establish a successful business career. He pursued a mercantile career, first in the firm of Gardner and Lowell with his cousin F.C. Lowell II and, after 1836, in partnership with his brother George Gardner in the John L. Gardner and Co.[8] Gardner's mercantile connections were as dense as his cousin's connections to the textile industry and to Boston's financial institutions. He married a daughter of the wealthy Salem merchant, Joseph Peabody, while two of his sisters married the sons of another wealthy merchant, William Gray.[9] As previously noted in chapter three, both John Lowell Gardner and his brother-in-law, Horace Gray, had financial affiliations, in addition to their wealth and family connections to the Lowell kin network that tied them to the institutional complex of the Boston elite. Eventually, with the fortune he had accumulated in mercantile trade in the first half of the nineteenth century, John Lowell Gardner turned to real estate investments in Boston and Brookline, and to management of the considerable property he had acquired through his wife and inherited from his father and paternal grandmother.[10]

The economic success of these three Lowell-Gardner cousins resulted from their involvements in both traditional and new fields of business, and through their affiliations to the financial institutions of Boston that had developed in the first half of the nineteenth century. While they were very successful as individual businessmen, it is their embeddedness in the Lowell kin network that is more noteworthy as a collective pattern. Their marriages produced the kind of tight network structure that served to reinforce the bonds within this kinship network.

John Amory Lowell first married Susan Cabot Lowell, his first cousin and the sister of Francis Cabot Lowell II. Francis Cabot Lowell II married Mary Lowell Gardner, his first cousin and the sister of John Lowell Gardner. Gardner's marriage to Catherine Endicott Peabody connected him to another wealthy mercantile family, and the marriages of two of his sisters, Elizabeth Pickering Gardner (1799-1879) and Sarah Russell Gardner (1807-1893), established a double link to the mercantile Gray family. When John Amory Lowell married for the second time in 1829 after the death of Susan Lowell, it was to Elizabeth Cabot Putnam (1809-1881), daughter of Judge Samuel Putnam of Salem. One of Elizabeth (Putnam) Lowell's brothers, Samuel R. Putnam (1797-1861), married Mary Traill Spence Lowell (1810-1898), another first cousin of John Amory Lowell, thus doubly establishing the Putnam connection to the Lowell kin network in this cohort.[11] It was therefore within this very tight network of intermarriage between the Lowells and Gardners, with connections to the Peabody, Gray, and Putnam families, that the close economic relationships and wealth of the Lowells and their kin were established and secured for most of the nineteenth century.

While the forging of this tight network pattern was initiated by the three principal Lowell economic leaders, all born around the turn of the nineteenth century but whose longevity ensured their influence through the 1870s, it was also a pattern that would be maintained by successive cohorts in the Lowell kin network with economic consequences. While there is no indication that the close intermarriages of the Lowell kin were motivated by the kind of highly conscious family-business organization favored by eighteenth-century mercantile families, these close intermarriages certainly produced patterns of a tightly organized kin network, with the concentration of individual fortunes as family wealth.

The structure of this kinship network also had other advantages for its members over its eighteenth-century counterpart, the family-business partnership. Under the new conditions of nineteenth-century economic institutionalization, the kin network allowed a much greater occupational diversity than the pursuit of business alone. The efforts of John Amory Lowell, Francis Cabot Lowell II, and John Lowell Gardner to solidify the Lowell economic base was thus only part of the picture of opportunities available within the kin network structure.

Occupational Diversity

In the nineteenth century, neither all sons nor all sons-in-law were directed toward business careers. The possibility of occupational diversity was one result of the changing structural conditions produced by economic differentiation and organizational change. In the past, the economic success of the mercantile family had depended on the recruitment of sons and sons-in-law to positions within the business partnership. The threat posed by sons who showed no aptitude for business was a serious one, and its potential for undermining the family's economic position was a major structural flaw in this form of economic organization.[12] With the development of a new industrial and financial infrastructure in Boston in the early nineteenth century, a family's economic success depended less on recruiting many sons into business than it did on establishing multiple directorship affiliations throughout the whole institutional complex.

As the Jackson case presented in chapter three suggested, having more than one successful businessman in the family system during this early period of economic transition may have been the minimum requirement for spreading economic risk and building significant connections throughout the kin network. But the absolute number of sons or sons-in-law required for economic continuity was certainly less than under the eighteenth-century conditions of the family partnership. A small number of successful businessmen in each cohort could wield a disproportionate amount of influence. The kin network was therefore able to be a more all-encompassing organizational structure than the family partnership. Its flexibility under new economic conditions is indicated by the greater individual choice over career and the broader range of occupational diversity among kin members it allowed.

Occupational diversity in the kin network increased career options for non-business-oriented sons and sons-in-law. It also had the positive effect of expanding a family's ties to new cultural, political, and professional arenas. Economic, political, and social-cultural sources of power could all overlap in the career of one prominent individual, as the case of John Amory Lowell in this cohort attests. Lowell's influence in the kin network not only grew out of his career as a successful businessman, but out of his leadership in education and culture as well. The overlap of these different spheres of influence in the career of one man suggests how readily economic success could be translated into social and cultural status in the nineteenth century. While individuals with such breadth of interests were relatively rare even in this era, the kin network commonly encompassed a diversity of talents and the potential for overlapping kinds of influence, power, and prestige among its members.

In the same 1780-1799 and 1800-1819 birth cohorts of Lowell kin that produced three significant leaders in business, there was a growing occupational diversity among the other members. As previously noted, Elizabeth Pickering Gardner (1799-1879), sister of John Lowell Gardner, made the first of the two Gardner marriages to sons of the merchant William Gray. John Chipman Gray (1793-1881) brought his substantial share of inherited mercantile wealth into the sphere of the Lowell kin network, but his political career as a representative to the Massachusetts General Court and state senate through the first half of the nineteenth century brought an added measure of political influence and professional prestige to the Lowells as well.[13] Gray was not the sole political representative of the Lowell kin network in the first half of the nineteenth century. Benjamin Gorham (1775-1855), uncle of John Amory Lowell, F.C. Lowell II, and John L. Gardner, also added to the family's political prominence, first as a member of the Massachusetts state legislature and later as a member of the House and the Senate of the U.S. Congress.[14]

The children of Charles and Harriet Traill (Spence) Lowell were the least prone of all Lowell cousins to follow business careers in this 1800-1819 cohort.[15] Their economic failures and cultural successes therefore serve as appropriate cases for an investigation of the flexibility of the kin network in allowing individual career choice, while at the same time providing these individuals with the security of a collective family identity.

The career of Charles Russell Lowell (1807-1870) represents the clearest case of the consequences of individual failure in business within the supportive structure of the collective kin network. Lowell's marriage to Anna C. Jackson, oldest and favorite daughter of Patrick Tracy Jackson, placed him in a potentially strategic position relative to the wealth and influence of that Boston Associate.[16] In building on the earlier strong connections between the Lowells and the Jacksons, this marriage might have merged two family fortunes and two circles of economic influence at the height of the two families' business success.

An indication that this marriage did result in an economic relationship between Lowell and his father-in-law, P.T. Jackson, is given in Jackson's journal of 1836. There he made note of the sum he had advanced to his daughter at the time of her marriage (which was to be deducted from her inheritance), as well as a substantial loan made to his son-in-law, Charles Russell Lowell.[17] Yet despite this connection to the family capital and the institutional affiliations of one of Boston's early economic elite members, Charles Russell Lowell lost his business and much of his father's property that had been placed under his management in the economic Panic of 1837. Lowell's lack of talent for business, rather than the unfavorable economic conditions of the era, was generally accepted as the reason for his failure by other members of the family.[18] After 1837 he left a career in business for the job of cataloguing the books of the Boston Athenaeum.

Although the chance for business success was missed in this particular case, the social contacts for economic opportunities that could lead to such success in the next generation were preserved in the structure of the kin network. The Lowell connections within the economic elite allowed Charles R. Lowell's eldest son, Charles Russell Lowell, Jr. (1835-1864), to establish himself as one of the rising young business leaders of his generation with interests in and established connections to industry and the railroads, before his untimely death in the Civil War.[19]

Other siblings of Charles Russell Lowell in this 1800-1819 cohort were active in a broader range of occupations and fields, particularly in the sphere of culture. As a poet, Harvard professor, the first editor of the *Atlantic Monthly*, and minister to the Court of St. James in London, James Russell Lowell (1819-1891) held a central place in Boston's intellectual and cultural life in the nineteenth century.[20] He achieved fame on the basis of his individual artistic merits; but as part of a family that valued and promoted its claims to culture, he was also a central figure in the Lowell kin network. While they never matched the reputation of James Russell Lowell, sister Mary Traill Spence (Lowell) Putnam (1810-1898) was recognized as a scholar, novelist, and accomplished linguist, and brother Robert Traill Spence Lowell (1816-1891), an ordained minister, headmaster, and professor, was also known as a minor novelist and poet. His great-grandson, Robert Lowell (1917-1977) would carry on this literary tradition in the twentieth century as the most renowned of all the Lowell poets.[21]

The personal histories of members of this 1800-1819 cohort, the first to survive beyond mid-century and the period of initial economic growth in Boston, are well-known through their individual biographies. The broader purpose of their presentation here is to trace the collective significance of the individual histories, and to place the patterns of individual social and cultural prominence and growing occupational diversity in the larger framework of the Lowell kin network. Members of the 1800-1819 cohort acted both as individuals and as members of their extended families. Over the nineteenth century, while individuals gained much more personal choice over careers and marriages than their eighteenth-century predecessors had experienced, the patterns of the family as a whole nevertheless reveal a tightening of the structure of the kin network, a collective pattern that had significant economic consequences. The two interrelated facets of this pattern were occupational diversity and intermarriage.

Occupational diversity was allowable and even necessary under the new economic conditions of the nineteenth century in which the family no longer directly controlled access to elite directorships, as it had to positions within the family-business partnership. The placement of some sons or sons-in-law in positions associated with the economic elite was crucial for the family's long-term economic continuity, but in the Lowell case, three key businessmen in the pool of fourteen siblings and cousins who made up this cohort were sufficiently successful to ensure the family's economic continuity through most of the nineteenth century.[22]

The occupational diversity of other sons and sons-in-law was made possible by the active efforts of the early economic elite to expand the scope and legitimacy of the professions and other cultural pursuits. The development of professional education at Harvard and the Massachusetts Institute of Technology, the sponsorship of the Lowell Institute, and the endowment of such institutional cornerstones of Boston cultural legitimacy as the Museum of Fine Arts were part of the attempt to channel economic power to the direction and control of social, political, and cultural life in Boston. The same conditions that promoted this occupational diversity among individual members of the kin group, however, also promoted a tightening of the boundaries of the network itself. The attempt to expand the sources of power and influence through individual members of the cohort could be most effective if wealth, elite position, and prestige were contained within the sphere of family control. The Lowell response, first evident among the 1800-1819 cohort, was to reinforce its network links through close intermarriage, thereby preserving the family's economic basis for success and promoting its social prestige through insularity.

In the group of fourteen siblings and cousins in the 1800-1819 cohort of the Lowell kin network, there were a total of thirteen marriages: two-thirds of these (9 of the 13) were made within the kin network itself or to four families closely identified with the mercantile and industrial/financial elite of Boston.[23] Only the marriages of George Gardner (1809-1884) to Helen Maria Read, of Robert Traill Spence Lowell (1816-1891) to Mary Ann Duane of Schenectedy, New York, and of James Russell Lowell (1819-1891) first to Maria White and, after her death, to Frances Dunlap were outside the well-defined circle of Boston's core of elite families.

The resulting tight network structure of the interconnected Lowells and Gardners and their kin, especially prevalent among the primary economic leaders of this cohort, generated the prestige characteristic of a closed social group while it preserved wealth within the extended family for much of the nineteenth century. Despite their prestige and the early concentration of the family fortune in the first half of the nineteenth century, the Lowells did not slide from the ranks of an active economic elite into a leisured social aristocracy after 1850, as has sometimes been argued.[24] The patterns established by the 1800-1819 cohort of Lowell kin members were maintained with surprising consistency, as other successful businessmen emerged to add to the family wealth and preserve the Lowell centrality in the economic upper class through the late nineteenth and early twentieth centuries.

Economic Persistence among the Lowells and Gardners

Patterns of continued economic success amid greater occupational diversity characterized the next three cohorts of the Lowell kin network: those born in the groups of 1820-1839, 1840-1859, and 1860-1879, whose careers overlapped throughout the late nineteenth and early twentieth centuries. The rapid branching out of the Lowell kin network from the seventeen siblings and cousins of the 1800-1819 cohort and the incompleteness of genealogical and career information make a precise account of membership in the kin network over time difficult. But although my attempt to trace the occupational and marital careers of Lowell kin and their descendants probably underestimates the positions they held and connections they forged, the pattern of economic continuity and of a sustained economic basis for social, cultural, and professional prominence is clear.

The most significant Lowell kin members in the three cohorts after 1820 are presented here in their line of descent from three members of the earlier cohorts: John Amory Lowell, John Lowell Gardner, and his brother, George Gardner. The collective picture this cohort analysis reveals is that of a tightly structured, yet adaptable, kin network, which incorporated some new businessmen, diversified and expanded its reaches into the sphere of culture and the professions, and yet maintained its prestige by means of considerable social insularity over the course of the late nineteenth century.

Descendants of John Amory Lowell. In the 1820-1839 cohort of the descendants of John Amory Lowell, two sons and a son-in-law stand out as the representatives of the family's capacity for economic continuity and professional leadership.

Augustus Lowell (1830-1901) took over active management of the family's textile interests after the Panic of 1857 as treasurer of the Boott Cotton Mills and treasurer and president of the Merrimack Manufacturing Co., the Massachusetts Mills, the Lowell Bleachery, the Lowell Machine Shop, and the Glendon Iron Co. In addition he was a director of the Everett Mills, the Middlesex Co., the Lawrence Mills, the Lowell Manufacturing Co., the Cranberry Iron Co., the Plymouth Cordage Co., and president of the Boston Gas Light Co. He served as a member of the executive committee of the MHLIC, as president of the Provident Institution for Savings, as director of the Suffolk National Bank, and as trustee of the Union Trust Co. of New York.[25] These positions gave him a central connection to the nexus of industrial and financial institutions in Boston. Augustus Lowell's business talents were reputed to have increased the family fortune by sixfold or sevenfold to "its most distended proportions."[26] An R.G. Dun & Co. credit report of 1873 for

Augustus Lowell read simply: "Is a rich man—and perfectly good for all contracts he would make."[27] Also following his father's lead, Augustus Lowell extended his economic influence to the spheres of culture, education, and the professions as the second trustee of the Lowell Institute, trustee of the Museum of Fine Arts, member of the Boston School Committee, member of the Corporation and Executive Committee of the Massachusetts Institute of Technology, and trustee of the Massachusetts Eye and Ear Infirmary, among other positions.[28]

His important place in the Lowell kin network as a key businessman was aided by his marriage in 1854 to Katharine Bigelow Lawrence (b. 1832), the youngest daughter of Abbott Lawrence. By this marriage, the key Lowell economic actor of the second half of the nineteenth century forged a link to the wealth and economic connections of one of the founding Boston Associate members of the Lawrence family. This first connection between the Lowells and Lawrences was thus made at the height of both families' economic success, and by a son whose business talents were fully equal to those of his father and father-in-law. Augustus Lowell's position in Boston's economic and social elite was assured by the combination of his own talents and his succession to a wide range of key directorships. It was doubly assured through this strategic link to a father-in-law whose wealth, power, and stature in Boston at mid-century were unrivaled.

Lowell continuity in the economic upper class through the late nineteenth century was also aided by the institutional affiliations established by Arthur T. Lyman (1832-1924) who married Ella B. Lowell, daughter of John Amory Lowell.[29] Following the lead of his brother-in-law Augustus Lowell, Lyman had turned from mercantile trade to cotton manufacturing after mid-century, at the time of his marriage into the Lowell kin network. Lyman served as president of nine textile mills in the course of his career. In addition, he held key positions in the cultural, educational, and financial institutions of Boston, a pattern characteristic of the other principal Lowell economic leaders. In this capacity, Arthur T. Lyman served as an overseer of Harvard between 1892 and 1899, as president of the Boston Athenaeum between 1899 and 1915, as trustee, member of the board of investment, and vice-president of the Provident Institution for Savings between 1875 and 1915, and as director (between 1878 and 1911) and president (between 1911 and 1915) of the MHLIC.[30] His influence as an officer and director was perpetuated by the institutional affiliations of his sons, Arthur H. Lyman (b. 1861) and Ronald T. Lyman (b. 1879), whose directorships in textile firms, old and new financial intermediaries, charitable, educational, and political organizations extended to the 1930s.[31]

In the 1820-1839 cohort, another son of John Amory Lowell, John Lowell (1824-1897), maintained the family tradition of prominent careers in law as a judge whose criticism of the Dred Scott decision and subsequent appointment to the Federal District Court by Lincoln brought the Lowells national political recognition.[32]

The 1840-1859 cohort in this line produced other famous Lowells whose leadership in the professions garnered even wider recognition for the Lowell kin network. The two eldest sons of Augustus and Katharine (Lawrence) Lowell, Percival Lowell (1855-1916) and Abbott Lawrence Lowell (1856-1943, president of Harvard between 1909 and 1933), left their marks respectively on astronomy and educational administration. Nearly twenty years later, Amy Lowell (1874-1925), the youngest daughter of Augustus Lowell, added to the family cultural tradition as a poet, the first woman in the Lowell kin network to receive such recognition on her own.[33]

Through the marriage of another of Augustus Lowell's daughters, an important economic actor was added to the Lowell kin network in the 1860-1879 cohort. Elizabeth Lowell (b. 1862) married a cousin, William Lowell Putnam (b. 1861), son of George and Harriet (Lowell) Putnam. The continuity of the tight network pattern promoted by this marriage is noteworthy in light of the economic affiliations it kept within the kin network. William Lowell Putnam served as a lawyer, as well as a director of the American Telephone and Telegraph Co., the American Bell Telephone Co., the Everett Mills, the Galveston-Houston Electric Co., the Houghton County Light Co., the Tampa Electric Co., the Salmon Falls Manufacturing Co., and the Plymouth Cordage Co. He was vice-president, chairman of the executive committee, and director of the Waltham Watch Co.; vice-president of the MHLIC; director and member of the executive committee of the State Street Trust Co.; and a trustee of the Suffolk Savings Bank. In the scope of his institutional affiliations within the economic upper class by the turn of the century, he was a fitting successor to his father-in-law, Augustus Lowell.[34] The economic continuity of the Lowell kin network was thus secured into the early twentieth century, as members of the kin network moved into a new range of significant corporate directorships and offices.

Descendants of John Lowell Gardner. In the line of John Lowell Gardner, all three sons followed careers in business in the second half of the nineteenth century. Joseph Peabody Gardner (1828-1875) started out in the mercantile business of his uncle, George Gardner. In 1854 he formed a partnership with Thomas Jefferson Coolidge in the firm of Gardner and Coolidge, commission merchants.[35] Four years later his sister Julia Gardner (1841-1921) married another Coolidge brother, Joseph Randolph Coolidge (1828-1925). Within this cohort, then, there were two Coolidge brothers who married into the Lowell-Gardner kin network, and one business partnership between a Gardner and a third Coolidge brother.[36] The tight network pattern maintained by close intermarriage between the Lowells and Gardners and other core Brahmin families was also supported by Joseph Peabody Gardner's marriage to Harriet Sears Amory in 1860.

Two other sons in this 1820-1839 cohort started out in their father's mercantile firm, but expanded their business interests to railroads, finance, and industry after the Civil War. John Lowell Gardner II (1837-1898) was a director and major stockholder in the Chicago, Burlington, and Quincy Railroad and a director of the Calumet and Hecla Mining Corporation, two companies with important links to Boston capital after the Civil War.[37] Gardner was also a trustee and member of the financial committee of the Suffolk Savings Bank and a trustee and treasurer of the Museum of Fine Arts. The connection between the worlds of finance and culture was most obviously made through his marriage to Isabella Stewart. Her prominent place in Boston society and her cultural project of founding the Isabella Stewart Gardner Museum at the turn of the century, sponsored by her husband's substantial fortune, was one of the more notorious examples in this kin network of high social status and cultural prominence resting on a solid material base.

At the same time, another son-in-law of John Lowell Gardner, Francis Skinner (1840-1905), helped ensure the continuity of Lowell-Gardner wealth by leaving much of his mercantile fortune to members of the family. With bequests to the Boston Public Library, the Museum of Fine Arts, the Massachusetts General Hospital, the Harvard Medical School, and the Arnold Arboretum of Harvard University, Skinner also contributed to the expansion of Lowell-Gardner cultural claims and cultural legitimacy.[38]

The longest surviving son of John Lowell Gardner born within this cohort established a line of descendants who perpetuated the Lowell-Gardner position in the economic upper class into the twentieth century. George Augustus Gardner (1829-1916) turned his accumulated mercantile fortune to investments in railroads, banking, and real estate after the Civil War. His directorships in textile manufacturing firms and in the established institutional cornerstones of Boston finance, the MHLIC and the Provident Institution for Savings, were by now part of the family tradition. In the early twentieth century, however, George A. Gardner was also a director of the Merchants National Bank, one of the five largest in Boston in this period. He gained his greatest recognition near the end of his life for sponsoring work projects among the unemployed in South Boston during the winters of 1913 and 1914. In his obituary in the *Boston Evening Transcript*, George A. Gardner was identified as one of the ten heaviest taxpayers in Boston.[39] That the annual tax on his personal real estate was $25,000, even before an accounting of the other family properties of which he was a trustee, is one indication of his great success in maintaining his family's wealth and economic position into the twentieth century.

In the next cohort, his son, George Peabody Gardner (1855-1939) and son-in-law, Augustus Peabody Loring (1857-1938), both maintained and expanded the institutional ties that secured their place in the economic upper class. Loring was a lawyer who took over many of the Lowell-Gardner directorships in textile and industrial firms and in several of the central Boston financial intermediaries. His directorship in the Second National Bank, another of the five largest banks in Boston at the turn of the century, is indication that membership often overlapped in both established and new financial organizations at the end of the nineteenth century. George P. Gardner, through his directorships in railroads, copper companies, and the General Electric Co., in addition to banks, insurance companies, trusts, and manufacturing firms, demonstrated this capacity to gain a foothold in new corporate enterprises even more clearly.[40]

Three other lines of descent from the 1800-1819 cohort support these general patterns of continued wealth, professional achievement, and social status that had characterized the Lowell kin network over the nineteenth century. But the following cases also demonstrate that, despite the fluctuation in career choice from one cohort to the next in one family line, the kin network had great flexibility in its capacity to create and preserve the structural opportunities for economic success throughout the extended family.

Francis Cabot Lowell II and Horace Gray had been two wealthy and prominent businessmen in the Lowell kin network of the 1800-1819 cohort. Yet in neither of their cases did they produce an economic successor among the sons or sons-in-law of the next three cohorts of descendants. One of Lowell's sons was a well-known historian and his Coolidge son-in-law was a physician. The Gray sons pursued careers in law, academia, and the insurance business.[41] But the importance of the kin network in the investigation of Lowell economic continuity is clearest in the case of one branch of the family where economic placement had not been fully established in the 1800-1819 cohort.

Descendants of George Gardner. George Gardner (1809-1884), the brother of John Lowell Gardner, had not been one of the principal businessmen of his cohort, although he had a mercantile career before 1850 and later turned to the management of family property.[42] Even his marriage to Helen Maria Read was noteworthy among the members of the 1800-1819 cohort for occurring on the periphery of the Boston elite. Nevertheless, it was in his family line that economic continuity in the late nineteenth century was most firmly established. Through the marriage of his daughter, Elizabeth Gardner (1843-1930) to Charles Walter Amory (1842-1913), another significant economic actor was added to the Lowell-Gardner kin network. Rather than the direct economic link between father and son or father and son-in-law, then, the less direct links within the kin network, between uncles, cousins, and in-laws, could instead be utilized to promote a business career.

Charles W. Amory was the son of William and Anna (Sears) Amory and brother of Harriet Sears Amory who also married into the Lowell-Gardner network.[43] He began his career in manufacturing after the Civil War. Starting as a treasurer in the Amory Manufacturing Co. and the Langdon Manufacturing Co., he became one of the leading men of his generation in the manufacturing and industrial concerns of the late nineteenth century. He served as president and director of the Amoskeag, Great Falls, Cocheco, and Lawrence Manufacturing companies, the Lyman Mills, and Fifty Associates. His ties to finance included his position as vice-president and trustee of the Provident Institution for Savings, the Old Colony Trust Co., the MHLIC, the Bay State Trust Co., the Boston Block Trust of Minneapolis, the Merchants National Bank, and the Boston Manufacturer's Mutual Fire Insurance Co. In addition he held important directorships in the major new industrial corporations of the late nineteenth and early twentieth century: the American Bell Telephone Co., the American Telephone and Telegraph Co., and the Western Telephone and Telegraph Co.[44]

His children built on these important industrial and financial positions through the turn of the century. Son William Amory (b.

1869) was also director of the Amory Manufacturing Co. (1892-1897) and the Amoskeag Manufacturing Co. (1897-1907); treasurer and president of the Pepperell Manufacturing Co. (1907-1919); president of the Lewiston Bleachery; director of the MHLIC, the Old Colony Trust Co., and the Suffolk Savings Bank for Seamen and Others; and on the board of directors of various Boston hospitals. His marriage to Mary Remington Stockton (b. 1872) provided a kinship connection to her father, Howard Stockton (b. 1842), who also held multiple directorships in textile companies, banks, and insurance companies in the early twentieth century.[45]

Clara Gardner Amory (b. 1872), daughter of Charles W. Amory, married Thomas Jefferson Coolidge, Jr. (1863-1912), cofounder and first president of the Old Colony Trust Co., president of the Bay State Trust Co., vice-president and director of the National Bank of Commerce, director of the Merchants National Bank, trustee of the Suffolk Savings Bank, director of the Lawrence and Amoskeag Manufacturing companies, as well as a director of A.T.&T., Western T.&T., the General Electric Co., the Edison Electric Illumination Co. of Boston, and the United Fruit Co.[46]

Consequences of the Tight Network Structure

The names of Putnam, Lyman, Loring, Amory, Coolidge would not be readily identified as linked to the Lowell kin network without the kind of genealogical investigation that has been developed here. It is the pattern of the Lowell and Gardner close intermarriages within a limited circle of Brahmin families and the economic access such intermarriage afforded each successive cohort in this family that marks this as a successful means of preserving the family's economic continuity.

By the end of the nineteenth and beginning of the twentieth centuries, the Lowells and members of their larger kin network had retained an important place in established positions and had a foothold in key new economic institutions of Boston. The tight network pattern they had maintained over the nineteenth century through close intermarriage with cousins and within a small circle of Boston's core elite families—the Lymans, Putnams, Amorys, and Coolidges—provided the basis for Lowell-Gardner continuity in the economic upper class at the same time as it enhanced their prominence in the social upper class.

Within every cohort of sons and sons-in-law over the nineteenth

TABLE 3
Lowell-Gardner Marriages

Birth Cohorts	First-Cousin Marriages	Core Brahmin Family Marriages	Other Marriages	Total
1780-1799; 1800-1819	2	7	4	13
1820-1839	1	8	0	9
1840-1859	1	4	8	13
1860-1879	0	7	9	16
Total:	4	26	21	51
	(t = 30) [58.8%]		[41.2%]	

century, the Lowell-Gardner kin network produced new business leaders who built on the family fortune and who maintained the family's interests in textile manufacturing and in the central financial intermediaries that continued to direct economic development in Boston. By the late nineteenth century there were members of this kin network with multiple directorships in the key organizations of the Boston corporate economy, which gave them positions from which family wealth could continue to wield economic influence and power.

At the same time, the relative boundedness of the Lowell kin network allowed the preservation of the collective family wealth. While much of this wealth was undoubtedly turned to conservative investments in family trusts and served to support many nonproductive members of the kin network rather than being turned to new capital investments, the older vintage wealth of the Lowells was also continually being supplemented by newer fortunes over the nineteenth century.

The argument that the economic leadership of the early nineteenth-century Lowell and Gardner businessmen was traded for a leisured social prominence by the second half of the nineteenth century is misleading on two counts.[47] First, investigation of the kin network shows that there were successive business leaders over the nineteenth century whose collective significance was to sustain Lowell-Gardner economic continuity. Second, the social and cultural prominence attained by the Lowells was not opposed to, but an outcome of, their collectively pursued economic activities. In the Lowell-

Gardner kin network, economic and social position complemented and sustained each other.

Side by side with Lowell and Gardner businessmen throughout the nineteenth century were kin who achieved fame or prominence in the literary arts, in the academic, legal, and medical professions, and in political careers. The insularity of the tight network structure promoted social prominence by fostering a closely bounded status group based on intermarriage within a small circle of other Boston families associated with the early economic elite.

Although insular in one sense, the kin network structure also allowed for a broadening of occupational diversity. By ensuring the advantage of access to education and the important social contacts such elite education could offer, the Lowells and Gardners promoted opportunities for the professional advancement of their younger members. The encouragement of occupational diversity and cultural pursuit was an opportunity afforded by institutional expansion under the new structural conditions of the nineteenth century, and it had the consequence of adding to the cultural power, influence, and social status of the extended Lowell family.

In addition to the economic capital that supported and sustained them, the Lowell kin network accumulated "cultural capital" through the success of its prominent members.[48] The cultural hegemony of the Lowell kin network rivaled its economic influence by the late nineteenth century, but these were two parts of the same collective family pattern. As trustees, benefactors, officers, and directors of Boston's cultural and educational establishments, members of the Lowell kin network played an important role in maintaining the family's social position in nineteenth and early twentieth-century Boston. With marked continuity throughout this whole period, however, this social prominence rested on the firm material foundation of an economic upper class.

Despite the success of the Lowell-Gardner kin network in maintaining economic continuity for its members, this was not the only economic strategy that worked effectively in the nineteenth century. Among the Lawrences and Appletons there was a different structure and organization to the kinship network, with a new approach to preserving the family's economic continuity through a period of major structural change.

THE EXPANDED NETWORK STRUCTURE:
LAWRENCE AND APPLETON CASES*

A different pattern characterized Lawrence and Appleton family continuity as they made the transition from an economic elite to an upper class over the course of the nineteenth century. Unlike the close intermarriages between Brahmin families, which produced the accumulated wealth and social-cultural insularity of the Lowell kin, the Lawrences and Appletons married much more widely among newer families on the periphery of Brahmin circles in every cohort born between 1820 and 1880. Rather than developing the tight network structure of the Lowell-Gardners, then, the Lawrences and Appletons shared a pattern of expanded kin networks.

My argument in chapter three was that the key to the Lawrence and Appleton economic success in the first half of the nineteenth century had not only been in the careers of the original Boston Associates, Abbott Lawrence and Nathan Appleton, but in their strong kin networks made up of the 1780-1799 and 1800-1819 cohorts whose multiple affiliations laced together the discrete institutions of the new economic elite complex. Given the economic position, wealth, and social status that these families had achieved by the 1820-1840 period, they could have solidified their respective networks through the kind of close intermarriages characteristic of the Lowells. Although there were certainly some marriages into other families of the core Boston Brahmin elite, as in the case of the marriage of Augustus Lowell to the youngest daughter of Abbott Lawrence, this was not as common a pattern among the Lawrence and Appleton descendants as it was among the Lowells and Gardners. The Lawrence and Appleton pattern of marriages into families on the periphery of the established Boston upper class must thus be investigated as another means by which continuity could be maintained in the changing economic context of nineteenth-century Boston.

Through a different strategy but with similar consequences to the Lowell-Gardners, the Lawrences and Appletons first consolidated their position in the established economic elite during the first half of the nineteenth century, then diversified their connections to key economic institutions in the second half. My argument rests not on evidence of a consciously planned and directed strategy, but on the outcome that this expanded network pattern produced in both cases. Although some Lawrence and Appleton sons became members of a leisured social aristocracy supported by their fathers' fortunes, and although there were relatively few Lawrences or Appletons listed by those surnames in elite directorship positions in Boston by the late nineteenth century, these were not signs of the long-term economic decline of the Lawrence and Appleton families as a whole.[49] Rather, an expanded network structure was another way through which family influence could be effectively spread throughout a diversified economy. It was one alternative means by which economic continuity could be achieved, even though the prestige associated with a more circumscribed and contained social status was often sacrificed in a more dispersed kinship network.

Through reconstruction of the kin networks of these two families by cohort over the second half of the nineteenth century, the longitudinal careers of the Lawrences, Appletons, and their significant in-law descendants may be connected as part of a collective, rather than an individual, history. In this case, as was also true for the Lowell-Gardners, sons-in-law and their descendants with different surnames maintained close economic and social relationships to the core Brahmin families through the marriage connections that linked them to the Lawrence and Appleton kin networks. Starting with a firm foundation of wealth and a network of important institutional affiliations in the early era of industrial capitalism, they rapidly enlarged the boundaries of their networks and expanded the scope of their economic connections over the nineteenth century.

Network Consolidation

The most striking pattern among the early cohorts of the Lawrences and Appletons was the consolidation of their positions in the established economic elite during the first half of the nineteenth century. In chapter three the data indicated that the strong network organization of brothers and collateral kin of the original Boston Associate entrepreneurs firmly grounded the Lawrence and Appleton families in the new complex of industrial and financial institutions established between 1820 and 1840. But there were other indications of this effort of consolidation in the 1800-1819 and 1820-1839 cohorts as well.

Descendants and In-Laws of the Lawrences and Appletons. One of the most significant examples of consolidation within the Brahmin establishment was the marriage in 1842 of the primary businessman of the Lawrence 1800-1819 cohort, Amos Adams Lawrence, to Sarah Elizabeth Appleton, daughter of William Appleton. This marriage gave a formal connection to these two families whose ties of friendship and business association had prevailed since the early nineteenth century. Appleton's assessment of his new son-in-law as a "young man of good common sense, with business habits, a very safe man to trust a daughter with" was perceptive.[50] By mid-century Amos A. Lawrence was a director of ten textile corporations, the Suffolk Bank, the Provident Institution for Savings, and the manager of the Lawrence family's extensive properties. By 1860 he had established a new industry in the manufacture of knit goods in his mill in Ipswich, Massachusetts, and by 1870 his total personal property was worth nearly half a million dollars, with his charitable donations and contributions to the support of his family doubling that amount.[51]

The firm grounding of the Lawrence and Appleton kin network in the established economic elite of the first half of the nineteenth century did not rest solely on this important connection, but was further established in the 1820-1839 cohort through other marriages within the circle of Boston's most prominent families. In the family of William Appleton, the marriage of daughter Harriet Cutler Appleton to Franklin Gordon Dexter, of daughter Hetty Sullivan Appleton to Thomas Jefferson Coolidge, and of son Francis Henry Appleton to Georgiana Silsbee were all connections that linked the Lawrences to established families of the traditional mercantile and early industrial elite.[52] Similar patterns were evident among the children of Abbott Lawrence in this cohort. One daughter, as noted previously, married Augustus Lowell, the key economic successor in the Lowell family in this period. Son James Lawrence married Elizabeth Prescott, daughter of William H. Prescott, a historian descended from a colonial Boston family, and son Abbott Lawrence, Jr., married Harriet Story White Paige, daughter of James W. Paige, business partner of Nathan Appleton.[53]

A pattern of marriages within the circle of Brahmin families was only part of the strategy of kin network consolidation. The economic roles of sons and sons-in-law also helped to consolidate the position and fortunes of Appleton and Lawrence families in the first half of the nineteenth century. Amos Adams Lawrence, Augustus Lowell, Franklin Gordon Dexter, and Thomas Jefferson Coolidge were important businessmen whose successful careers as merchants and textile manufacturers ensured Lawrence and Appleton economic continuity throughout most of the nineteenth century. Among the direct Lawrence descendants, Abbott Lawrence, Jr. (1828-1893), and Francis William Lawrence (1839-1903), grandson of Amos Lawrence, also maintained affiliations with the manufacturing and industrial concerns central to the family's economic interests. Abbott Lawrence, Jr., graduated from Harvard in 1849 and received a law degree in 1863, then chose to pursue a career in business as the president and director of several corporations. In the last two years before his death in 1893 he served in the important position of actuary of the MHLIC. Francis William Lawrence was a director of the Ipswich mills of his uncle, Amos A. Lawrence, as well as a director of the Merrimack Chemical and the Globe Gaslight companies, and president of the Brookline National Bank.[54]

Economic consolidation of the Lawrences and Appletons within the ranks of the established economic elite was thus the pattern that marked these kinship networks through the first half of the nineteenth century. If this pattern of close intermarriage in the circle of prominent Boston families had predominated among all members of this and subsequent cohorts, the structure of their kin networks would have been similar to that of the Lowells by the late nineteenth century. But even as the consolidation process was underway, there were initial signs among other members of the 1820-1839 cohort of Lawrences and Appletons of a new, expanded network pattern that became increasingly important through the second half of the nineteenth century. In addition to marriages within the Boston families most closely identified with the early Brahmin elite, members of the 1820-1839 cohort began to widen the circles of their marriage connections with links to the Banker, Tucker, Sprague, Whitney, Rotch, Chapman, Daniels, Train, and Oliver families.[55]

The career of one son-in-law in the Lawrence network, Henry Austin Whitney (1826-1889), married to Fanny Lawrence, daughter of William Lawrence, best illustrates the consequences that this kind of wider marriage pattern could have. Whitney started his business career as a member of his father's large firm in the wholesale boot and shoe trade. The leather shoe industry, also native to Massachusetts and New England, was developed by entrepreneurs outside the immediate sphere of the Boston Associate textile and banking interests. Besides pioneering in this new industry, Henry A. Whitney was also instrumental in developing the steamship business between Boston and Baltimore, an important part of the expanding transportation network in the 1860s and 1870s.[56] As a director and vice-president of the Merchants and Miners' Transportation Co., and as a director of the Shoe and Leather Dealer's National Bank, Whitney belonged to the new economic institutional elite developing in this period. But in his other affiliations, as director and president for thirteen years of the Boston and Providence Railroad Corporation, director of the New England Trust Co., director (1874-1889) and president (1847-1876) of the Suffolk National Bank, and vice-president and trustee of the Provident Institution for Savings, he had important connections to established elite institutions in Boston as well.[57] Through his multiple directorships, Whitney bridged the old and new institutional structures of an expanding industrial economy.

The example of Henry A. Whitney's career is cited here as an illustration of how the expanded networks of the Lawrences and Appletons may have worked in promoting economic continuity throughout the nineteenth century. The textile industry and financial intermediaries, which were the foundation of the new elite structure in the early nineteenth century, were supplemented by the rise of new corporate industries and financial institutions throughout the nineteenth century. This expanding elite institutional complex was permeable by "new men," many of whom were from Boston families on the periphery of established Brahmin circles. While the emerging Boston social and cultural complex helped to produce a more circumscribed upper-class world over the course of the nineteenth century, the sphere of economic activities in which the upper class was involved continued to widen with the great diversification of the economy after the Civil War.

The Lawrence and Appleton pattern of wide intermarriage among these families who were linked to newer economic concerns, while they simultaneously maintained a strong center in established elite institutions in Boston, allowed them to expand the scope of their network interconnections in the second half of the nineteenth century. This is the pattern that was most characteristic of the 1840-1859 and subsequent cohorts of the Appleton and Lawrence kin networks, and it is therefore a pattern worthy of more detailed investigation.

The Widening Sphere of Intermarriage

The broad scope of the expanded network marriage patterns of the Lawrences and Appletons, and the latitude for economic continuity such a marriage strategy allowed within the kin network, was most evident in the 1840-1859 cohorts within these families. While the Lowell-Gardner network drew its new sons-in-law from within the well-defined circles of the most prominent Brahmin families of the established economic and social upper class in the second half of the nineteenth century, the Lawrence and Appleton networks expanded outward. It is within the 1840-1859 cohort that the difference between these two intermarriage strategies was most pronounced. While the outcome of one was to contain wealth and social/cultural prestige within its tight network boundaries, the other resulted in an expansion of its reach outward, maximizing affiliations to established elite institutions and, at the same time, establishing a foothold in the diversified corporate industries and financial intermediaries of the new economic complex that had developed by the late nineteenth century.

The consolidation of the Lawrence and Appleton networks in established elite institutions of the early nineteenth century provided a firm foundation for the families' economic continuity. As the lists of institutional affiliations of sons and sons-in-law attest, directorships in the textile industry and in such Brahmin establishment financial intermediaries as the Provident Institution of Savings and the MHLIC were effectively inherited over the course of the nineteenth century. But members of the Lawrence and Appleton kin networks, particularly in the 1840-1859 cohort, developed affiliations to new business enterprises in Boston over the second half of the nineteenth century as well. The diversity of marriages and careers that built this expanded network structure and contributed to long-term continuity may best be illustrated through individual representatives of this cohort. The following case study of Lawrence sons, in-laws, and their various descendants born in the 1840-1859 and 1860-1879 cohorts reflect in their collective careers the extensive spread of interconnections established throughout Boston's economy by the late nineteenth century.

Descendants of Amos Lawrence. Amory Appleton Lawrence (1848-1911), son of Amos A. Lawrence and grandson of Amos Lawrence, represented the direct line of Lawrence continuity in the economic upper class within the 1840-1859 cohort. Son of a leading businessman, he inherited directorships in the textile industry and principal Boston financial intermediaries that his father, grandfather, and great-uncles had developed and held through the first half of the nineteenth century. After his graduation from Harvard in 1870, he entered the family firm of Lawrence and Co., dry goods commission merchants, and he continued as a senior partner in this firm through the first decade of the twentieth century. In the course of his successful business career, Amory A. Lawrence was president and director of the Salmon Manufacturing Co. and the Ipswich and Gilmanton mills; a director of the Dwight, Cocheco, and Boston Manufacturing companies, the Pacific

Mills, and the Waltham Bleachery and Dye Works; a director of the Boston and Maine Railroad Co., the Maine Central Railroad, and the New York, New Haven, and Hartford Railroad Co.; a director of the Massachusetts Bank and the National Union Bank; vice-president of the Provident and of the MHLIC; an overseer of Harvard College; and an officer and director of a variety of Boston charities and associations.[58]

As this list shows, Amory A. Lawrence maintained affiliations to many of the same key industries and financial intermediaries as had his Lawrence predecessors. But his marriages reflected the expanded network pattern of the later Lawrence cohorts, even as he maintained the family's centrality in the traditional elite institutional complex. His first marriage in 1871 was to Emily Fairfax Silsbee, daughter of John Boardman and Martha Mansfield (Shepard) Silsbee. Marriage into this prominent mercantile family was a predictably appropriate match for one of the key economic successors of the Lawrence family. But Amory A. Lawrence's second marriage in 1900 to Gertrud M. Rice, daughter of Francis Blake and Sallie Blake (Austin) Rice, linked him to the wider economic interests of the Rice family, most notably in the boot and shoe manufacturing industry. His third marriage to Laura Amory Dugan was even further outside the circles of the socially recognizable Brahmin upper class.[59]

While the oldest son of Amos A. Lawrence branched out from the Brahmin establishment in his marriages, other members of the 1840-1859 cohort, in the line of descent from Amos Lawrence, demonstrated that the Lawrences remained centrally connected to families of the Boston upper class through their marriages to core Brahmin families. In the same A.A. Lawrence family, daughter Marianne Appleton Lawrence married Robert Amory, a physician and lecturer at the Harvard Medical School who retired from his practice in 1887 to serve for the next ten years as president of the Brookline Gas Co.[60] Another daughter, Sarah Lawrence, married Peter Chardon Brooks, grandson of the entrepreneur who made a fortune in marine insurance and was reputed to be the "richest man in New England" by mid-century. Peter Chardon Brooks II was a director of the Merchants Exchange Co. and Cocheco Mills, but his inherited wealth allowed him to retire from active business pursuits to lead a gentleman's life of raising horses, cattle, and sheep on his 3,000-acre estate in Medford, Massachusetts.[61]

The youngest daughter in the family of Amos A. Lawrence also married an heir to another early nineteenth-century Boston fortune that had been made through investments in Cuban sugar plantations and

Chilean copper mines and in merchandising and real estate. Harriet Dexter Lawrence's marriage to Augustus Hemenway II (b. 1853) brought an estate estimated at $3 million in real estate into the circles of the Lawrence kin network.[62]

Two other sons-in-law and a son among the children of Amos A. Lawrence in the 1840-1859 cohort had distinguished careers in the professions. William Lawrence (b. 1850) was an Episcopal minister and bishop. He married Julia Cunningham, whose brother, Frederick Cunningham (b. 1854), reciprocally married William's sister, Hetty Sullivan Lawrence, introduced previously in chapter four through the personal revelations of her journal. Cunningham practiced marine law in Boston after his graduation from the Harvard Law School in 1877.[63] From another prominent Boston family, William Caleb Loring (b. 1851) entered the Lawrence kin network in this cohort through his marriage to Susan Mason Lawrence. He was the Assistant Attorney General of Massachusetts between 1875 and 1878, a lawyer with the firm of Ropes, Gray, and Loring, general solicitor of the New York and New England Railroad between 1882 and 1885, and an Associate Justice of the Supreme Judicial Court of Massachusetts between 1899 and 1917.[64]

This pattern of marriages of Lawrence daughters into families of the Brahmin establishment undoubtedly had a similar impact on the Lawrences as it had had on the Lowell kin network: that of enhancing the prestige of the family and of ensuring its economic, social, and cultural continuity. But the Lawrences continued to marry more widely, as well.

Also included in this cohort of Lawrences through his marriage to a granddaughter of Amos Lawrence, Howard Stockton (1842-1932) combined a career as a lawyer with a wide range of directorships in institutions spread throughout the manufacturing, corporate, and financial sectors of the Boston economy in the late nineteenth century. Stockton was treasurer of the Cocheco, Salmon Falls, Merrimack, and Essex manufacturing companies; president of the Nashua and Jackson manufacturing companies; president of the American Bell Telephone Co. between 1887 and 1889; actuary of the MHLIC between 1901 and 1932; director of the Merchants National Bank, the Old Boston National Bank, the Old Colony Trust Co., the City Trust Co., and the Boston Manufacturers' Mutual Insurance Co.; as well as vice-president and director of the American Mutual Liability Insurance Co. In these positions, he secured a well-established place in the new corporate and financial institutions of Boston. As an estate trustee, a trustee of the Boston

Athenaeum, and as a member of the executive committee of the corporation of the Massachusetts Institute of Technology, Stockton also brought his legal and financial expertise to the cultural and educational institutions traditionally linked to Brahmin Boston.[65]

Lawrence economic continuity extended into the twentieth century through Stockton's children born in the 1860-1879 cohort. Lawrence Mason Stockton (b. 1871) was a lawyer with the firm of Stimson and Stockton, a director of the New England Trust Co. and the State Street Trust Co., and a clerk of the Essex Co. His brother, Philip Stockton (b. 1874), a civil engineer, held directorships in the Boston and Worcester Electric Co. and the Fall River Gas Works, in addition to directorships in several trust companies, banks, and insurance companies in Boston and, in one case, in New York.[66] Their brother-in-law, William Amory, was previously cited as a member of the Lowell kin network of this cohort. This overlap between the Lawrence and Lowell families in the late nineteenth century is another indication that, while the Lawrence network expanded outward, it also retained connections to the families in the inner circles of the Brahmin establishment.

Descendants of Samuel Lawrence. Among the in-law descendants in the line of Samuel Lawrence, Malcolm Graeme Haughton was a prime representative of the kind of "new men" who were incorporated into the Lawrence kin network in this cohort. Born in Ireland, he came to the United States and pursued a successful mercantile career in New Orleans and New York before establishing a business in Boston as a cotton buyer. His marriage to Mary Nisbet Lawrence in 1863 brought him into direct contact with the Lawrence textile interests. In this case, it is highly likely that the kin network provided effective channels for the conduct of business. Whatever the source of his business success, his firm was still thriving at the turn of the century. Two sons, Lawrence Haughton (b. 1864) and Malcolm Graeme Haughton, Jr. (b. 1864), were employed as cotton buyers in Haughton and Co. in Boston and in its expanded branches in Mississippi and Texas. Another son, Percy Duncan Haughton (b. 1876), a member of the Harvard class of 1899, was employed as a bond salesman and dealer in investment securities with the firm of E.H. Rollins and Sons. As an example of how far Boston economic interests extended in this period, it is noteworthy that the Rollins descendants, who were the principal officers in this firm at the turn of the century, also held directorships in gas and electric companies and railroads in Montana, Colorado, and Illinois.[67]

Descendants of William Lawrence. In the line of the in-law descendants of William Lawrence in the 1840-1859 cohort, Alanson Tucker (b. 1848) maintained Lawrence textile interests in the Ocean Cotton Mills of Newburyport and later as a commission merchant in the firm of Dana, Tucker, and Co.[68] Also in this line, two of the sons of Seth E. and Harriet (Lawrence) Sprague followed careers as physicians in Boston, while a third, Charles Franklin Sprague, had a distinguished career in politics as a state senator and U.S. congressman.[69] The careers of these Sprague in-law descendants added to the general professional prestige of the 1840-1859 and 1860-1879 cohorts of the Lawrence kin network. But the Lawrence connection to the Sprague family through this particular relationship also opened the kin network to a broader range of economic interests and institutional affiliations. By the turn of the century, various descendants in the Sprague family were officers and directors in new industries as diverse as shoe machinery companies, coal companies, life insurance companies, and the Boston Stock Exchange.[70] In such a case as this, the expanded kin network provided the Lawrences with personal ties to new business opportunities in a diversifying industrial economy.

Also included in this cohort and in the line of descendants from William Lawrence were the sons of Henry Austin Whitney, whose inclusion in the Lawrence kin network in the 1820-1839 cohort was previously cited as an early indication of the expanded network strategy. Son Joseph Cutler Whitney (b. 1856) was engaged in the wool commission business in Boston as a partner of George B. Drake, who was also a director of the Quartette Mining Co. In addition to Whitney's role in the management of real estate and trust properties for his family, he had interests in mining as the secretary, treasurer, and director of the Melones Mining Co. His brother, Ellerton Pratt Whitney (b. 1858), was vice-president and director of the Merchants and Miners Transportation Co., thus building on his father's lead in the transportation industry.[71]

Even more prominent as an officer and director in the transportation, mining, iron and steel, and land development industries of the early twentieth century was another Whitney relative, Henry Melville Whitney (b. 1860), who was listed as one of the millionaires of Massachusetts in 1892 and 1902 with a fortune made in railroad development and steamships.[72] The list of Whitney's positions in the first decade of the twentieth century included his presidency and directorship in the American Asbestos Co., the Kings Asbestos Mines, the New England Granite Co., the Dominion Iron and Steel Co., the Boston and

Gloucester Steamboat Co., and the Metropolitan Steamship Co.[73] Although this Whitney was not directly tied to the Lawrence network through his own marriage connection, he was part of the general dispersed network that linked the Lawrence and Whitney extended families. While such general kinship connections between two families did not necessarily have direct economic consequences, they did create a dense web of personal relationships, which could still be a potential basis for business affiliations and economic influence.

The effectiveness of the expanded network strategy was in its capacity to extend its reach into a diversified economy while retaining connections to the inner circle of Boston Brahmin families. The case of one other child of Henry A. and Fanny (Lawrence) Whitney illustrates that connection to the Lawrence kin network continued to provide access to the most prominent and well-established Boston families in the late nineteenth century. A daughter, Elizabeth Whitney, married Dr. James Jackson Minot in 1884. This marriage was an affirmation of the Whitneys' social acceptance into inner Brahmin family circles in an era when the courtship market was subject to greater institutional closure, and it was therefore a reaffirmation of the Lawrences' place in Boston's economic upper class. In the early twentieth century, members of the Minot family had substantial investments in real estate, trusts, and banking. Two of the sons of James Jackson and Elizabeth (Whitney) Minot, James Jackson Minot, Jr. (b. 1891) and Henry Whitney Minot (b. 1896), were in business respectively as an investment banker with multiple and varied directorships in industry and finance, and as a commodity importer.[74]

Descendants of Abbott Lawrence. Finally, in the line of descent from Boston Associate Abbott Lawrence, several additional in-law members of the 1840-1859 cohort may be added to this picture of the Lawrences' expanded kinship network in the late nineteenth and early twentieth centuries. Horatio Appleton Lamb (b. 1850) was in the dry good commission business in Boston, a director of the Essex Co., a financial officer in several industries and banks, a treasurer of the New England Fiber Co. and the Riverside Water Co., a trustee of the Dix Fund and the Suffolk Savings Bank, and a vice-president of the MHLIC between 1915 and 1926. His father, Thomas Lamb, descendant of a mercantile family, had been the president of the Washington Insurance Co. at mid-century. Another Lamb descendant who was a contemporary of Horatio Appleton Lamb had an even more prominent position in the institutional structure of Boston finance by the late nineteenth century. Roland O. Lamb worked his way up from bookkeeper, clerk, and secretary to become president of the John Hancock Mutual Life Insurance Co. by the first decade of the twentieth century.[75]

Strong connections to such important positions in the world of finance were crucial to Lawrence economic continuity at the turn of the century. Through the marriages of two of Abbott Lawrence's granddaughters in the 1840-1859 cohort, two sons-in-law from the Peabody family brought the full range of Peabody financial connections into the sphere of the Lawrence kin network. John Endicott Peabody (b. 1853), son of Samuel Endicott and Marianne Cabot (Lee) Peabody, graduated from Trinity College, Cambridge, in 1874. He worked for sixteen months in a commission house in Antwerp, Belgium, before beginning employment with Drexel, Morgan in New York.[76] Ties between Boston and New York financial circles were increasingly important in this period. This Peabody connection to the powerful New York bankers suggests that the Lawrence kin network was successful in expanding its geographical reach in a period in which membership in the economic upper class was increasingly interregional rather than local.

Another Peabody son in the Lawrence network, Francis Peabody, Jr. (b. 1854), also had extensive ties to finance through his directorships in New England trust companies. His father and a third brother held directorships in banks, as well as trust and insurance companies, through the turn of the century. Brother George Lee Peabody (1865-1911) was also a member of the important Boston investment banking firm of Lee, Higginson, and Co. The marriage of another Peabody in this same family, Martha Endicott Peabody, to John Lawrence (b. 1861), grandson of Abbott Lawrence, created an unusually tight kinship connection between these two families.[77] The importance of the financial connections made through the Peabody family in an era of financial capitalism should not be underestimated. As a means of maintaining economic continuity in a viable upper class, the expanded network pattern of the Lawrences provided the coordination between a wide variety of corporate industrial interests and the most important institutions of financial control at the turn of the century.

A final case among the 1860-1879 cohort of in-law descendants of Abbott Lawrence illustrates the scope of directorships across industrial and financial institutions, which provided for the economic continuity of the Lawrence kin network into the twentieth century. Reginald Foster (b. 1863) married Henrietta Story Lawrence in 1893. A graduate of

Yale and the Boston University Law School, he entered the practice of law in Boston in the firm of Foster and Turner. By the end of the first decade of the twentieth century, Reginald Foster was a director of the Boston and Albany Railroad and the Pacific Mills; a trustee of the Boston Terminal Co. and Massachusetts Electric Co., as well as of the Central Building Trust and the Pemberton Building Trust; a director of the New England Mutual Life Insurance Co. and the Old Colony Trust Co.; and a director of the United Fruit Co. His brother, Alfred Dwight Foster (b. 1852), was a lawyer and professor of law in Boston whose range of affiliations included the presidencies of the New England Mutual Life Insurance Co. and the Boston Northwest Real Estate Co., and directorships in the Fall River Gasworks Co., the New Hampshire Electric Railway, the Norwich and Worcester Railroad, the State National Bank, and the State Street Trust Co.[78]

Consequences of an Expanded Network Structure

Taken collectively, these case studies show that by the late nineteenth and early twentieth centuries the Lawrence kin network had expanded to include in-laws from a wide variety of families, in diverse occupations, with multiple institutional positions in the old and new economic organizations in Boston. The broad marital and career patterns of the Lawrences and their kin have been documented in detail here as an illustration of another kind of family strategy for continuity in the economic upper class. The pattern of an expanded network simultaneously allowed families to retain a foothold in the established elite institutions of Brahmin Boston while they expanded their reach outward to incorporate new members and their families with broader based economic interests and newer institutional affiliations.

This pattern characterized the Appleton economic continuity in addition to that of the Lawrences, and it was most likely characteristic of other Boston families in the nineteenth century as well. Patterns of wider intermarriage often render the structure of kinship networks less visible, however, with the consequence that "old families"—measured through the persistence of a single surname only—seem to disappear over time from the ranks of the economic upper class. It is only through an intensive search of genealogical records, catalogues of occupational careers, and directories of institutional affiliations that such kin networks can be reconstructed. At the beginning of this chapter, I noted that the 1905 *Directory of Directors in the City of Boston and Vicinity* lists

TABLE 4
Lawrence Marriages

Birth Cohorts	First-Cousin Marriages	Core Brahmin Family Marriages	Other Marriages	Total
1780-1799; 1800-1819	0	1	3	4
1820-1840	0	2	11	13
1840-1859	1	11	10*	22
1860-1879	0	5	6	11
Total:	1	19	30	50
	(t = 20) [40%]		[60%]	

* Seven Whitney, Sprague, Stockton, and Haughton marriages in this and the following cohort have been difficult to trace. I have counted them here as "other" because marriages that these families made within the Brahmin core are, in all other cases, readily identifiable.

only eighteen individuals with the surnames of Lowell, Jackson, Appleton, or Lawrence, one apparent indication of the decline of these families from important economic positions by the beginning of the twentieth century. In fact, however, this list includes at least one hundred ten individuals with surnames that can be linked through genealogical reconstruction to the extended Lawrence kin network alone. The processes through which the paths of the kinship network were used to channel important advice, make decisions, or use influence are much more elusive in the historical record. Nevertheless, the structure of such an expanded kinship network as that of the Lawrences provided the potential that it could be used, particularly to further family-based class interests during a period of significant social change.

In response to another frequently cited argument about the eclipse of family-based or class-based power in the United States, the expanded network pattern of the Lawrences suggests how continuity in the economic upper class could be fully consistent with an expanding economy and increased opportunities for social mobility into the ranks of the economic elite. New industries brought "new men" into positions of economic power and influence through the nineteenth century and into the twentieth, and a kinship network such as that of the Lawrences adapted by expanding to incorporate them. The consistency with which sons, sons-in-law, and their descendants in successive cohorts of the

Lawrence kin network retained a position in the economic upper class speaks more to a collective pattern of economic placement than it does to the independent success of individuals. Such sustained placement among the Lowells, Lawrences, and Appletons was a sign of an effective class strategy, produced through different family responses to nineteenth-century economic change.

Despite the differentiation process, which increasingly separated the institutional spheres of family and economy in the nineteenth century, Boston Brahmin families retained a means of economic control through their overlapping kinship and business interconnections. The ability of some of the descendants of the original Boston Associates to retain positions in the economic upper class through the second half of the nineteenth century, a period of major structural transformation in the U.S. economy, suggests the crucial role that families, as viable economic units, played in forging a more entrenched kind of class continuity. This analysis provides one piece of the larger genealogical research necessary for understanding the structures and processes through which an industrial capitalist economy developed. The continuing importance of the family as an economic institution in a corporate economy is suggested by looking at the Brahmin connections to some new industries in early twentieth-century Boston.

Chapter 6

KINSHIP AND CLASS:
INTO THE TWENTIETH CENTURY

Boston Brahmin families were remarkably successful in securing their place in the economic upper class through the end of the nineteenth century. As new corporate industries with more complex organizational forms developed in the early twentieth century, however, it seemed less likely that they could continue to play a significant role in economic development. It is in this era, in particular, that the managerial revolution seemed to threaten the capacity of upper-class families to maintain control over the direction of economic development. The rise of new corporate, Boston-based industries and the development and expansion of a new kind of financial intermediary institution, the investment banking firm, are two important examples of new organizations that emerged in this era, and it is in their history that the continued economic function of upper-class Boston families should be assessed.

THE BOSTON UPPER CLASS IN A CORPORATE ECONOMY

In the late nineteenth century, Boston took the lead in the development of several new corporate industries in the American economy.

After World War I the leading role in industrial development would be taken over by New York and other cities, although Boston would maintain its economic importance as a center of finance.[1] In the early development of such new corporations as the American Bell Telephone Co. and General Electric, however, there were still important patterns of family and business interconnections to be seen.

The telephone industry developed in progressive stages through a series of companies: National Bell Telephone in 1878, American Bell Telephone in 1880, and a major new subsidiary with long-distance lines, American Telephone and Telegraph, in 1885.[2] At the center of this development was the Boston Brahmin, William Hathaway Forbes (1840-1896), son of John Murray Forbes who had made a family fortune in the China trade and in the development of the railroads. William Forbes was a friend and associate of Henry Lee Higginson and other men at the center of the Boston economic upper class in the late nineteenth century.[3] When the original investors in the Bell patent, Gardiner Greene Hubbard and Thomas Sanders, needed funds for the national expansion of the New England telephone system they had developed, they turned to William Forbes who coordinated the funds from Boston investors and became president of the company. By 1880 the American Bell Telephone Co. had a monopoly on the nation's telephone industry, and this monopoly was effectively controlled by the Boston officers and directors and their relatives who owned over fifty percent of the stock.[4]

The officers and directors of the company were all men who were firmly rooted in Boston's established economic upper class with many ties of kinship to one another. President and director William H. Forbes was connected through an intricate kin network to vice-president and director, Charles Pickering Bowditch (1842-1921), and to director Charles Elliot Perkins (1840-1907). Within the 1860-1879 Forbes cohort, another son married a daughter of Alexander Cochrane (1840-1919), thus linking this Bell Telephone Co. director to the Forbes family by ties of kinship as well as business.[5]

Several sons-in-law in the Lowell-Gardner kin network, Charles Walter Amory, William Lowell Putnam, Charles Pickard Ware, and Howard Stockton, were directors in the new telephone industry and representative of the Brahmin capitalists and financiers who led the development of this industry in its formative decades.[6] The institutional centrality of many sons, sons-in-law, cousins and nephews in industry and finance at the turn of the century suggests that wealth and family ties still helped provide access to economic power, even under the new institutional conditions that characterized the transformation to an advanced industrial economy.

Through the first decades of the twentieth century, even as new managers such as Theodore N. Vail (1845-1920) took over the presidency of American Bell Telephone and A.T.& T. with the financial backing of New York financiers, Bostonians continued to hold over half of the directorships in A.T.& T., which had been reorganized as the parent company of the telephone industry.[7] In the scope of their individual industrial and financial connections spread throughout the new corporate economy, these Bostonians represented much more economic influence and control over the development of the new institutional structure of the corporate economy than the group of Boston Brahmins have usually been granted. The leadership role of Boston financiers was a significant one in a number of other new industrial corporations in the last decades of the nineteenth and first decade of the twentieth centuries.

In the General Electric Co. and the United Fruit Co., two additional Boston-based corporations, there were also members of the Boston upper class on the boards, although in these cases they were in the minority. General Electric, which was incorporated in 1892 from the merger of the Edison General Electric Co. and the Thomson-Houston Co., was headed by Charles A. Coffin (1844-1926) who had started his career in shoe manufacturing in Lynn, Massachusetts.[8] Coffin was not a member of the inner circle of the Boston economic upper class, but through the presidency of General Electric he coordinated the new administrative means of corporate control. Directors Henry Lee Higginson, Thomas Jefferson Coolidge, Jr., and Oliver Ames were the representatives of the well-entrenched Boston upper class who served as advisors on the board of this new corporation. Their knowledge of administrative methods in the development of the railroad industry was crucial in helping to organize the administrative structure of this company.

Of the sixteen men who served as directors of this company for five or more years between 1893 and 1910, eight were prominent members of the Boston economic upper class.[9] More important than their numbers on the board of directors were their multiple affiliations, especially to Boston banks and financial intermediary institutions. Six of the eight men were officers or directors of the Old Colony Trust Co.; two were directors of the National Shawmut Bank, the largest Boston bank in terms of capital assets between 1900 and 1915; two were directors of the Merchants National Bank; one was a director of the State National Bank.[10] In addition to these interlocks between Boston banks and General Electric, this group of eight men held positions in a variety of trust companies, insurance companies, and savings banks in Boston and Massachusetts more generally, which spread their access to other financial intermediaries even wider. If the channels of access to sources of Boston capital are measured by kin networks, rather than by individual financial affiliations only, this pattern of interlocks was even denser and more extensive.

While New York financiers were the dominant controlling interests on the board of General Electric, then, the institutional base of the Boston financiers should not be underestimated. In addition to the internal links of their Boston business affiliations, there were other signs of the overlap between the circles of Boston and New York finance. By the first decades of the twentieth century, most of these Bostonians belonged to New York as well as to Boston social clubs, and there were more marriages into New York and Washington families, in addition to Boston alliances.[11] Such patterns suggest that the financial institutional base of a corporate economy was becoming more national in scope in this period.

Similar patterns of connections to Boston financial intermediaries were true of directors of the United Fruit Co., organized by the merger of New York and Boston fruit importers in 1899. Thomas Jefferson Coolidge, Jr., had been one of the key men in creating the merger. Thus the overlapping connections between the United Fruit Co. and the Old Colony Trust Co., which Coolidge had cofounded with his father in 1890, were very extensive by 1905, with six of United Fruit's fourteen directors linked to this important financial intermediary institution.[12]

There were other such direct ties to Boston financial institutions through multiple directorships, as well as to Brahmin families through intermarriage. Reginald Foster was one such in-law member of the Lawrence kin network who served as a director in the United Fruit Co. The directorships within American Bell Telephone and A.T.& T., General Electric, and the United Fruit companies suggest that the traditional bases of economic power and control—wealth and family connections—had not been fully replaced by new managerial criteria in the shift to a new corporate economy.

Some indication of the combined significance of multiple institutional affiliations and kin relationships within this new corporate economy of early twentieth-century Boston may be suggested by the overlapping ties in the ten largest corporations and five largest banks in Boston in 1905.[13] Sidney Wilmot Winslow (1854-1917) was president of the United Shoe Machinery Co. and a director of the U.S. Mining Co. and the First National Bank. As the officer and director in many gas and electric companies, principal owner of the *Boston Herald* and *Boston Traveller* newspapers, and a director of Old Colony Trust, he had a foothold in new and old institutions in Boston's economy. He was cited, at the time of his death, as "a conspicuous figure in the economic affairs of the nation."[14] He represented many Bostonians in this period whose multiple positions as officers and directors interlocked some of the largest corporate industries and financial institutions in the region.

The well-established pattern of dense corporate and financial interlocks created by the multiple positions of upper-class individuals and kin members was still characteristic of the new institutional structure of the economy in the early twentieth century. But Boston Brahmins also created a new institutional response to the demands of a more rationalized economy. The organization of the investment banking firm was one such institutional development through which Boston's position as an important center of finance into the twentieth century may be seen.

THE NEW INSTITUTIONAL RESPONSES OF BOSTON FINANCE

By 1880 Boston was one of the most important centers of finance in the United States. The development of a financial infrastructure, which had been the institutional response of the Boston Associates to changing economic conditions in the 1820s, had successfully supported the growth of the textile industry, railroads, midwestern mining, and real estate development. But in the last two decades of the nineteenth century there were strong indications that this financial institutional base was no longer adequate to the needs of a changing economy.

The great proliferation of commercial banks, numbering sixty-two in Boston's population of four hundred fifty thousand in 1889, as contrasted with forty-five New York banks in a population of a million and a half, led to increased competition, more speculative policies, and bank failures in the decade of the 1890s.[15] The earlier strategy for the mobilization of capital, through which men in key positions in Boston's financial intermediaries were able personally to direct the flow of institutional funds to the textile industry, was no longer fully viable in a

greatly expanded and diversified economy, despite the personal interconnections that continued to link discrete organizations in the economy. The growth of the economy through most of the nineteenth century had depended on the assurance of fixed capital.[16] With the
structural transformation and new expansive capacity of the corporate
economy by the end of the nineteenth century, the need for a new basis
of capital accumulation and more flexible means of capital mobilization became paramount.

One response was the growth of an industrial securities market.
By the early 1890s, industrial securities began to be listed on the Stock
Exchange and leading brokerage houses began trading them. Public
confidence in this securities market was enhanced by the reliability of
preferred stock, which also ensured that owner control could be maintained intact.[17] But the key institutional innovation in this industrial
securities market was the investment banking firm that mediated
between investors and companies and offered a greatly expanded
capacity for capital accumulation and mobilization. In Boston, where
public confidence in industrial securities had been well-established in
railroad investments, investment banking firms met the new economic
needs of the era with an institutional response that combined innovative
and traditional aspects of the financial intermediary organization.[18]

The two most important investment banking firms in Boston, Lee,
Higginson and Co., and Kidder, Peabody and Co., had been organized
in an earlier period as family-run firms. In the case of Lee, Higginson,
John Clarke Lee and his cousin by marriage, George Higginson, formed
a partnership as brokers in 1848. By 1868 they had expanded to include
their sons, George Cabot Lee, Henry Lee Higginson, Francis Lee Higginson, and a brother-in-law, Henry Lee.[19] In the years after the Civil
War, the firm's business of marketing securities was expanded to
include the important banking function of extending capital for economic growth and expansion, in addition to investment advising. With
such multiple functions, the investment banking firm promoted a new,
more fluid, flow of capital through the corporate economy.[20]

According to the historian of Lee, Higginson, and Co., two prin-
ciples guided the company's purchase of new securities: the determi-
nation of real economic need in a new project or company, and the cal-
iber and trustworthiness of the men involved in it.[21] Given the central
position of the Lees and the Higginsons in Boston's economic upper
class, trustworthiness could be assessed on the basis of personal knowledge through ties of kinship and friendship. Lee, Higginson's involve-

ment in the profitable Calumet and Hecla Copper Mine, for example, was assured by Henry Lee Higginson's close relationship as the brother-in-law of the organizers of this venture, Quincy Adams Shaw and Alexander Agassiz.[22]

In this period the firm also helped finance two railroads: the Chicago, Burlington, and Quincy, whose development had been led by Bostonian John Murray Forbes, and the Atchinson, Topeka, and Santa Fe. Lee, Higginson's involvement in the American Bell Telephone Co. and General Electric was led by Henry Lee Higginson and his new partner, Gardiner Martin Lane, who maintained a close association with other directors on these boards. In 1908, Lee, Higginson, and Co., under the direction of another new manager and Boston Brahmin, James Jackson Storrow, led in the development of the automobile industry through the financing of General Motors. Kidder, Peabody, and Co., with close ties to New York and European finance, was also at the forefront of the major industrial development of the period.[23]

The combination of astute investments in new industries and the interconnections between Lee, Higginson partners and other members of the economic upper class in this period led to a new use of family and personal ties in the conduct of business. There are examples of the use of these personal ties to promote economic influence and control in the manuscript collection of the Lee, Higginson company papers. In an exchange of letters between Henry Lee Higginson and William Madison Wood (director, treasurer, and vice-president of the American Woolen Co.), for example, there was strong indication of Higginson's attempt to influence the composition of the board of directors of that company. The attempt in this case was unsuccessful, as Wood's response indicated:

> My board of directors is full and as far as I know a vacancy is not likely to occur at present, and should a vacancy exist I can give you no assurance that it will be agreeable to the members of my board of directors to add any person of my selection. In my experience, I have never known such persistent efforts to acquire a seat on a board of directors where no vacancy exists.[24]

But in other cases these channels of personal influence proved more effective as a means of influencing decisions. In a letter to C.A. Coffin, president of General Electric, Henry L. Higginson threatened withdrawal from the board if "a very objectionable man . . . a regular wirepuller, not to be trusted" were included among the G.E. directors.[25] Higginson's letters of recommendation, written in confidence to close friends, kin, and business associates in Boston's principal economic institutions, also attempted to promote the entrance of young men into elite institutional positions, based solely on their Brahmin family connections. Of Augustus P. Gardner he wrote:

> He is a gentleman of means, thirty years old, a member of the Gardner family here. He lives at Hamilton, has no regular business, but has a very regular business mind and much wishes work. Whenever he gets it, he does it well—has a hard head, a pleasant manner, absolute integrity, great courage and calmness, and is constantly in company with his two uncles, who are really able men of business. He is the kind of man who will serve you well as a director.

Charles Francis Adams II, as well, was worthy of Higginson's recommendation as: "a man of mark—both on account of his brain and his character. He also would absolutely fill the bill. You manage so well that I wish to help you in all ways—and I believe in young men."[26] In these sons of Boston Brahmin families, Henry Lee Higginson found the appropriate personal qualities and social and economic connections that he had reason to believe were effective resources in business.

While an investment banking firm such as Lee, Higginson, and Co. used the traditional lines of kinship and personal influence to gain wider leverage over economic development in Boston, its institutional centrality to the Boston economic upper class was also important in another respect. Boston families had confidence in the financial advice and investment strategies of this firm, and they began to diversify their holdings in the late nineteenth century, in particular by selling the companies in which their family fortunes had been made.[27] While this trend has been variously interpreted as the final stage in the progressive undermining of family capitalism or the transfer of family ownership to managerial control and widespread stock ownership, it could also be interpreted as a rational response to the new requirements of a diversified corporate economy and as part of a broader economic strategy.

For families of the economic upper class who had established such a firm foothold in this new corporate economy through their own directorships and positions of influence, the strategy of making their assets more readily available for investments in large-scale, expanding industries was well within the scope of their economic interests. Although the economic upper class lacked the kind of direct means of shaping this new economic institutional structure that they had had in the 1820s, the continued pattern of indirect control through networks of family and friends had proved to be an effective way to act in the interests of their continuity as a class.

The corporate growth of Boston-based industries and the mediation of economic change by Brahmin financiers in investment banking firms was the background against which Brahmin families such as the Lowells and Lawrences maintained their economic continuity. In this period of fundamental structural change in the American economy, between 1880 and 1910, there were both traditional and new institutional responses forged by the Boston economic upper class. Inheritance of wealth and property was not the sole means of gaining access to positions of power and control under these new economic conditions. But inherited wealth and family background did continue to provide an important measure of access to positions of economic power and influence—one that has been underestimated in the case of many of the sons and sons-in-law of Boston Brahmin families. The economic upper class, made up of those families who had maintained their continuity through the first decade of the twentieth century, coexisted with the rise of a new economic elite. In the growth of a diversified economy there was always room and need for "new men" in the expanded elite structure.[28] Some of these new businessmen were incorporated into the ranks of established upper-class families through intermarriage, with the consequence that established Brahmin families gained a wider access to new business opportunities and fortunes.

A fuller account of the means by which Boston Brahmins maintained their viability as an economic upper class well into the twentieth century would require another study, with access to different kinds of sources than have been used to trace this history through the nineteenth century. Most family genealogies were produced by descendants in the late nineteenth and early twentieth centuries, a period in which intense concern with family and class solidarity was also reflected in the publication of numerous memoirs and such catalogues of upper-class membership as *The Social Register*. Tracing intermarriages and kinship interconnections forward into the present, rather than backward to an original ancestor, would require the use of sources other than genealogies. Similarly, many contemporary business records are closed to researchers, while family assets are notoriously difficult to trace. Ultimately, what this study can do is to point to the importance of under-taking the challenge of continued research on twentieth-century family and class patterns. What it does suggest is that, despite the new require-ments and changing opportunity structure produced by the transition to an advanced industrial economy in the early twentieth century, kin-ship remained an important basis of class position and economic conti-nuity in Boston.

CONCLUSION

The dynamics of family strategies, consolidation of a class structure, and economic transformation are all analytically distinguishable and autonomous aspects of the process of social change. But the subject of this book has been their interrelationship, which generally has been ignored in the sociological literature on stratification, in economic models of business organization, and in the historical study of American society.

The standard periodization and interpretation of economic change in the nineteenth century adopted by economic historians has most often followed the model of structural differentiation in which there was a "traditional" period of family and business overlap, a "transitional" period in the early nineteenth century in which a new institutional structure was developed to meet the expanded needs of entrepreneurs and family firms in an early industrial economy, and a "modern" period in the late nineteenth century in which the family was seen as irrevocably severed from its command over the process of economic production and over other forms of power and control. Other historians and sociologists have referred to periods of "family capitalism," "financial capitalism," and "managerial capitalism," usually following the logic of an economic imperative directing these stages of social change.

The emphasis in this book has been on reinterpreting this model from the perspective that Boston's most economically powerful families were active and autonomous participants in this process of change. They were active agents because they shared consolidated group interests, which made them likely to attempt to direct or exploit the opportunities such new conditions presented. The structural mechanism that allowed for some autonomy in the family's economic response to new conditions was the kin network.

In the early period of economic development, the kin network laced together new, discrete organizations as the basis of continued family control and influence. Reconstruction of these kin networks over time makes visible the patterned ways in which families attempted to turn their position in the economic elite in one period into economic continuity rooted in the structure of an economic upper class.

Not all Boston Brahmin families were successful in this attempt, nor did all successful families produce the same pattern as they worked to preserve their economic position. At least two patterns by which the economic continuity of the Lowell and Lawrence kin networks was achieved through the early twentieth century may be identified. Reconstructed kin networks illustrate different patterns, with different consequences, which may have been representative of other families of Boston in this period as well. By marrying closely within an identifiable core elite group to preserve wealth and social status or by marrying more widely to attract new businessmen into the family circle, Brahmin families retained a solid material base for their social and cultural status.

In their successful patterns of economic continuity, Boston families not only held onto a place in the established institutional structure, but they also moved into positions as officers and directors of new industries and financial intermediaries by the period of transition to a new corporate economy, between 1880 and 1910. This is not to claim that all members of the new economic elite in that period were drawn from the ranks of an entrenched economic upper class. But the capacity of sons, sons-in-law, nephews, cousins, and grandsons of Boston Brahmin families to gain a foothold in the new corporate economy was greater than has generally been conceded. In two kinds of institutional transformation characteristic of the early twentieth century—the growth of new corporate industries and the coordination of economic control by investment banking firms as powerful financial intermediaries—kinship and personal ties continued to play an important role, even under conditions of administrative changes in the organization of business firms and of rationalized demands for an expanded and more fluid basis of capital formation.

Two types of networks connected the institutions and individual members of the economic elite in Boston in the late nineteenth century. Interlocking directorates, created by one individual's multiple positions, were one source of personal coordination between institutions. But the significance of even these dense webs of connections linked through one individual has been an ongoing debate in the stratification literature, subject to considerable difference of interpretation. Thus, the second type of network—one created by extended family ties—which laced together a complex economic, social, and cultural institutional structure by weaving kinship connections within and among organizations is significant on two counts.

First, the kin network coordinated economic alliances, which were even more extensive than the multiple affiliations of any one individual. The channels of personal interconnections it created were often less visible than interlocking directorates, but more crucial to an understanding of the kind of economic power and control that could be maintained through the structure of the family.

Second, kin networks are significant in showing how patterns of elite control could be extended over time. They add a dynamic aspect to the analysis of power and influence as rooted in the multigenerational structure of the family rather than in the career of one individual. The kin network, complementing and overlaying the picture of interlocking directorates in one period, allows us to move beyond the analysis of the behavior of individuals to the significant patterns of groups and their collective strategies. To return to Schumpeter's insight noted in chapter one, genealogical research on families contributes to a more nuanced understanding of the structures and processes through which a capitalist class has developed.

Study of family alliances and continuity plays an important role in terms of expanding our understanding of social class and power as well. The critique of the importance of social class and family continuity in American society has rested on two claims: that of a revolution in the mode of access to power, and that of a revolution in the nature of power-holding itself. Although family background did not and could not fully determine access to the most important directorships and officer positions in a period of economic expansion and transformation, wealth and family position did continue to matter in economically significant ways throughout the nineteenth century and into the twentieth. At the very least, wealth and family connections were resources that lubricated access to power and economic control in the new economy. The entrance of sons and sons-in-law of wealthy and well-connected Boston families into new elite institutions at the turn of the century was evidence of the family's capacity to make use of these changing economic circumstances in the interests of its own continuity as part of an economic upper class.

The second claim, that power began to depend more on technical skill than on property by the late nineteenth century, is undeniably true, but overstated, as a claim for the fundamental revolution in the class structure of American society. Technical skills were also prevalent among sons and sons-in-law of the Boston upper class, as many of the occupational histories of later cohorts in these families showed. Access to elite educational institutions, which was still the prerogative of sons and sons-in-law of the wealthy in the nineteenth century, ensured that they would continue to be trained for leadership roles in new and old professional specializations. The organizational changes in managerial hierarchies and administrative structures of business firms, which were increasingly necessary in the new corporate economy of the late nineteenth century, have been overstated, at least in the case of Boston, as representing the severing of management from ownership control. The important Boston financiers in the 1880 to 1910 period, often men whose interests were also based on a concern for family persistence, mediated the development of the corporate economy with some new institutional responses, which expanded their potential for influence and control.

Finally, the structural analysis of kinship networks also requires complementary investigation of the process through which they were maintained. The resiliency of families as economic units was not inevitable, but one consequence of women's important but little recognized role as kin-keepers. Relegated to their "separate sphere," women have frequently been missing from the accounts of economic history. Analysis of both the public and private uses of the family shows how these were mutually reinforcing spheres, rather than separate ones. Men and women of the upper class, in particular, shared an interest in using the family as a resource for economic continuity, and they worked in complementary ways toward this end. The scholarly research of family historians and women's historians over the past several decades has great potential for transforming the traditional approaches of sociologists and economists, particularly in illuminating how private life penetrated even the most public arenas.

The significance of patterns within a particular community ultimately rests on the capacity to generalize from that one case. Boston undoubtedly had unique features that encouraged its longer persistence of kinship control over economic activities. Its early industrial base supported an older, well-established economic elite. Its importance as a center of finance led to different requirements under conditions of structural economic transformation. But as a single case, it illustrates the extent to which kinship and class have been underestimated as important variables in the process of economic change over the course of the nineteenth century. From this perspective, the structure of kin networks and the kind of economic strategies that promoted the class continuity of Boston families have a broader significance as part of a more complex model of the dynamics of social change in American society.

Appendix

GENEALOGICAL CHARTS OF THE LOWELLS, LAWRENCES, APPLETONS, AND JACKSONS

LOWELL GENEALOGY

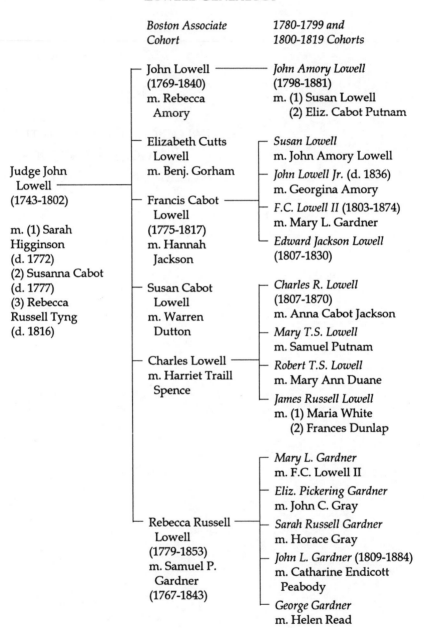

Boston Associate
Cohort

1780-1799 and
1800-1819 Cohorts

John Lowell ——— *John Amory Lowell*
(1769-1840)   (1798-1881)
m. Rebecca   m. (1) Susan Lowell
Amory   (2) Eliz. Cabot Putnam

Elizabeth Cutts   *Susan Lowell*
Lowell   m. John Amory Lowell
m. Benj. Gorham   *John Lowell Jr.* (d. 1836)
                                     m. Georgina Amory

Judge John
Lowell
(1743-1802)

Francis Cabot ———   *F.C. Lowell II* (1803-1874)
Lowell   m. Mary L. Gardner
(1775-1817)
m. Hannah   *Edward Jackson Lowell*
Jackson   (1807-1830)

m. (1) Sarah
Higginson
(d. 1772)
(2) Susanna Cabot
(d. 1777)
(3) Rebecca
Russell Tyng
(d. 1816)

Susan Cabot   *Charles R. Lowell*
Lowell   (1807-1870)
m. Warren   m. Anna Cabot Jackson
Dutton
                                Mary T.S. Lowell
                                 m. Samuel Putnam

Charles Lowell ———   *Robert T.S. Lowell*
m. Harriet Traill   m. Mary Ann Duane
Spence
                                  James Russell Lowell
                                   m. (1) Maria White
                                        (2) Frances Dunlap

Mary L. Gardner
m. F.C. Lowell II

Eliz. Pickering Gardner
m. John C. Gray

Rebecca Russell ———   *Sarah Russell Gardner*
Lowell   m. Horace Gray
(1779-1853)
m. Samuel P.   *John L. Gardner* (1809-1884)
Gardner   m. Catharine Endicott
(1767-1843)   Peabody

George Gardner
m. Helen Read

Lowell-Gardners: 1820-1839 Cohort

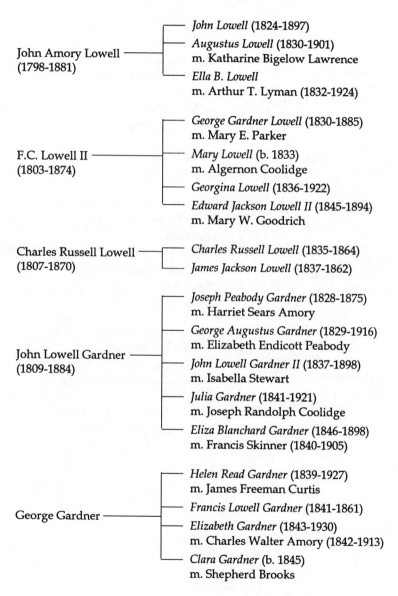

John Amory Lowell
(1798-1881)

- *John Lowell* (1824-1897)
- *Augustus Lowell* (1830-1901)
  m. Katharine Bigelow Lawrence
- *Ella B. Lowell*
  m. Arthur T. Lyman (1832-1924)

F.C. Lowell II
(1803-1874)

- *George Gardner Lowell* (1830-1885)
  m. Mary E. Parker
- *Mary Lowell* (b. 1833)
  m. Algernon Coolidge
- *Georgina Lowell* (1836-1922)
- *Edward Jackson Lowell II* (1845-1894)
  m. Mary W. Goodrich

Charles Russell Lowell
(1807-1870)

- *Charles Russell Lowell* (1835-1864)
- *James Jackson Lowell* (1837-1862)

John Lowell Gardner
(1809-1884)

- *Joseph Peabody Gardner* (1828-1875)
  m. Harriet Sears Amory
- *George Augustus Gardner* (1829-1916)
  m. Elizabeth Endicott Peabody
- *John Lowell Gardner II* (1837-1898)
  m. Isabella Stewart
- *Julia Gardner* (1841-1921)
  m. Joseph Randolph Coolidge
- *Eliza Blanchard Gardner* (1846-1898)
  m. Francis Skinner (1840-1905)

George Gardner

- *Helen Read Gardner* (1839-1927)
  m. James Freeman Curtis
- *Francis Lowell Gardner* (1841-1861)
- *Elizabeth Gardner* (1843-1930)
  m. Charles Walter Amory (1842-1913)
- *Clara Gardner* (b. 1845)
  m. Shepherd Brooks

Lowell-Gardner Family: 1840-1859 and 1860-1879 Cohorts

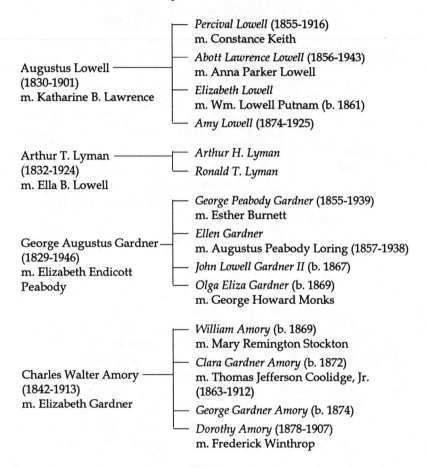

Augustus Lowell
(1830-1901)
m. Katharine B. Lawrence

- *Percival Lowell (1855-1916)*
  m. Constance Keith
- *Abott Lawrence Lowell (1856-1943)*
  m. Anna Parker Lowell
- *Elizabeth Lowell*
  m. Wm. Lowell Putnam (b. 1861)
- *Amy Lowell (1874-1925)*

Arthur T. Lyman
(1832-1924)
m. Ella B. Lowell

- *Arthur H. Lyman*
- *Ronald T. Lyman*

George Augustus Gardner
(1829-1946)
m. Elizabeth Endicott
Peabody

- *George Peabody Gardner (1855-1939)*
  m. Esther Burnett
- *Ellen Gardner*
  m. Augustus Peabody Loring (1857-1938)
- *John Lowell Gardner II (b. 1867)*
- *Olga Eliza Gardner (b. 1869)*
  m. George Howard Monks

Charles Walter Amory
(1842-1913)
m. Elizabeth Gardner

- *William Amory (b. 1869)*
  m. Mary Remington Stockton
- *Clara Gardner Amory (b. 1872)*
  m. Thomas Jefferson Coolidge, Jr.
  (1863-1912)
- *George Gardner Amory (b. 1874)*
- *Dorothy Amory (1878-1907)*
  m. Frederick Winthrop

LAWRENCE GENEALOGY

Boston Associate Cohort   *1800-1819 and 1820-1839 Cohorts*

Luther Lawrence
(1778-1839)

William Lawrence ———————— *Fanny Lawrence*
(1783-1848)   m. Henry Austin Whitney (1826-1889)

Amos Lawrence ———————┬— *William Richards Lawrence* (1812-1885)
(1786-1852)   │   m. Susan Coombs Dana
m. Sarah Richards   ├— *Amos Adams Lawrence* (1814-1886)
                                               │   m. Sarah Elizabeth Appleton
                                               └— *[daughter?]*

                                               ┌— *Anna Lawrence*
                                               │   m. Benjamin Rotch
Abbott Lawrence ———————┼— *James Lawrence*
(1792-1855)   │   m. Elizabeth Prescott
m. Katharine Bigelow   ├— *Abbott Lawrence, Jr.* (1828-1893)
                                               │   m. Harriet Story White Paige
                                               └— *Katharine Bigelow Lawrence* (b. 1832)
                                                   m. Augustus Lowell (1830-1901)

Samuel Lawrence
(1801-1880)

Lawrence Family: 1840-1859 Cohort

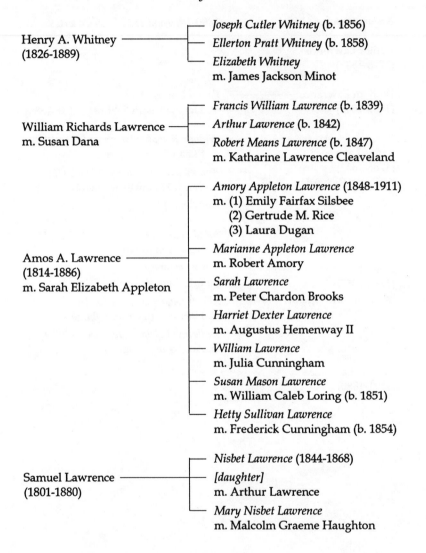

Henry A. Whitney
(1826-1889)
— *Joseph Cutler Whitney* (b. 1856)
— *Ellerton Pratt Whitney* (b. 1858)
— *Elizabeth Whitney*
  m. James Jackson Minot

William Richards Lawrence
m. Susan Dana
— *Francis William Lawrence* (b. 1839)
— *Arthur Lawrence* (b. 1842)
— *Robert Means Lawrence* (b. 1847)
  m. Katharine Lawrence Cleaveland

Amos A. Lawrence
(1814-1886)
m. Sarah Elizabeth Appleton
— *Amory Appleton Lawrence* (1848-1911)
  m. (1) Emily Fairfax Silsbee
     (2) Gertrude M. Rice
     (3) Laura Dugan
— *Marianne Appleton Lawrence*
  m. Robert Amory
— *Sarah Lawrence*
  m. Peter Chardon Brooks
— *Harriet Dexter Lawrence*
  m. Augustus Hemenway II
— *William Lawrence*
  m. Julia Cunningham
— *Susan Mason Lawrence*
  m. William Caleb Loring (b. 1851)
— *Hetty Sullivan Lawrence*
  m. Frederick Cunningham (b. 1854)

Samuel Lawrence
(1801-1880)
— *Nisbet Lawrence* (1844-1868)
— *[daughter]*
  m. Arthur Lawrence
— *Mary Nisbet Lawrence*
  m. Malcolm Graeme Haughton

Lawrence Family: 1860-1879 Cohort and Beyond

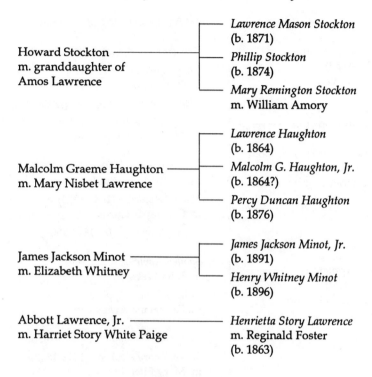

Howard Stockton
m. granddaughter of
Amos Lawrence

— *Lawrence Mason Stockton*
(b. 1871)

— *Phillip Stockton*
(b. 1874)

— *Mary Remington Stockton*
m. William Amory

Malcolm Graeme Haughton
m. Mary Nisbet Lawrence

— *Lawrence Haughton*
(b. 1864)

— *Malcolm G. Haughton, Jr.*
(b. 1864?)

— *Percy Duncan Haughton*
(b. 1876)

James Jackson Minot
m. Elizabeth Whitney

— *James Jackson Minot, Jr.*
(b. 1891)

— *Henry Whitney Minot*
(b. 1896)

Abbott Lawrence, Jr.
m. Harriet Story White Paige

— *Henrietta Story Lawrence*
m. Reginald Foster
(b. 1863)

Appleton Genealogy

Boston Associate Cohort	*1800-1819 and 1820-1839 Cohorts*

Samuel Appleton
(1766-1853)
m. Mary Gore

Nathan Appleton ————
(1779-1861)
m. (1) Maria Theresa Gold
(1786-1833)
(2) Harriet Coffin Sumner

Eben Appleton ————
(1784-1829)
m. Sarah Patterson

William Appleton ————
(1786-1862)
m. Mary Anne Cutler

Thomas Gold Appleton (1812-1884)

Mary Appleton (1813-1889)
m. Robert J. Mackintosh

Charles Sedgwick Appleton (1815-1835)

Fanny Elizabeth Appleton (1817-1861)
m. Henry W. Longfellow

Wm. Sumner Appleton (1840-1903)
m. Edith Stuart Appleton

Harriot Appleton (1841-1923)
m. Greeley S. Curtis

Nathan Appleton, Jr. (1843-1906)

Samuel Appleton
m. Julia Webster

William Stuart Appleton
m. Georgiana Armistead

Wm. Sullivan Appleton (1815-1836)

James Amory Appleton (1818-1843)
m. Mary Ellen Lyman

Warren (William) Appleton
m. Emily Warren

Marianne Appleton
m. John Singleton Copley Greene

Frank Appleton
m. Georgianna Silsbee

Harriet Cutler Appleton
m. Franklin Gordon Dexter

Mehitable Sullivan Appleton (1831-1920)
m. T. Jefferson Coolidge

Sarah Elizabeth Appleton
m. Amos Adams Lawrence (1814-1886)

JACKSON GENEALOGY

Boston Associate Cohort   *1800-1819 and 1820-1839 Cohorts*

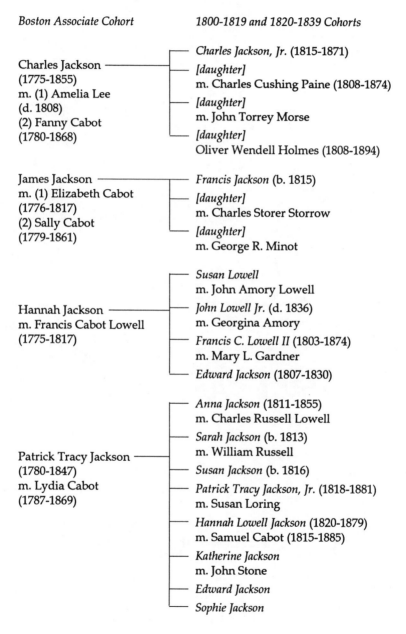

Charles Jackson
(1775-1855)
m. (1) Amelia Lee
(d. 1808)
(2) Fanny Cabot
(1780-1868)

Charles Jackson, Jr. (1815-1871)

[daughter]
m. Charles Cushing Paine (1808-1874)

[daughter]
m. John Torrey Morse

[daughter]
Oliver Wendell Holmes (1808-1894)

James Jackson
m. (1) Elizabeth Cabot
(1776-1817)
(2) Sally Cabot
(1779-1861)

Francis Jackson (b. 1815)

[daughter]
m. Charles Storer Storrow

[daughter]
m. George R. Minot

Hannah Jackson
m. Francis Cabot Lowell
(1775-1817)

Susan Lowell
m. John Amory Lowell

John Lowell Jr. (d. 1836)
m. Georgina Amory

Francis C. Lowell II (1803-1874)
m. Mary L. Gardner

Edward Jackson (1807-1830)

Patrick Tracy Jackson
(1780-1847)
m. Lydia Cabot
(1787-1869)

Anna Jackson (1811-1855)
m. Charles Russell Lowell

Sarah Jackson (b. 1813)
m. William Russell

Susan Jackson (b. 1816)

Patrick Tracy Jackson, Jr. (1818-1881)
m. Susan Loring

Hannah Lowell Jackson (1820-1879)
m. Samuel Cabot (1815-1885)

Katherine Jackson
m. John Stone

Edward Jackson

Sophie Jackson

NOTES

INTRODUCTION

1. The terms "elite" and "upper class" are confusing in the sociological literature since they are sometimes used interchangeably. In this study, I use "elite" or "economic elite" to refer to individuals holding central positions of power in the local economy at any one point in time. An "economic upper class" is a more rooted and established group of families who have maintained key economic positions over more than one generation and who have developed a distinct class consciousness and style of life. An economic elite in one period may or may not have the staying power to become an economic upper class over time. Unraveling these terms—and, more importantly, grounding them in the historical record—is the task of this project. For a general discussion of the varied uses and meanings of elite(s), see Raymond Boudon and Francois Bourricaud, *A Critical Dictionary of Sociology*, Chicago: University of Chicago Press, 1989, 155-62. For a similar use of terms to mine, see E. Digby Baltzell, "'Who's Who in America' and 'The Social Register': Elite and Upper Class Indexes in Metropolitan America," in Reinhard Bendix and Seymour Martin Lipset (eds.), *Class, Status, and Power: Social Stratification in Comparative Perspective*, New York: Free Press, 1966, 2nd edition, 266-75.

2. Oliver Wendell Holmes, *Elsie Venner: A Romance of Destiny*, Boston: Houghton, Mifflin, 1861.

3. Cleveland Amory, *The Proper Bostonians*, New York: Dutton, 1947, 14.

4. Studies showing differences among working class families include: Tamara K. Hareven, *Family Time and Industrial Time: The Relationship Between the Family and Work in a New England Industrial Community*, Cambridge: Cambridge University Press, 1982; Leslie Woodcock Tentler, *Wage-Earning Women*, New

York: Oxford University Press, 1979; Christine Stansell, *City of Women: Sex and Class in New York, 1789-1860*, Urbana: University of Illinois Press, 1987. Studies of the middle class include: Mary P. Ryan, *Cradle of the Middle Class: The Family in Oneida County, New York, 1790-1865*, Cambridge: Cambridge University Press, 1981; Stuart M. Blumin, *The Emergence of the Middle Class: Social Experience in the American City, 1760-1900*, Cambridge: Cambridge University Press, 1989.

5. Steven Birmingham, *Our Crowd: The Great Jewish Families of New York*, New York: Harper and Row, 1967; idem, *The Right People: A Portrait of the American Social Establishment*, Boston: Little, Brown, 1968; idem, *Real Lace: America's Irish Rich*, New York: Harper and Row, 1973; Russell B. Adams, Jr., *The Boston Money Tree: How the Proper Men of Boston Made, Invested and Preserved Their Wealth from Colonial Days to the Space Age*, New York: Thomas Y. Crowell, 1977; John E. Harr and Peter J. Johnson, *Rockefeller Century: Three Generations of America's Greatest Family*, New York: Scribner's, 1988; John H. Davis, *Guggenheims, 1848-1988: An American Epic*, New York: Shapolsky Publishers, 1989; Nelson W. Aldrich, Jr., *Old Money: The Mythology of America's Upper Class*, New York: Vintage Books, 1989.

6. Typical of this genre are: Paul Fussell, *Class: A Painfully Accurate Guide Through the American Status System*, New York: Ballantine, 1983; Lewis H. Lapham, *Money and Class in America*, New York: Ballantine, 1988. An older tradition of books on the upper class as collective biographies included: Gustavus Myers, *History of the Great American Fortunes*, New York: Modern Library, 1936; Anna Rochester, *Rulers of America: A Study of Finance Capital*, New York: International Publishers, 1936; Ferdinand Lundberg, *America's Sixty Families*, New York: Citadel Press, 1960; Ferdinand Lundberg, *The Rich and the Super-rich: A Study in the Power of Money Today*, New York: L. Stuart, 1968.

CHAPTER ONE

1. Claude Lévi-Strauss, "Reciprocity, the Essence of Social Life," in Rose L. Coser (ed.), *The Family: Its Structure and Functions*, New York: St. Martin's Press, 1964; *Elementary Structures of Kinship*, Boston: Beacon Press, 1969. Talcott Parsons also developed this theoretical argument in "The Incest Taboo in Relation to Social Structure," in Coser (ed.), *The Family*.

2. Max Weber, *Economy and Society*, New York: Bedminster Press, 1968; idem, *General Economic History*, New Brunswick, N.J.: Transaction Books, 1981.

3. Jack Goody, *The Development of the Family and Marriage in Europe*, Cambridge: Cambridge University Press, 1983.

4. Lawrence Stone, *The Family, Sex and Marriage in England, 1500-1800*, New York: Harper and Row, 1979.

5. Max Weber, *General Economic History*, 355-69.

6. A recent review article on the state of family sociology begins: "Reviews of research on the family typically define it by relating its functions to the environment. The definitions represent a search for theory; the field rests on a weak base. Macro theory has been slighted. Micro theory, having neglected comparative and historical data, remains mute on the topic of change" (Joan Huber and Glenna Spitze, "Trends in Family Sociology," in Neil J. Smelser [ed.], *Handbook of Sociology*, Newbury Park, Calif.: Sage Publications, 1988).

7. Lawrence Stone, *The Crisis of the Aristocracy, 1558-1641*, New York: Oxford University Press, 1967, is the model for studies of intermarriage as an economic strategy. For studies of family business dynasties under capitalism, see John Scott, *Corporations, Classes, and Capitalism*, London: Hutchinson, 1979.

8. Alfred D. Chandler, Jr., *The Visible Hand: The Managerial Revolution in American Business*, Cambridge: Harvard University Press, 1977, 3-6.

9. Ibid., 50-78.

10. Ibid., 4.

11. Maurice Zeitlin, "Corporate Ownership and Control: The Large Corporation and the Capitalist Class," *American Journal of Sociology*, 79, no. 5 (March 1974): 1073-19. Reprinted in Zeitlin, *The Large Corporation and Contemporary Classes*, New Brunswick: Rutgers University Press, 1989.

12. Maurice Zeitlin, "Corporate Ownership and Control," provides a review of the literature critical of the Berle and Means study (pp. 1081-89). Among the studies he cites is the comprehensive reassessment by Philip H. Burch, Jr., *The Managerial Revolution Reassessed*, Lexington, Mass.: Heath, 1971.

13. Michael Useem, *The Inner Circle: Large Corporations and the Rise of Business Political Activity in the U.S. and U.K.*, New York: Oxford University Press, 1984.

14. Herbert G. Gutman, "Work, Culture and Society in Industrializing America, 1815-1919," in *Work, Culture and Society in Industrializing America: Essays in American Working-Class and Social History*, New York: Vintage Books, 1977, 3-78.

15. Tamara Hareven, *Family Time and Industrial Time: The Relationship Between Family and Work in a New England Industrial Community*, Cambridge: Cambridge University Press, 1982.

16. Joseph Schuympeter, "Social Classes in an Ethnically Homogeneous Environment," in *Imperialism and Social Classes*, New York: Augustus M. Kelley, 1951, 148, 169.

17. Anthony M. Orum, "Political Sociology," in Neil J. Smelser (ed.), *Handbook of Sociology*, Newbury Park, Calif.: Sage Publications, 1988, 403-8.

18. Daniel Bell, "The Breakup of Family Capitalism," *The End of Ideology*, New York: Free Press, 1965, 39-45.

19. Talcott Parsons and Neil J. Smelser, *Economy and Society*, New York: Free Press, 1956.

20. David Riseman, *The Lonely Crowd*, New Haven: Yale University Press, 1954.

21. C. Wright Mills, *The Power Elite*, New York: Oxford University Press, 1959.

22. G. William Domhoff, *Who Rules America?*, Englewood Cliffs, N.J.: Prentice-Hall, 1967; *The Higher Circles*, New York: Random House, 1970; *The Powers That Be: Process of Ruling-Class Domination in America*, New York: Random House, 1978; *Who Rules America Now?: A View for the '80s*, Englewood Cliffs, N.J.: Prentice-Hall, 1983.

23. Nancy F. Cott, *The Bonds of Womanhood: "Woman's Sphere" in New England, 1780-1835*, New Haven: Yale University Press, 1977; Mary P. Ryan, *Cradle of the Middle Class: The Family in Oneida County, New York, 1790-1865*, Cambridge: Cambridge University Press, 1981.

24. Mary P. Ryan, "Creating Woman's Sphere: Gender in the Making of American Industrial Capitalism: 1820-1865," chapter three in *Womanhood in America: Colonial Times to the Present*, 3rd edition, New York: Franklin Watts, 1983, 113-65.

25. Catherine Beecher, *A Treatise on Domestic Economy*, New York: Schocken Books, 1977; Maxine L. Margolis, *Mothers and Such: Views of American Women and Why They Changed*, Berkeley: University of California Press, 1984.

26. Carroll Smith-Rosenberg, "The Female World of Love and Ritual: Relations Between Women in Nineteenth-Century America," *Signs: A Journal of Women in Culture and Society*, 1 (Autumn 1975), 1-29; Ellen Carol DuBois, *Feminism and Suffrage: The Emergence of an Independent Women's Movement in America, 1848-1869*, Ithaca: Cornell University Press, 1978; Sara M. Evans, *Born for Liberty: A History of Women in America*, New York: Free Press, 1989.

27. Nancy Hewitt, "Beyond the Search for Sisterhood: American Women's History in the 1980s," *Social History*, 10 (October 1985), 299-322; Linda Kerber, "Separate Spheres, Female Worlds, Woman's Place: The Rhetoric of Women's History," *Journal of American History*, 75 (June 1988).

28. Alice Kessler-Harris, "Gender Ideology in Historical Reconstruction: A Case Study from the 1930s," *Gender and History*, vol. 1, no. 1 (Spring 1988), 31-49.

29. Bonnie G. Smith, *Ladies of the Leisure Class: The Bourgeoisies of Northern France in the Nineteenth Century*, Princeton: Princeton University Press, 1981.

30. Mary P. Ryan, *Women in Public: From Banners to Ballots, 1825-1880*, Baltimore: Johns Hopkins University Press, 1989.

CHAPTER TWO

1. Harriet Martineau, *Society in America* (1837), quoted in Louis Coser, *Sociology Through Literature*, Englewood Cliffs, N.J.: Prentice-Hall, 1963, 142.

2. See Henry James, *The American Scene*, Bloomington: Indiana University Press, 1968 (originally 1907), 226-55; H. G. Wells, *The Future of America*, 1906; Frederic Cople Jaher, *Doubters and Dissenters: Cataclysmic Thought in America, 1885-1918*, New York: Free Press, 1964, 141-87.

3. Walter Muir Whitehill, *Boston: A Topographical History*, Cambridge: Belknap Press of Harvard University Press, 1968; Bainbridge Bunting, *Houses of Boston's Back Bay: An Architectural History, 1840-1917*, Cambridge: Belknap Press of Harvard University Press, 1967.

4. Census figures cited by Bunting, *Houses*, p. 463, note 1 to chapter two.

5. Harold and James Kirker, *Bulfinch's Boston, 1787-1817*, New York: Oxford University Press, 1964.

6. Cited in Whitehill, *Boston*, p. 71.

7. Ibid., 79-84, 105-12.

8. A. Forbes and J. W. Greene, *The Rich Men of Massachusetts: Containing a Statement of the Reputed Wealth of About 1500 Persons, with Brief Sketches of More than 1000 Characters*, Boston: W.V. Spencer, 1851.

9. Mrs. Charles Pelham Curtis, *Memories of Fifty Years*, pp. 11-12, quoted in Whitehill, *Boston*, 137.

10. Oscar Handlin, *Boston's Immigrants: A Study in Acculturation*, Cambridge: Harvard University Press, 1959, 88-123.

11. William Dean Howells, *The Rise of Silas Lapham*, New York: Penguin Books, 1983 (originally 1885), 24.

12. John Modell and Tamara K. Hareven, "Urbanization and the Mal-

leable Household: An Examination of Boarding and Lodging in American Families," in Tamara K. Hareven (ed.), *Family and Kin in Urban Communities, 1700-1930*, New York: New Viewpoints, 1977, 164-86.

13. Whitehill, *Boston*, 88-94.

14. Bunting, *Houses of Boston's Back Bay*, 33.

15. Ibid., 15, 67-68. The class significance, and political implications, of this architectural style in the case of Paris is revealing in terms of Boston's imitation of it, as well. In carving out the grand boulevards of Paris, Louis Napoleon and Haussmann consciously introduced a new style of urban public life. Leisure and entertainment amid this architectural grandeur were wielded as instruments of policy, simultaneously enhancing the prestige of the government and siphoning off political discontent to Napoleon III's increasingly autocratic rule. The class divisions between rich and poor were brought into ever-sharper relief in comparisons between the renovated grand boulevards of the new Paris and the slums of the old neighborhoods. See Robert L. Herbert, *Impressionism: Art, Leisure and Parisian Society*, New Haven: Yale University Press, 1988. In Boston, as well, the markers of social class can be read in the uses of urban space and architectural styles.

16. Howells's intimate understanding of the status hierarchy within Boston Society in the late nineteenth century is characterized in such passages as the following:

> Yes, sir, it's about the sightliest view I know of. I always did like the water side of Beacon. Long before I owned property here, or even expected to, m'wife and I used to ride down this way, and stop the buggy to get this view over the water. When people talk to me about the Hill, I can understand 'em. It's snug, and it's old-fashioned, and it's where they've always lived. But when they talk about Commonwealth Avenue, I don't know what they mean. It don't hold a candle to the water side of Beacon. You've got just as much wind over there, and you've got just as much dust, and all the view you've got is the view across the street. No sir! When you come to the Back Bay at all, give me the water side of Beacon. [William Dean Howells, *The Rise of Silas Lapham*, 55-56]

Howells also captures a sense of the process through which the Back Bay was being *socially* constructed as an area of elegance and refinement, along with its physical construction:

> The neighborhood smelt like the hold of a ship after a three years' voyage. People who had cast their fortunes with the New Land went by professing not to notice it; people who still "hung on to the

Hill" put their handkerchiefs to their noses, and told each other the old terrible stories of the material used in filling up the Back Bay. [43]

17. Bunting, *Houses of Boston's Back Bay*, 400-458. Appendix A, "Buildings Constructed in the Back Bay," provides a complete list of buildings, date of construction, owners, and architects for the key streets of the Back Bay, allowing documentation of the social history, as well as the architectural history, of this area.

18. Sam Bass Warner, Jr., *Streetcar Suburbs: The Process of Growth in Boston, 1870-1900*, Cambridge: Harvard University Press, 1978.

19. Whitehill, *Boston*, 159.

20. Bunting, *Houses of Boston's Back Bay*, 3.

21. Walter Firey, *Land Use in Central Boston*, Cambridge: Harvard University Press, 1947, 269.

22. Ronald Story, *Harvard and the Boston Upper Class: The Forging of an Aristocracy, 1800-1870*, Middletown: Wesleyan University Press, 1985.

23. Story, *Harvard*, 41-134.

24. Paul DiMaggio, "Cultural Entrepreneurship in Nineteenth-Century Boston: The Creation of an Organizational Base for High Culture in America," *Media, Culture and Society*, vol. 4., no. 1 (1982), 33-50, and idem, "Cultural Entrepreneurship in Nineteenth-Century Boston, part II: the Classification and Framing of American Art," *Media, Culture and Society*, vol. 4, no. 4 (1982), 303-22. DiMaggio argues persuasively that the cultural consolidation of Boston's upper class was effected by completing three tasks: the creation of appropriate organizational forms, followed by the classification and framing of the art they promoted as "high culture."

25. DiMaggio, "Cultural Entrepreneurship in Nineteenth-Century Boston, part II," 316-18.

26. The fullest account of the Boston Brahmins' class authority in politics and culture is in the comprehensive and comparative study by E. Digby Baltzell, *Puritan Boston and Quaker Philadelphia*, New York: Free Press, 1979. See also Frederic Cople Jaher, "The Politics of the Boston Brahmins: 1800-1860," in Ronald P. Formisano and Constance K. Burns (eds.), *Boston 1700-1980: The Evolution of Urban Politics*, Westport, Conn.: Greenwood Press, 1984, 67-69.

27. Jaher, "Politics of the Boston Brahmins," 75.

28. Support of the tariff and the regulation of incorporation are clear

examples of laws that support particular economic interests. Jaher also notes that more municipal concerns with social order were also linked to economic interests:

> It was the Brahmins who had the most property to lose from lower class violence, deficient fire and police organizations and high taxes and the most to gain from a better business district, a House of Industry, a formidable jail house and a beautiful Common that would raise property values in Beacon Hill. Less privileged Bostonians participated marginally, if at all, in these urban benefits. [Jaher, "Politics of the Boston Brahmins," 78.]

29. Geoffrey Blodgett, "Yankee Leadership in a Divided City: Boston, 1860-1910," *Journal of Urban History*, vol. 8, no. 4 (August 1982), 371-96.

30. Peter K. Eisinger, *The Politics of Displacement: Racial and Ethnic Transition in Three American Cities*, New York: Academic Press, 1980, 50.

31. Roger Lane, *Policing the City: Boston 1822-1885*, Cambridge: Harvard University Press, 1967, 180-224.

32. Geoffrey Blodgett, *The Gentle Reformers: Massachusetts Democrats in the Cleveland Era*, Cambridge: Harvard University Press, 1966, 120.

33. Eisinger, *Politics of Displacement*, 45-47.

34. Frederic Cople Jaher, *The Urban Establishment: Upper Strata in Boston, New York, Charleston, Chicago, and Los Angeles*, Urbana: University of Illinois Press, 1982, 44-87.

35. Frederic Cople Jaher, "The Boston Brahmins in the Age of Industrial Capitalism," in Jaher (ed.), *The Age of Industrialism in America*, New York: Free Press, 1968, 188-262.

36. Frederic Cople Jaher, "Nineteenth Century Elites in Boston and New York," *Journal of Social History*, Fall 1972, no. 1; Frederic Cople Jaher, "Style and Status: High Society in Late Nineteenth Century New York," in Jaher (ed.), *The Rich, the Well-Born, and the Powerful: Elites and Upper Classes in History*, 258-84.

37. Jocelyn M. Ghent and Frederic Cople Jaher, "The Chicago Business Elite: 1830-1930, A Collective Biography," *Business History Review*, vol. 50, no. 3, Autumn 1976, 288-328.

38. Jaher, "Boston Brahmins," 237; also Jaher, *The Urban Establishment*, 87-125. The period from 1870 to 1970 is described as the "twilight" of Brahmin families.

39. Although Jaher does not place his analysis in a theoretical perspective, the logic of his argument is close to that of Pareto's concern with the circulation of elites in *The Mind and Society: A Treatise on General Society*, New York: Dover, 1963, originally c. 1935.

40. Jaher, "Boston Brahmins," 228.

41. Jaher, "Businessman and Gentleman: Nathan and Thomas Gold Appleton—An Exploration in Intergenerational History," *Explorations in Entrepreneurial History*, vol. 4 (Fall 1966), 17-40.

42. Frederic J. Stimpson, *My United States*, New York: Scribner's, 1931, 76-77; also quoted in Bunting, *Houses of Boston's Back Bay*, 16-17. Bunting accepts this interpretation and incorporates it in his analysis of Back Bay architectural styles, which he argues became more conservative between 1876 and 1890. The revival of Georgian architecture in this period "illustrates the effort of the latter-day Bostonian to identify himself with his family-founding, seafaring ancestor. Now, in the 1890s, despite ample wealth, Back Bay residents chose to build homes of substantially the same size and architectural style as had their ancestors a hundred years earlier" [19].

43. Alfred Kazin, *On Native Grounds*, New York: Reynal and Hitchcock, 1942, 3-50; Van Wyck Brooks, introduction to William Dean Howells, *A Hazard of New Fortunes*.

44. On the relation between class and status, as variables of group power, Max Weber has argued: "When the bases of the acquisition and distribution of goods are relatively stable, stratification by status is favored. Every technological repercussion and economic transformation threatens stratification by status and pushes the class situation into the foreground. Epochs and countries in which the naked class situation is of predominant significance are regularly the periods of technical and economic transformations. And every slowing down of the shifting of economic stratifications leads, in due course, to the growth of status structures and makes for a resuscitation of the important role of social honor" (H. H. Gerth and C. Wright Mills [eds.], *From Max Weber: Essays in Sociology*, New York: Oxford University Press, 1946, 193-94).

45. Gabriel Kolko made such an argument about the continuity of the Brahmins in he second half of the nineteenth century in his article, "Brahmins and Business, 1870-1914: A Hypothesis on the Social Basis of Success in American History," in Kurt Wolff and Barrington Moore, *The Critical Spirit*, Boston: Beacon Press, 1967, 343-63. He has also argued that a national upper class developed in late nineteenth-century America, in *Wealth and Power in America: An Analysis of Social Class and Income Distribution*, New York: Praeger, 1962, and *Main Currents in Modern American History*, New York: Harper and Row, 1976.

CHAPTER THREE

* See Appendix for genealogical charts.

1. Cleveland Amory, *The Proper Bostonians*, New York: Dutton, 1947, 36-60.

2. Hannah Josephson, *The Golden Threads: New England's Mill Girls and Magnates*, New York: Russell and Russell, 1949. Josephson traces the origin of the term to a group of fifty merchants who joined together to secure Boston real estate. But the term is used more frequently by later writers to refer to those textile manufacturers who started the large firms in the Merrimack River valley. The most extensive historical account of this group is in Robert F. Dalzell, Jr., *Enterprising Elite: The Boston Associates and the World They Made*, Cambridge: Harvard University Press, 1987.

3. Ferris Greenslet, *The Lowells and Their Seven Worlds*, Boston: Houghton Mifflin, 1946, 43; *Genealogy of the Lowell Family*, Boston: William Huse and Co., 1876.

4. Greenslet, *The Lowells and Their Seven Worlds*, 125.

5. Nathan Appleton, "The Introduction of the Power Loom and the Origin of Lowell," Boston: B. H. Penhallow, 1858. Dalzell, in *Enterprising Elite*, discusses the new industrial influences on F. C. Lowell, dating from his experience of residing in Scotland, pp. 5-25.

6. Kenneth Wiggins Porter, *The Jacksons and the Lees: Two Generations of Massachusetts Merchants, 1765-1844*, New York: Russell and Russell (Atheneum), 1937, vol. 1, 746-47; Frances W. Gregory, *Nathan Appleton: Merchant and Entrepreneur, 1779-1861*, Charlottesville: University Press of Virginia, 1975, 37-71.

7. Dr. James Jackson, "Notes on the Life and Character of Patrick Tracy Jackson," in James Jackson Putnam, M.D., *A Memoir of Dr. James Jackson*, Boston: Houghton Mifflin, 1905, 142.

8. Frances W. Gregory, *Nathan Appleton*, 199.

9. Kishichi Wantanabe, "The Business Organization of the Boston Manufacturing Company—The Early Development of Modern Management in the U.S.," *Economic and Business Review*, Kyoto: Sangry University, vol. 1 (May 1979).

10. William Hickling Prescott, *Memoir of the Hon. Abbott Lawrence*, printed for private distribution, 1856; Robert Means Lawrence, *The Descendants of Major Samuel Lawrence*, Cambridge: Riverside Press, 1904.

11. Russell B. Adams, Jr., *The Boston Money Tree*, New York: Thomas Y. Crowell, 1977, 83-88; *Dictionary of American Biography*, vol. 11, 44-46.

12. Hamilton Andrews Hill, *Memoir of Abbott Lawrence*, Boston, printed for private distribution, 1883, 24; *Dictionary of American Biography*, vol. 11, 44-46.

13. Hannah Josephson, *The Golden Threads*, 96-114; Caroline F. Ware, *The Early New England Cotton Manufacture: A Study in Industrial Beginnings*, New York: Russell and Russell, 1966.

14. Lance E. Davis, "Sources of Industrial Finance: The American Textile Industry, A Case Study," *Explorations in Entrepreneurial History*, vol. 9, no. 4, April 1957.

15. Lance E. Davis, "Stock Ownership in the Early New England Textile Industry," *Business History Review*, vol. 32, no. 2, 1958.

16. Alfred D. Chandler, Jr., *The Visible Hand: The Managerial Revolution in American Business*, Cambridge: Harvard University Press, 1977, 67-72; Kishichi Wantanabe, "The Business Organization of the Boston Manufacturing Company."

17. Records of the Boston Manufacturing Company, Index File, Baker Library, Harvard University Graduate School of Business Administration; A. Forbes and J. W. Greene, *The Rich Men of Massachusetts*, Boston: W. V. Spencer, 1851; *Our First Men: A Calendar of Wealth, Fashion, and Gentility; Containing a List of Those Persons Taxed in the City of Boston, Credibly Reported to be Worth $100,000, with Biographical Notices of the Principal Persons*, Boston: Booksellers, 1846; Thomas L. V. Wilson, *The Aristocracy of Boston: Who They Are and What They Were*, Boston, 1848.

18. Gregory, *Nathan Appleton*, 171; "History of the Boston Manufacturing Company and Lowell," typescript in the Index File of the Boston Manufacturing Company records, Baker Library, Harvard University Graduate School of Business Administration.

19. Wantanabe, "The Business Organization of the Boston Manufacturing Company," 57-59; Frances W. Gregory, "The Office of President in the American Textile Industry," *Bulletin of the Business Historical Society*, vol. 26, 1954.

20. "History of the Boston Manufacturing Company": list of treasurers and directors, ex-officio, presidents, and directors, Baker Library, Harvard University Graduate School of Business Administration.

21. "History of the Boston Manufacturing Company": original subscription list of the Merimack Manufacturing Company, Baker Library, Harvard University Graduate School of Business Administration.

22. Caroline F. Ware, *The Early New England Cotton Manufacture*; "History of the Boston Manufacturing Company," Baker Library, Harvard University Graduate School of Business Administration.

23. Robert Dalzell's history of the Boston Associates, *Enterprising Elite: The Boston Associates and the World They Made*, Cambridge: Harvard University Press, 1987, is a comprehensive account of the motivations of this group. He is persuasive in arguing that they were fundamentally cautious men, intent on harnessing the forces of social change in their own interests. Yet I disagree with the interpretation that their role as key economic actors declined over the nineteenth century. As Dalzell points out, the Boston Associates were successful in achieving their goal of solidifying their families' place in the upper class. This was not just a social position, but an economically grounded one, as well. The Boston Associates' economic activities must be analyzed as a *class* strategy, not simply as the motivations of a socially conservative group of individual men.

24. Peter Dobkin Hall, whose work on an earlier era of New England family and business interconnections has been very important in shaping my own, argues that in the nineteenth century private organizations took over the economic functions of the family. See *The Organization of American Culture, 1700-1900: Private Institutions, Elites, and the Origins of American Nationality*, New York: New York University Press, 1982. I believe that kinship continued to have an importance in this era, especially in linking these private institutions. This is the argument I make in this chapter.

25. Naomi R. Lamoreaux, "Banks, Kinship, and Economic Development: The New England Case," *Journal of Economic History*, vol. 46, no. 3 (September 1986), 647-67.

26. David Rice Whitney, *The Suffolk Bank*, Cambridge: Riverside Press, 1878; Edward Weeks, *The Lowells and Their Institute*, Boston: Little Brown, 1966, 39-40.

27. Bray Hammond, *Banks and Politics in America*, 549-56.

28. Ibid., 549ff.; Harold F. Williamson, "Money and Commercial Banking, 1789-1861," in Harold F. Williamson (ed.), *The Growth of the American Economy*.

29. Edward C. Kirkland, *Men, Cities, Transportation: A Study in New England History, 1820-1900*, Cambridge: Harvard University Press, 1948.

30. Arthur M. Johnson and Barry E. Supple, *Boston Capitalists and Western Railroads: A Study in the Nineteenth Century Railroad Investment Process*, Cambridge: Harvard University Press, 1967.

31. N.S.B. Gras, *The Massachusetts First National Bank*, 108.

32. Krooss, *American Economic Development*, 210; Lance E. Davis, "Sources of Industrial Finance: The American Textile Industry, A Case Study."

33. Walter Muir Whitehill, *The Provident Institution for Savings in the Town*

of Boston, 1816-1966: A Historical Sketch, Boston: published by the Provident, 1966, 12.

34. Harold F. Williamson, *The Growth of the American Economy,* 269-71.

35. Alan Olmstead, "Mutual Savings Bank Depositors in New York," *Business History Review,* vol. 49, no. 3, Autumn 1975, 289.

36. Alan Olmstead, "Mutual Savings Bank Depositors," 299.

37. Lance E. Davis and Peter L. Payne, "From Benevolence to Business: The Story of Two Savings Banks," *Business History Review,* vol. 32, no. 4, Winter 1958, 402-4.

38. Whitehill, *The Provident Institution for Savings,* Appendix, 114-21.

39. Paul Goodman, "Ethics and Enterprise: the Values of the Boston Elite, 1800-1860," *American Quarterly,* vol. 18, no. 3, Fall 1966.

40. Gerald T. White, *A History of the Massachusetts Hospital Life Insurance Company,* Cambridge: Harvard University Press, 1955, 3-5.

41. White, *History of the MHLIC,* 5; Appendix I, 169-76.

42. White, *History of the MHLIC,* 34-39, 77.

43. Donald Holbrook, *The Boston Trustee,* Boston: Marshall Jones, 1937; Natalie R. Grow, "The Boston-Type Open-End Fund: Development of a National Financial Institution, 1924-1940," Ph.D. dissertation, Harvard University, 1977, chapter one, part three, "Boston, the Home of Money Management," 26-38.

44. Frederic Cople Jaher, "The Boston Brahmins in the Age of Industrial Capitalism," in Frederic Cople Jaher (ed.), *The Age of Industrialism in America,* New York: Free Press, 1968, 188-96.

45. Lance E. Davis, "Sources of Industrial Finance: The American Textile Industry, A Case Study."

46. White, *A History of the Massachusetts Hospital Life Insurance Company,* Appendix I, 169-76.

47. White, *History of the MHLIC,* 10-13.

48. Ibid., 66-67.

49. Ibid., 48-50, 89-97.

50. Lance E. Davis, "Stock Ownership in the Early New England Textile Industry," 211-13.

51. Lance E. Davis, "Capital Mobility and American Growth," 296-99.

52. Frederic Cople Jaher, "Nineteenth-Century Elites in Boston and New York," *Journal of Social History*, no. 1, Fall 1972.

53. Ronald Story, "Harvard and the Boston Brahmins: A Study in Institutional and Class Development, 1800-1865," *Journal of Social History*, vol. 8, Spring 1975.

54. Kin networks of the Appletons were compiled primarily through the use of Gregory, *Nathan Appleton*; Isaac Appleton Jewett, *Memorial of Samuel Appleton*; and T. Frank Waters, *A Genealogy of the Ipswich Descendants of Samuel Appleton*, Salem, Mass.: Salem Press, 1907. The kin network of the Lawrences was compiled through the use of Robert Means Lawrence, *The Descendants of Major Samuel Lawrence*, Cambridge: Riverside Press, 1904.

55. Frances Gregory, *Nathan Appleton*, 198, 281-86.

56. Information on affiliations with financial institutions was compiled from *The Boston City Directory: Containing Names of the Inhabitants, their Occupations, Places of Business and Dwelling Houses, with List of the Streets, Lanes, Wharves, the Town Officers, Public Offices and Banks and Other Useful Information*, Boston: John H. A. Frost and Charles Stimpson, Jr., publishers, 1820-1840.

57. Walter Muir Whitehill, *The Provident Institution for Savings in the Town of Boston, 1816-1966*, Boston: published by the Provident Institution for Savings, 1966, 111-22; White, *A History of the Massachusetts Hospital Life Insurance Company*, Appendix I, 169-76.

58. White, *History of the MHLIC*, 48.

59. *Boston City Directories*, 1820-1840; White, ibid., 173.

60. Robert Means Lawrence, *The Descendants of Major Samuel Lawrence*, 13-16, 20-22; *Boston City Directories*, 1820-1840.

61. William Lawrence, *The Life of Amos A. Lawrence*, 11-57.

62. Gregory, *Nathan Appleton*, 270.

63. Ibid., 272, 283.

64. *Will of Abbott Lawrence*, Suffolk County Probate Court, Boston, 1855, Number 39964, Articles 2-10.

65. *Will of Abbott Lawrence*, articles 17-18.

66. "Our First Men: A Calendar of Wealth, Fashion, and Gentility, Containing a List of Those Persons Taxed in the City of Boston, Credibly Reported

to be Worth $100,000, with Biographical Notices of the Principal Persons," Boston, 1846; Thomas L. V. Wilson, "The Aristocracy of Boston: Who They Are and What They Were," Boston, 1848; and A. Forbes and J. W. Greene, *The Rich Men of Massachusetts: Containing a Statement of the Reputed Wealth of About 1500 Persons with Brief Sketches of More than 1,000 Characters*, Boston: W. V. Spencer, 1851.

67. Ferris Greenslet, *The Lowells and Their Seven Worlds*, Boston: Houghton Mifflin, Riverside Press, 1946; *Genealogy of the Lowell Family: The One Hundred and Fiftieth Anniversary of the Foundation of the First Religious Society of Newburyport*, Boston: William Huse and Co., printers, 1876; and Robert Means Lawrence, *The Descendants of Major Samuel Lawrence*, 176-83.

68. *Boston City Directories*, 1820-1825.

69. Edward Weeks, *The Lowells and Their Institute*, Boston: Little, Brown, 1966, 36-54; Greenslet, *The Lowells and Their Seven Worlds*, 221.

70. Robert Means Lawrence, *The Descendants of Major Samuel Lawrence*, 179-80; Kishichi Wantanabe, "The Business Organization of the Boston Manufacturing Company—The Early Development of Modern Management in the U.S.," *Kyoto Sangry University Economic and Business Review*, no. 1, May 1974, 51-69.

71. Greenslet, *The Lowells and their Seven Worlds*, 221; Ella Lyman Cabot, *Arthur T. Lyman and Ella Lyman*, Boston, privately printed, 1932, 91.

72. Whitehill, *The Provident Institution for Savings*, 112, 118.

73. White, *A History of the Massachusetts Hospital Life Insurance Company*, 175; *Boston City Directories*, 1820-1840.

74. Weeks, *The Lowells and Their Institute*, 36-57; Greenslet, *The Lowells and Their Seven Worlds*, 235.

75. *Boston City Directories*, 1820-1840; Whitehill, *The Provident Institution for Savings*, 112; White, *A History of the Massachusetts Hospital Life Insurance Company*, 173, 175.

76. Greenslet, *The Lowells and Their Seven Worlds*, 237.

77. David Heymann Clemens, *American Aristocracy: The Lives and Times of James Russell Lowell, Amy Lowell, and Robert Lowell*, New York: Dodd, Mead, 1980.

78. Delmar Lowell, *The Historic Genealogy of the Lowells in America*, published by the author, 1899; Frank Augustine Gardner, M.D., *Gardner Memorial*, Salem, Mass.: privately printed, 1933.

79. *Boston City Directories*, 1820-1840; Whitehill, *Provident Institution for Savings*, 111-22; White, *History of the Massachusetts Hospital Life Insurance Company*, 169-76.

80. Kenneth W. Porter, *The Jacksons and the Lees: Two Generations of Massachusetts Merchants, 1765-1844*, New York: Russell and Russell, 1937, 2 volumes; *Dictionary of American Biography*, vol. 9, 534-35, 545-46, 552-53.

81. James Jackson Putnam, M.D., *A Memoir of Dr. James Jackson*, Boston: Houghton Mifflin, 1905.

82. James Jackson Putnam, *A Memoir*, 96-117, 199-220.

83. L. Vernon Briggs, *History and Genealogy of the Cabot Family, 1475-1927*, Boston: Charles E. Goodspeed, 1927, 2 volumes, 155, 169-71, 266-67, 270-75.

84. Peter Dobkin Hall, "Family Structure and Class Consolidation Among the Boston Brahmins," Ph.D. dissertation, State University of New York at Stonybrook, 1974; Peter D. Hall, "Marital Selection and Business in Massachusetts Merchant Families, 1700-1900," in Rose Coser (ed.), *The Family: Its Structures and Functions*, New York: St. Martin's Press, 1974, 226-40; Peter D. Hall, "Family Structure and Economic Organization: Massachusetts Merchants 1700-1850," in Tamara K. Hareven (ed.), *Family and Kin in Urban Communities, 1700-1930*, New York: New Viewpoints, 1977, 38-61.

85. Putnam, *A Memoir of Dr. James Jackson*, 350-77; *Boston City Directories*, 1820-1840; Whitehill, *The Provident Institution for Savings*, 111-22; White, *A History of the Massachusetts Hospital Life Insurance Company*, 169-76.

86. "Journal of P. T. Jackson," Jan. 1, 1836 to Sept. 13, 1837, Lee Family Papers, Massachusetts Historical Society, Boston, Massachusetts.

87. Porter, *The Jacksons and the Lees*, 766-70.

88. Putnam, *A Memoir of James Jackson*, 128-56.

89. "Our First Men," Boston, 1846.

90. Suffolk County Probate Records (Boston, Massachusetts), #35363, vol. 145, p. 161.

91. Suffolk County Probate Records, #49632.

92. Ibid., #88663.

93. Sidney Ratner, *New Light on the History of Great American Fortunes: American Millionaires of 1892 and 1902*, New York: Augustus M. Kelley, 1953.

94. Cleveland Amory, *The Proper Bostonians*, New York: Dutton, 1947;

Russell B. Adams, Jr., *The Boston Money Tree*, New York: Thomas Y. Crowell, 1977; *Directory of Directors in the City of Boston and Vicinity*, Boston: Banker's Service Co., 1905, 121; John William Leonard (ed.), *Who's Who in Finance, Banking, and Insurance*, New York: Joseph and Sefton, 1911, 270-348.

CHAPTER FOUR

1. Pierre Bourdieu, "Marriage Strategies as Strategies of Social Reproduction," in Robert Forster and Orest Ranum (eds.), *Family and Society, Selections from the Annales: Economies, Sociétés, Civilisations*, Baltimore: Johns Hopkins University Press, 1976, 120-21.

2. Nancy A. Hewitt, *Women's Activism and Social Change: Rochester, New York, 1822-1872*, Ithaca: Cornell University Press, 1984.

3. *Bacon's Dictionary of Boston*, Boston: Houghton, Mifflin, 1886, 85-89, 439-40.

4. Examples of historical studies include Hewitt, *Women's Activism*, Ryan, *Women in Public*, and Marsha Wedell, *Elite Women and the Reform Impulse in Memphis, 1875-1915*, Knoxville: University of Tennessee Press, 1991. The primary contemporary studies are Arlene Daniels, *Invisible Careers: Women Community Leaders in the Volunteer World*, Chicago: University of Chicago Press, 1988; Susan A. Ostrander, *Women of the Upper Class*, Philadelphia: Temple University Press, 1984; and Teresa Odendahl, *Charity Begins at Home: Generosity and Self-Interest Among the Philanthropic Elite*, New York: Basic Books, 1990.

5. Mary L. Gardner Lowell, Line-a-Day Journals, 1825-1849, January 1, 1836, F. C. Lowell II Papers, Massachusetts Historical Society, Boston, Massachusetts.

6. Idem, January 1 and 2, 1845, F. C. Lowell II Papers.

7. Mary Gardner Lowell Invitation List, 1840, F. C. Lowell II Papers.

8. Journals of Hetty S. Lawrence Cunningham, 1876-1881, Monday, August 14, 1876, Marian Lawrence Peabody Papers, Massachusetts Historical Society (MHS), Boston, Massachusetts.

9. Among historical studies, Lawrence Stone's, *The Crisis of the Aristocracy, 1558-1641*, New York: Oxford University Press, 1967, best demonstrates the significance of marriage as a tool of political alliance-building. Kathleen Gough's study of the Nayar of South India, in David Schneider and Kathleen Gough (eds.), *Matrilineal Kinship*, is also a classic in the anthropological literature on this subject. Among sociologists, William J. Goode [*The Family*, Englewood Cliffs, N.J.: Prentice-Hall, 1964, 1982] has been the theorist most consistently inter-

ested in explaining the macrostructural influences on family processes, including courtship systems. But there have been few detailed studies in the subfield of family sociology or stratification that have made intermarriage strategies their focus.

10. Anna Sears Amory Letters, excerpts from vols. 1-10, 1820s-1880s; "Diaries and Letterbooks," Sears Family Papers, Massachusetts Historical Society, Boston, Massachusetts.

11. "Biography of David Sears," vol. 10 (April 22, 1865 to December 17, 1885), 159-61, Anna Sears Amory Letters, MHS.

12. Miriam Mason Sears to Anna Sears Amory, July 30, 1837, Anna Sears Amory Letters, MHS.

13. Ibid., July 30, 1837, Anna Sears Amory Letters, MHS.

14. Ibid., September 1837, Anna Sears Amory Letters, MHS.

15. Ibid.

16. Ellen Sears d'Hauteville to Anna Sears Amory, October 25, 1837, Anna Sears Amory Letters, MHS.

17. Anna Sears Amory to Miriam Mason Sears, November 15, 1837, Anna Sears Amory Letters, MHS.

18. David Sears to Gonzalve d'Hauteville, November 22, 1837, Sears Family Papers, MHS.

19. Letter of David Sears to Ellen Sears D'Hauteville, January 1, 1838, attached to the D'Hauteville Marriage Contract of August 1837, MHS.

20. David Sears to Gonzalve d'Hauteville, January 12, 1838, Sears Family Papers, MHS.

21. "Answers of Dr. John C. Warren to Interrogatories on the state of Madame Ellen d'Hauteville's health in Paris, in the Spring of 1838," January 16, 1839, Anna Sears Amory Letters, MHS.

22. David Sears to Monsieur Frederic Couveau, February 4, 1839, Sears Family Papers, MHS.

23. Letter from Jean Charles Sismondi to William Ellery Channing, April 1840, William Ellery Channing Papers, MHS.

24. Michael Grossberg, *Governing the Hearth: Law and the Family in Nineteenth-Century America*, Chapel Hill: University of North Carolina Press, 1985, 241-42; endnote 14, p. 382.

25. "Memoranda," April 2, 1850, Sears Family Papers, MHS.

26. David Sears to Monsieur Genton-Doge, December 31, 1845, Sears Family Papers, MHS.

27. Typescript of the Elizabeth R. Mason Diaries, vols. 1-3, 1854-1864, Massachusetts Historical Society, Boston, Massachusetts. The recent publication of P.A.M. Taylor (ed.), *More Than Common Powers of Perception: The Diary of Elizabeth Rogers Mason Cabot*, Boston: Beacon Press, 1991, has brought together diary collections beginning in 1844 when Elizabeth was ten years old to 1906 when she was 82, located in both the Massachusetts Historical Society and the Schlesinger Library at Radcliffe College. The introduction to this volume, pp. 1-37, provides a comprehensive and useful background to the social-historical milieu of this Boston Brahmin woman.

28. Elizabeth R. Mason Diaries, July 15, 1849, MHS; also quoted in Taylor (ed.), *More than Common Powers of Perception*, p. 65.

29. Elizabeth R. Mason Diaries, April 1, 1857, MHS.

30. Ibid., September 15, 1855; September 12, 1856; September 5, 1858; March 28, 1859, MHS.

31. Elizabeth R. Mason Diaries, November 22, 1855; July 19, 1857, MHS.

32. Ibid., September 12, 1856, MHS.

33. Many of the proposals came in the form of notes delivered to Elizabeth's family home, some clearly unanticipated. On the subject of one such suitor, she wrote:

> Wednesday early I came to town, but before leaving Edward C. put in my hands a note which astonished me as much as if he had struck me on the spot. It really made my brain reel. Are the men all mad, some to act everything and feel nothing, some to feel and show no sign. Am I the butt of every man who comes near me, that one should after an acquaintance of a few evengs. offer me his hand forsooth, as if I must be greatly honored thereby. [June 1, 1859]

For other engagement proposals, see diary entries of March 29, 1856; June 30, 1856. Entries on October 7, 1856, March 31, 1857, April 17, 1858, and July 14, 1858, provide accounts of her most persistent suitor, Josiah Quincy. For an account of her courtship and engagement proposal from Walter Cabot, see entries of December 17, 1857; May 8, 15, and 25, 1859; and especially December 21, 1859. P.A.M. Taylor notes that Elizabeth had received eight proposals of marriage in addition to that of Walter Cabot. He cites, among her suitors, the shadowy figures of Phillip, Hubbard, Kerl, Delano, and Van Schaick (pp. 20, 109).

34. Elizabeth R. Mason Diaries, May 14, 1858, MHS.

35. Ibid., June 6, 1854, MHS.

36. Ibid., July 19, 1856, MHS.

37. Ibid., April 7, 1857; November 6, 1857, MHS.

38. Ibid., March 20, 1859, MHS.

39. Ibid., April 17, 1858, MHS.

40. Ibid., May 3, 1858, MHS.

41. Ibid., December 21, 1859, MHS.

42. Ibid., March 25, 1860, MHS. P.A.M. Taylor also notes the extent of Elizabeth R. Mason's inherited wealth—about $600,000—at the time of the death of her father in 1867. After the settlement of the legal fees of the estate, it was estimated that she would have an income of $30,000 to 40,000 per year; see *More Than Common Powers*, 8.

43. Elizabeth R. Mason Diaries, January 14, 1860, MHS.

44. Journals of Hetty S. Lawrence Cunningham, 1876-1878, 1881, Marian Lawrence Peabody Papers, Massachusetts Historical Society, Boston, Massachusetts.

45. Journals of Hetty S. Lawrence Cunningham, Tuesday, August 15, 1876, M. L. Peabody Papers, MHS.

46. Ibid., Wednesday, August 2, 1876, M. L. Peabody Papers, MHS.

47. Ibid., Sunday, January 7, 1877, M. L. Peabody Papers, MHS.

48. Ibid., Saturday, February 10, 1877, M. L. Peabody Papers, MHS.

49. Ibid., Tuesday, March 13, 1877 and Sunday, March 18, 1877, M. L. Peabody Papers, MHS.

50. Ibid., Sunday, May 13, 1877, M. L. Peabody Papers, MHS.

51. Ibid., Thursday, May 24, 1877, M. L. Peabody Papers, MHS.

52. Ibid., Thursday, June 28, 1877, M. L. Peabody Papers, MHS.

53. Ibid., Friday, August 31, 1877, M. L. Peabody Papers, MHS.

54. Ibid., Thursday, September 20, 1877, M. L. Peabody Papers, MHS.

55. Ibid., December 11, 1877, M. L. Peabody Papers, MHS.

56. Ibid., Thursday, January 17, 1878, M. L. Peabody Papers, MHS.

57. Ibid., Tuesday, December 18, 1877, M. L. Peabody Papers, MHS.

58. Ibid., Thursday, June 28, 1877, and Saturday, October 6, 1877, M. L. Peabody Papers, MHS.

59. Ibid., Wednesday, November 15, 1876; Saturday, June 9, 1877; Friday, August 31, 1877; Thursday, October 18, 1877, M. L. Peabody Papers, MHS.

60. Ibid., December 11, 1885, M. L. Peabody Papers, MHS.

61. Mary Beth Norton, *Liberty's Daughters: The Revolutionary Experience of American Women, 1750-1800*, Boston: Little, Brown, 1980. See especially chapter two: "The Important Crisis Upon Which Our Fate Depends," 40-70.

62. Marian Lawrence Peabody, *To Be Young Was Very Heaven*, Boston: Houghton Mifflin, 1967, especially chapter 1, "Boston Beginnings," and chapter 3, "Schooldays in Boston;" Robert Means Lawrence, *The Descendants of Major Samuel Lawrence*, Cambridge: Riverside Press, 1904, 217-19.

63. M. L. Peabody, *To Be Young*, p. 31.

64. Ibid., 34.

65. Ibid., 35.

66. Ibid., 42-43.

67. Ibid., 58-59.

68. Ibid., 59-60.

69. Ibid., 66-67.

70. Ibid., 361.

71. Ibid.

72. Ibid., 362.

73. Ibid., 366.

CHAPTER FIVE

* See Appendix for genealogical charts.

1. *Directory of Directors in the City of Boston and Vicinity*, Boston: Bankers' Service Company, 1905.

2. Edward Pessen, "The Social Configuration of the Antebellum City: An Historical and Theoretical Inquiry," *Journal of Urban History*, vol. 2, no. 3, May 1976, 278-80.

3. Samuel Eliot Morison, *Three Centuries of Harvard, 1636-1936*, Cambridge: Harvard University Press, 1965; Edward Weeks, *The Lowells and Their Institute*, Boston: Little, Brown, 1966, 51, 75-76.

4. Weeks, *The Lowells and Their Institute*, 36-78.

5. Ibid., 55, 65.

6. Walter Muir Whitehill, *The Museum of Fine Arts, Boston: A Centennial History*, 2 vols., Cambridge: Harvard University Press, 1970; Josiah Quincy, *The History of the Boston Athenaeum*, Cambridge: Metcalf and Co., 1851.

7. Ferris Greenslet, *The Lowells and Their Seven Worlds*, Boston: Houghton Mifflin, 1946, 222.

8. Frank Augustine Gardner, M.D., *Gardner Memorial: A Biographical and Genealogical Record of the Descendants of Thomas Gardner, Planter*, Salem, Mass.: privately printed, 1933, 148-51.

9. Gardner, *Gardner Memorial*, 134-36; "Our First Men: A Calendar of Wealth, Fashion, and Gentility Containing a List of Those Persons Taxed in the City of Boston, Credibly Reported to be Worth $100,000, with Biographical Notices of the Principal Persons," Boston, 1846; Thomas L. V. Wilson, "The Aristocracy of Boston: Who They Are and What They Were," Boston, 1848.

10. Gardner, *Gardner Memorial*, 151.

11. Delmar Lowell, *The Historic Genealogy of the Lowells in America*, published by the author, 1899; Greenslet, *The Lowells and Their Seven Worlds*, 239; Ella Lyman Cabot, *Arthur T. Lyman and Ella Lyman*, Boston: by the author, 1932, 114.

12. Peter Dobkin Hall, "Family Structure and Economic Organization: Massachusetts Merchants, 1700-1850," in Tamara K. Hareven, *Family and Kin in Urban Communities, 1700-1930*, New York: New Viewpoints, 1977, 38-61.

13. Gardner, *Gardner Memorial*, 134.

14. *The Gorham Family*, Winterpark, Fla.: Alfred Averill Knapp, 1961.

15. Greenslet, *The Lowells and Their Seven Worlds*, 238-58.

16. Ibid., 238.

17. "Journal of P. T. Jackson, Jan. 1, 1836-Sept. 13, 1837," Lee Family Papers, Massachusetts Historical Society, Boston, Massachusetts.

18. Greenslet, *The Lowells and Their Seven Worlds*, 239.

19. Ibid., 272-300.

20. Martin Duberman, *James Russell Lowell*, Boston: Beacon Press, 1966; David Heymann Clemens, *American Aristocracy: The Lives and Times of James Russell Lowell, Amy Lowell, and Robert Lowell*, New York: Dodd, Mead, 1980, 55-154.

21. Greenslet, *The Lowells and Their Seven Worlds*, 239-41; Clemens, *American Aristocracy*, 283-513.

22. There is no information on three Dutton sons who were members of this cohort. One graduated in the Harvard class of 1829; another in 1831. There are, however, no Harvard class books from these years that would provide career information on these men. There are no Duttons listed in any of the directories of the economic elite of this period; because of lack of information they have been excluded from analysis of the Lowell kin network: *Yale Biographies and Annals, 1792-1805*, 277.

23. Greenslet, *The Lowells and Their Seven Worlds*, 422-43; Gardner, *Gardner Memorial*, 134-36.

24. Jaher, "Boston Brahmins"; Jaher, *The Urban Establishment*.

25. Robert Means Lawrence, *The Descendants of Major Samuel Lawrence*, Cambridge: Riverside Press, 1904, 180-83; *Dictionary of American Biography*.

26. Greenslet, *The Lowells and Their Seven Worlds*, 320.

27. Massachusetts vol. 84, p. 427, R. G. Dun & Co. Collection, Baker Library, Harvard University Graduate School of Business Administration.

28. Edward Weeks, *The Lowells and Their Institute*, 79-100.

29. Ella Lyman Cabot, *Arthur T. Lyman and Ella Lyman*, 115-289; Coleman, *Genealogy of the Lyman Family in Great Britain and America*, Albany, N.Y.: J. Munsell and Co., 1872.

30. Gerald T. White, *History of the Massachusetts Hospital Life Insurance Company*, Cambridge: Harvard University Press, 1955, 169; Walter Muir Whitehill, *The Provident Institution for Savings in the Town of Boston*, Boston: published by the Provident, 1966, 113; *Boston City Directories*.

31. John William Leonard (ed.), *Who's Who in Finance, Banking, and Insurance*, New York: Joseph and Sefton, 1911, 318-19.

32. Greenslet, *The Lowells and Their Seven Worlds*, 263, 317-18.

33. Ibid., 357-67, 381-409; Weeks, *The Lowells and Their Institute*, 136; Clemens, *American Aristocracy*, 157-279.

34. Leonard, *Who's Who in Finance*, 330; *Directory of Directors in the City of Boston and Vicinity*, Boston: Bankers' Service Co., 1905, 176-77.

35. Gardner, *Gardner Memorial*, 187.

36. Gardner, *Gardner Memorial*, 155-60; Joseph Coolidge and Marguerite Olivier, *Genealogy of Some of the Descendants of John Coolidge of Watertown, Massachusetts, 1630*, Boston: privately printed, 1903, 26-29.

37. Gardner, *Gardner Memorial*, 200; Johnson and Supple, *Boston Capitalists and Western Railroads*; William B. Gates, Jr., *Michigan Copper and Boston Dollars*.

38. Gardner, *Gardner Memorial*, 160-61, 202-11.

39. Ibid., 190-96; Leonard, *Who's Who in Finance*, 301; *Boston Evening Transcript*, August 7, 1916.

40. *Directory of Directors in the City of Boston and Vicinity*, 92, 136-37; Leonard, *Who's Who in Finance*, 301, 318.

41. Greenslet, *The Lowells and Their Seven Worlds*, 324-28; Gardner, *Gardner Memorial*, 135-36.

42. Gardner, *Gardner Memorial*, 161-65.

43. John William Linzee, *The Linzee Family*, Boston: privately printed, 1917, vol. 2, 121-28.

44. Leonard, *Who's Who in Finance*, 272; *Directory of Directors in the City of Boston and Vicinity*, 13; Gardner, *Gardner Memorial*, 167-68.

45. Gardner, *Gardner Memorial*, 168; Leonard, *Who's Who in Finance*, 338; *Directory of Directors*, 207-8.

46. Leonard, *Who's Who in Finance*, 288; *Directory of Directors*, 57, 550; Gardner, *Gardner Memorial*, 168-69; Coolidge, *Genealogy of Descendants of John Coolidge*, 29.

47. Adams, *The Boston Money Tree*, 217, 220-21.

48. Pierre Bourdieu, "Cultural Reproduction and Social Reproduction," in Richard Brown (ed.), *Knowledge, Education, and Cultural Change*, London: 1973.

49. Thomas Gold Appleton, eldest son of Nathan Appleton, held this distinction in the Appleton kin network. Frederic Cople Jaher, "Businessman and

Gentleman: Nathan and Thomas Gold Appleton—An Exploration in Intergenerational History," *Explorations in Entrepreneurial History*, vol. 4, no. 1, Fall 1966, 17-39.

50. Adams, *The Boston Money Tree*, 151.

51. *Memorials of the Harvard Class of 1835*, Boston: David Clapp and Son, 1886, 40; *Dictionary of American Biography*, vol. 11, 47-48; Adams, *The Boston Money Tree*, 152; William Lawrence, *The Life of Amos A. Lawrence, With Extracts from His Diary and Correspondence*, Boston: Houghton Mifflin, Riverside Press, 1899.

52. *New England Historic Genealogical Register*, vol. 17, 293-304.

53. Lawrence, *Descendants of Major Samuel Lawrence*, 153-71.

54. White, *History of the Massachusetts Hospital Life Insurance Company*, 175; Lawrence, *Descendants of Major Samuel Lawrence*, 96-100, 163.

55. Lawrence, *Descendants*, 81-96.

56. Ibid., 88-90.

57. David Rice Whitney, *The Suffolk Bank*, Cambridge: Riverside Press, 1878.

58. *Harvard College Class of 1870, Tenth Report, Fiftieth Anniversary*, Houghton Library, Harvard University.

59. Leonard, *Who's Who in Finance*, 315; Lawrence, *Descendants of Major Samuel Lawrence*, 211ff.

60. Lawrence, *Descendants of Major Samuel Lawrence*, 106, 196-202; *Harvard Class of 1863*, Houghton Library, Harvard University.

61. "Aristocracy of Boston," 8; Lawrence, *Descendants*, 202-7; Grace Williamson Edes, *Annals of the Harvard Class of 1852*, Cambridge: privately printed, 1922.

62. Ratner, *Millionaires*, 21; Adams, *The Boston Money Tree*, 169-71; *Harvard Class of 1875*, Houghton Library, Harvard University.

63. Lawrence, *Descendants of Major Samuel Lawrence*, 217-23; *Harvard Class of 1871, First and Seventh Reports*; *Harvard Class of 1874*, Houghton Library, Harvard University.

64. Lawrence, *Descendants*, 106-10; *Harvard CLass of 1872*.

65. Lawrence, *Descendants*, 131-34; *Directory of Directors in the City of Boston and Vicinity*, 207-8; Leonard, *Who's Who in Finance*, 338.

66. Lawrence, *Descendants*, 131-32; *Directory of Directors in the City of Boston and Vicinity*, 208.

67. Lawrence, *Descendants of Major Samuel Lawrence*, 183-84; *Harvard Class of 1899*, Houghton Library, Harvard University; *Directory of Directors in the City of Boston and Vicinity*, 186.

68. *Harvard Class of 1872, Fourth Report*, Houghton Library, Harvard University.

69. Lawrence, *Descendants of Major Samuel Lawrence*, 83-84; *Harvard Class Report of 1871 and 1879*, Houghton Library, Harvard University; William Bradford Weston, *Hon. Seth Sprague of Duxbury, Plymouth County, Massachusetts, His Descendants Down to the Sixth Generation*, privately printed, 1915, 90-92.

70. *Directory of Directors in the City of Boston and Vicinity*, 203-4.

71. Lawrence, *Descendants of Major Samuel Lawrence*, 85-87; *Harvard Class Report of 1878*, Houghton Library, Harvard University; *Directory of Directors in the City of Boston and Vicinity*, 72, 235.

72. Sidney Ratner, *New Light on the History of Great American Fortunes: American Millionaires of 1892 and 1902*, New York: Augustus M. Kelley, 1953, 22.

73. *Directory of Directors in the City of Boston and Vicinity*, 235; Leonard, *Who's Who in Finance*, 346.

74. *Directory of Directors in the City of Boston and Vicinity*, 150; Leonard, *Who's Who in Finance*, 320; Ratner, *Millionaires*, 21; *Harvard Class of 1874, First Report*, Houghton Library, Harvard University.

75. Lawrence, *Descendants*, 148-49; *Harvard Class of 1871*, Houghton Library, Harvard University; "Aristocracy of Boston," 23; *Directory of Directors in the City of Boston and Vicinity*, 128; Leonard, *Who's Who in Finance*, 314.

76. Lawrence, *Descendants*, 239-242.

77. Lawrence, *Descendants*, 244-47; *Directory of Directors in the City of Boston and Vicinity*, 166; Leonard, *Who's Who in Finance*, 327.

78. *Directory of Directors in the City of Boston and Vicinity*, 87-88; Leonard, *Who's Who in Finance*, 299; Lawrence, *Descendants*, 247-50; Frederick Clifton Pierce, *Foster Genealogy: Being the Record of the Posterity of Reginald Foster; Also the Record of All Other American Fosters*, Chicago: W. B. Conkey, 1899, vol. 1, 401-3, 470-71.

CHAPTER SIX

1. Frederic H. Curtiss, "Fifty Years of Boston Finance, 1880-1930," Boston: n.p., 1930.

2. John Brooks, *Telephone: The First Hundred Years*, New York: Harper and Row, 1975.

3. Arthur S. Pier, *Forbes—Telephone Pioneer*, New York: Dodd, Mead, 1953.

4. Adams, *The Boston Money Tree*, 205.

5. Ralph E. Forbes, *The Forbes Family*, Milton, Mass.: privately printed, 1934; *New York Times*, obituaries, April 11, 1919, 11:3.

6. *Directory of Directors in the City of Boston and Vicinity*, 83; Leonard, *Who's Who in Finance*, 296-97; *Marriage Records of Massachusetts*, 1880, vol. 317, p. 55.

7. *Annual Reports*, American Telephone and Telegraph Co., 1880-1919, Baker Library, Harvard University Graduate School of Business Administration.

8. John Winthrop Hammon, *Men and Volts: The Story of General Electric*, Philadelphia: Lippincott, 1941.

9. *Annual Reports* of the General Electric Co., January 31, 1893-1901, Baker Library, Harvard University Graduate School of Business Administration.

10. Gordon Abbott: director of the State National Bank and Old Colony Trust Co. (Leonard, *Who's Who in Finance*, 270; *Harvard Class of 1884*, Houghton Library, Harvard University). Oliver Ames: Old Colony Trust Co., and the National Shawmut Bank (Leonard, *Who's Who*, 272; *Harvard Class of 1886*, Houghton Library, Harvard; *Boston Evening Transcript*, June 19, 1929, obituary). Thomas Jefferson Coolidge, Jr.: Old Colony Trust Co. and Merchants National Bank (*Boston Evening Transcript*, April 15, 1912, obituary). W. Murray Crane (Ratner, *Millionaires*, 22). Frederick Perry Fish: Old Colony Trust Co. (*Annual Reports*, Baker Library, Harvard Business School). George P. Gardner: Old Colony Trust and Merchants National Bank (Leonard, *Who's Who*, 301; *Harvard Class of 1877*, Houghton Library, Harvard; Gardner, *Gardner Genealogy*). Henry Lee Higginson: National Shawmut Bank (Leonard, *Who's Who*, 308). Robert Treat Paine, II: Old Colony Trust Co. (Leonard, *Who's Who*, 324).

11. Abbott belonged to the Knickerbocker and Brook Clubs of New York; he married Katharine Tiffany of Baltimore, Maryland. Ames belonged to the Knickerbocker and University Clubs of New York; Coolidge to the Knickerbocker, Brook, and Metropolitan. Crane married two women from outside the Boston circle: first, Mary Benner of New York, and second, Josephine Porter Boardman of Washington, D.C. Fish was a member of the Union, University,

Grolier, and American Art Clubs of New York; Gardner, of the University and Harvard Clubs of New York; Higginson, of the Knickerbocker and Harvard Clubs of New York; and Paine, of the Harvard and University Clubs.

12. Six directors of the United Fruit Co. were also directors in the Old Colony Trust Co. They were: John Stephen Bartlett (*Boston Evening Transcript*, January 27, 1925); T. J. Coolidge, Jr., Reginald Foster, and Francis Russell Hart (Leonard, *Who's Who in Finance*, 288, 299, 306); Andrew Woodbury Preston (*Boston Evening Transcript*, September 27, 1924; Leonard, *Who's Who*, 329); and Henry Oliver Underwood (Leonard, *Who's Who*, 341; *Harvard Class of 1879*). Others held directorships in Boston's financial intermediaries, as well. (*Annual Reports*, United Fruit Co., Baker Library, Harvard Business School; Charles M. Wilson, *Empire in Green and Gold: The Story of the American Banana Trade*, New York: Holt, 1947.)

13. The ten largest corporations in terms of capital assets in Boston in 1905 were, in order of size: A.T.&T., the American Woolen Co., General Electric Co., American Agricultural Chemical Co., Copper Range Consolidated Co., New England Telephone and Telegraph, American Bell Telephone Co., United Shoe Machinery Corporation, and the U.S. Mining Co. The five largest banks were: the First National, Merchants National, National Shawmut, Second National, and State National banks. *Directory of Directors in the City of Boston and Vicinity*.

14. Leonard, *Who's Who in Finance*, 348; *Boston Evening Transcript*, June 19, 1917.

15. Curtiss, "Fifty Years of Boston Finance," 2-3; Fritz Redlich, *The Molding of American Banking, Men and Ideas*, New York: Johnson Reprint Corporation, 1968, 2 volumes; Muriel Hidy, "The Capital Markets, 1789-1860," in Harold F. Williamson (ed.), *The Growth of the American Economy*, New York: Prentice-Hall, 1944.

16. Thomas R. Navin and Marian V. Sears, "The Rise of a Market for Industrial Securities, 1887-1902," *Business History Review*, vol. 29, no. 2, June 1955, pp. 105-38.

17. Navin and Sears, "The Rise of a Market," 116, 120, 136.

18. Vincent P. Carosso, *Investment Banking in America: A History*, Cambridge: Harvard University Press, 1970.

19. Marshall Wilkins Stevens, *History of Lee, Higginson and Company*, Boston: privately printed, December 15, 1927, pp. 5-6; Appendix A, p. 37.

20. Edward Weeks, *Men, Money and Responsibility: A History of Lee, Higginson Corporation, 1848-1962*, Boston: privately printed, 1962.

21. Stevens, *History of Lee, Higginson*, 23.

22. Weeks, *Men, Money and Responsibility*, 11-12; Stevens, *History*, 23; Thomas Wentworth Higginson, *The Descendants of the Reverend Francis Higginson (1630)*, privately printed, 1910, 34.

23. Henry Greenleaf Pearson, *Son of New England: James Jackson Storrow, 1864-1926*, Boston: Thomas Todd, 1932; Weeks, *Men, Money*, 19-22; Carosso, *Investment Banking in America*, 1-50.

24. Lee, Higginson, and Company Papers, items #279 and #281: letters of February 20, 1906, and February 21, 1906, between Henry Lee Higginson and William Wood. Baker Library, Harvard University Graduate School of Business Administration.

25. Letter from Henry Lee Higginson to C. A. Coffin, items, #412-414, Lee, Higginson, and Company Papers, Baker Library, Harvard Business School. This letter contains the very revealing pencilled notation: "This letter is indiscreet and should be showed to nobody."

26. Letter from Henry Lee Higginson to Lucius Tuttle, December 8, 1896, item #149, Lee, Higginson, and Company Papers, Baker Library, Harvard Business School.

27. Carosso, *Investment Banking in America*, 49-50.

28. Studies of the social origins of business leaders in the late nineteenth century have found a consistency in social class composition of these men. Frances W. Gregory and Irene D. Neu, "The American Industrial Elite in the 1870s" and William Miller, "The Business Elite in Business Bureaucracies," in William Miller (ed.), *Men in Business: Essays on the Historical Role of the Entrepreneur*, New York: Harper and Row, 1962.

BIBLIOGRAPHY

BOOKS, ARTICLES, AND THESES: GENERAL SOURCES

Adams, Henry. *The United States in 1800*. Ithaca, New York: Cornell University Press, 1955.

Aldrich, Nelson W., Jr. *Old Money: The Mythology of America's Upper Class*. New York: Vintage Books, 1989.

Allen, Michael Patrick. *The Founding Fortunes: A New Anatomy of the Super-Rich Families in America*. New York: Dutton, 1989.

Amory, Cleveland. *The Last Resorts*. New York: Harper and Row, 1952.

——— . *The Proper Bostonians*. New York: Dutton, 1947.

——— . *Who Killed Society?* New York: Harper and Row, 1960.

Appleton, Nathan. "Correspondence Between Nathan Appleton and John A. Lowell in Relation to the early history of Lowell." Boston, 1848.

——— . "An Examination of the Banking System of Massachusetts, in reference to the renewal of Bank Charters." Boston: Stimpson and Clapp, 1831.

——— . "Introduction of the Power Loom and the Origin of Lowell." Boston: B.H. Penhallow, 1858.

Back Bay Boston: The City as a Work of Art. Boston: Museum of Fine Arts, 1969.

Bailyn, Bernard. *The New England Merchants in the Seventeenth Century*. Cambridge: Harvard University Press, 1979.

Baltzell, E. Digby. *Philadelphia Gentlemen: The Making of a National Upper Class*. Glencoe, Ill.: Free Press, 1958.

————. *The Protestant Establishment: Aristocracy and Caste in America.* New York: Vintage Books, 1984.

————. *Puritan Boston and Quaker Philadelphia: Two Protestant Ethics and the Spirit of Class Authority and Leadership.* New York: Free Press, 1979.

Barron, Clarence Walker. *The Boston Stock Exchange, with Sketches of Prominent Brokers, Bankers, Banks, and Moneyed Institutions of Boston.* Boston: Hunt and Bell, 1893.

Baxter, W.T. *The House of Hancock: Business in Boston, 1724-1775.* Cambridge: Harvard University Press, 1945.

Bell, Daniel. "The Breakup of Family Capitalism," in *The End of Ideology.* New York: Free Press, 1965.

Berle, Adolf A. *Power Without Property: A New Development in American Political Economy.* New York: Harcourt, Brace, and World, 1959.

Berle, Adolf A., and Means, Gardiner, C. *The Modern Corporation and Private Property.* New York: Harcourt, Brace, and World, 1968, revised edition.

Bining, Arthur C., and Cochran, Thomas C. *The Rise of American Economic Life.* New York: Charles Scribner's Sons, 1964.

Blodgett, Geoffrey, T. *The Gentle Reformers: Massachusetts Democrats in the Cleveland Era.* Cambridge: Harvard University Press, 1966.

Bourdieu, Pierre. "Cultural Reproduction and Social Reproduction," in Richard Brown (ed.), *Knowledge, Education, and Cultural Change.* London: 1983.

————. "Marriage Strategies as Strategies of Social Reproduction," in Robert Forster and Orest Ranum (eds.), *Family and Society, Selections from the Annales: Economies, Sociétés, Civilisations.* Baltimore: Johns Hopkins University Press, 1976.

Brooks, John. *Telephone: The First Hundred Years.* New York: Harper and Row, 1975.

Bunting, Bainbridge. *Houses of Boston's Back Bay: An Architectural History, 1840-1917.* Cambridge: Harvard University Press, 1967.

Burch, Philip H., Jr. *Elites in American History.* New York: Holmes and Meier, 1980-81, 3 volumes.

————. *The Managerial Revolution Reassessed: Family Control in America's Large Corporations.* Lexington, Mass.: D.C. Heath, 1972.

Carosso, Vincent P. *Investment Banking in America: A History.* Cambridge: Harvard University Press, 1970.

Chandler, Alfred D., Jr. *Strategy and Structure: Chapters in the History of the American Industrial Enterprise.* Cambridge: Massachusetts Institute of Technology Press, 1962.

————. *The Visible Hand: The Managerial Revolution in American Business.* Cambridge: Harvard University Press, 1977.

Cochran, Thomas C. *Railroad Leaders, 1845-1890: The Business Mind in Action.* Cambridge: Harvard University Press, 1953.

————. *Two Hundred Years of American Business.* New York: Basic Books, 1977.

Cochran, Thomas, and Miller, William. *The Age of Enterprise: A Social History of Industrial America.* New York: Macmillan, 1942.

Conference on Research in Income and Wealth. *Trends in the American Economy in the Nineteenth Century.* New York: Arno Press, 1975.

Curtiss, Frederic H. *Fifty Years of Boston Finance, 1880-1930.* Boston: n.p., 1930.

Dalzell, Robert F., Jr. *Enterprising Elite: The Boston Associates and the World They Made.* Cambridge: Harvard University Press, 1987.

Daniellan, N.R. *A.T.&T.: The Story of Industrial Conquest.* New York: Vanguard Press, 1939.

Davidoff, Leonore. *The Best Circles: Society Etiquette and The Season.* London: Cresset Library, 1986.

Davidoff, Leonore, and Catherine Hall. *Family Fortunes: Men and Women of the English Middle Class, 1780-1850.* Chicago: University of Chicago Press, 1987.

Davis, Lance E. "Capital Mobility and American Growth," in Robert Fogel and Stanley L. Engerman (eds.), *The Reinterpretation of American Economic History.* New York: Harper and Row, 1971.

————. "The New England Textile Mills and the Capital Markets: A Study of Industrial Borrowing, 1840-60," *Journal of Economic History,* 20, March 1960.

————. "Sources of Industrial Finance: The American Textile Industry, A Case Study." *Explorations in Entrepreneurial History,* 9, April 1957.

————. "Stock Ownership in the Early New England Textile Industry." *Business History Review,* 32, 1958.

Davis, Lance E., and Payne, Peter L. "From Benevolence to Business: The Story of Two Savings Banks." *Business History Review,* 32, Winter 1958.

DiMaggio, Paul. "Cultural Entrepreneurship in Nineteenth-Century Boston: The Creation of an Organizational Base for High Culture in America." *Media, Culture and Society*, vol. 4, no. 1, 1982.

—————. "Cultural Entrepreneurship in Nineteenth-Century Boston, Part II: The Classification and Framing of American Art." *Media, Culture and Society*, vol. 4, no. 4, 1982.

Domhoff, G. William. *The Higher Circles*. New York: Random House, 1970.

—————. *The Powers That Be: Processes of Ruling-Class Domination in America*. New York: Random House, 1978.

—————. *Who Rules America?* Englewood Cliffs: N.J.: Prentice-Hall, 1967.

—————. *Who Rules America Now?: A View for the '80s*. Englewood Cliffs, N.J.: Prentice-Hall, 1983.

Domhoff, G. William, and Ballard, Hoyt B. (eds.). *C. Wright Mills and the Power Elite*. Boston: Beacon Press, 1968.

Eisinger, Peter K. *The Politics of Displacement: Racial and Ethnic Transition in Three American Cities*. New York: Academic Press, 1980.

Farber, Bernard. *Guardians of Virtue: Salem Families in 1800*. New York: Basic Books, 1972.

—————. *Kinship and Class*. New York: Basic Books, 1971.

Firey, Walter. *Land Use in Central Boston*. Cambridge: Harvard University Press, 1947.

Gates, William B., Jr. *Michigan Copper and Boston Dollars: An Economic History of the Michigan Copper Mining Industry*. Cambridge: Harvard University Press, 1951.

Gibb, George Sweet. *The Saco-Lowell Shops: Textile Machinery Building in New England, 1813-1949*. Cambridge: Harvard University Press, 1950.

Goodman, Paul. "Ethics and Enterprise: The Values of the Boston Elite, 1800-1860." *American Quarterly*, 18, Fall 1966.

Goody, Jack. *The Development of the Family and Marriage in Europe*. Cambridge: Cambridge University Press, 1983.

Gras, N.S.B. *The Massachusetts First National Bank of Boston, 1784-1934*. Cambridge: Harvard University Press, 1937.

Green, Martin. *The Problem of Boston*. New York: Norton, 1966.

Gregory, Frances W. "The Office of President in the American Textile Industry." *Bulletin of the Business Historical Society*, 26, 1954.

Grossberg, Michael. *Governing the Hearth: Law and Family in Nineteenth-Century America.* Chapel Hill: University of North Carolina Press, 1985.

Grow, Natalie R. "The Boston-Type Open-End Fund: Development of a National Financial Institution, 1924-1940." Ph.D. dissertation, Harvard University, 1977.

Hall, Peter Dobkin. "Family Structure and Class Consolidation Among the Boston Brahmins." Ph.D. dissertation, State University of New York at Stonybrook, 1974.

————. "Family Structure and Economic Organization: Massachusetts Merchants, 1700-1850," in Tamara K. Hareven (ed.), *Family and Kin in Urban Communities, 1700-1930.* New York: New Viewpoints, 1977.

————. "Marital Selection and Business in Massachusetts Merchant Families, 1700-1900," in Rose Coser (ed.), *The Family: Its Structures and Functions.* New York: St. Martin's Press, 1974, 2nd edition.

————. *The Organization of American Culture, 1700-1900: Private Institutions, Elites, and the Origins of American Nationality.* New York: New York University Press, 1982.

Hamabata, Matthews Masayuki. *Crested Kimono: Power and Love in the Japanese Business Family.* Ithaca: Cornell University Press, 1990.

Hammond, Bray. *Banks and Politics in America: From the Revolution to the Civil War.* Princeton: Princeton University Press, 1957.

Hammond, John Winthrop. *Men and Volts: The Story of General Electric.* Philadelphia: Lippincott, 1941.

Handlin, Oscar. *Boston's Immigrants, 1790-1865: A Study in Acculturation.* Cambridge: Harvard University Press, 1959, revised edition.

Hareven, Tamara. *Family Time and Industrial Time: The Relationship Between Family and Work in a New England Industrial Community.* Cambridge: Cambridge University Press, 1982.

Hays, Samuel P. *The Response to Industrialism, 1885-1914.* Chicago: University of Chicago Press, 1957.

Hidy, Muriel. "The Capital Markets, 1789-1860," in Harold F. Williamson (ed.), *The Growth of the American Economy.* New York: Prentice-Hall, 1944.

"History of the Boston Manufacturing Company and Lowell," in the Index File of the BMC Records (typewritten). Archives, Baker Library, Harvard Business School.

Holbrook, Donald. *The Boston Trustee*. Boston: Marshall Jones, 1937.

Howe, Mark Anthony DeWolfe. *The Boston Symphony Orchestra—An Historical Sketch*. Boston: Houghton Mifflin, 1914.

Huthmacher, J. Joseph. *Massachusetts People and Politics, 1919-1933*. Cambridge: Harvard University Press, 1959.

Jaher, Frederic Cople. *The Age of Industrialism in America: Essays in Social Structure and Cultural Values*. New York: Free Press, 1968.

———. "Businessman and Gentleman: Nathan and Thomas Gold Appleton— An Exploration in Intergenerational History." *Explorations in Entrepreneurial History*, 4, Fall 1966.

———. *Doubters and Dissenters: Cataclysmic Thought in America, 1885-1918*. New York: Free Press, 1964.

———. "Elites and Equality in Antebellum America." *Reviews in American History*, 2, March 1974.

———. "Nineteenth Century Elites in Boston and New York." *Journal of Social History*, Fall 1972.

——— (ed.). *The Rich, the Well-Born, and the Powerful: Elites and Upper Classes in History*. Urbana: University of Illinois Press, 1974.

———. *The Urban Establishment: Upper Strata in Boston, New York, Charleston, Chicago, and Los Angeles*. Urbana: University of Illinois Press, 1982.

Jaher, Frederic Cople, and Ghent, Jocelyn M. "The Chicago Business Elite: 1830-1930—A Collective Biography." *Business History Review*, 50, Autumn 1976.

Johnson, Arthur M., and Supple, Barry E. *Boston Capitalists and Western Railroads: A Study in the Nineteenth Century Railroad Investment Process*. Cambridge: Harvard University Press, 1967.

Josephson, Hannah. *The Golden Threads: New England's Mill Girls and Magnates*. New York: Russell and Russell, 1949.

Keller, Morton. *The Life Insurance Enterprise, 1885-1910: A Study in the Limits of Corporate Power*. Cambridge: Harvard University Press, 1963.

Kirkland, Edward C. *A History of American Economic Life*. New York: Appleton-Century-Crofts, 1969, 4th edition.

Kolko, Gabriel. "Brahmins and Business, 1870-1914: A Hypothesis on the Social Basis of Success in American History," in Kurt Wolff and Barrington Moore, Jr. (eds.), *The Critical Spirit*. Boston: Beacon Press, 1967.

———. *Main Currents in Modern American History*. New York: Harper and Row, 1976.

———. *Wealth and Power in America: An Analysis of Social Class and Income Distribution*. New York: Praeger, 1962.

Lamoreaux, Naomi R. "Banks, Kinship, and Economic Development: The New England Case." *Journal of Economic History*, vol. 46, no. 3, September 1986.

Lane, Roger. *Policing the City: Boston 1822-1885*. Cambridge: Harvard University Press, 1967.

Lundberg, Ferdinand. *America's Sixty Families*. New York: Citadel Press, 1960.

———. *The Rich and the Super-Rich: A Study in the Power of Money Today*. New York: Stuart, 1968.

Lystra, Karen. *Searching the Heart: Women, Men and Romantic Love in Nineteenth-Century America*. New York: Oxford University Press, 1989.

Mann, Arthur. *Yankee Reformers in the Urban Age*. Cambridge: Harvard University Press, 1954.

Marcus, George (ed.). *Elites: Ethnographic Issues*. Albuquerque: University of New Mexico Press, 1983.

Marcus, George E., with Peter Dobkin Hall. *Lives in Trust: The Fortunes of Dynastic Families in Late Twentieth Century America*. Boulder: Westview Press, 1992.

McLachlan, James. *American Boarding Schools: A Historical Study*. New York: Charles Scribner's Sons, 1970.

Miller, William. *Men in Business: Essays on the Historical Role of the Entrepreneur*. New York: Harper and Row, 1962.

Mills, C. Wright. "The American Business Elite: A Collective Portrait." *The Tasks of Economic History: Journal of Economic History*, 5 (1945).

———. *The Power Elite*. New York: Oxford University Press, 1959.

Morison, Samuel Eliot. *The Maritime History of Massachusetts, 1783-1860*. Boston: Northeastern University Press, 1979.

———. *Three Centuries of Harvard, 1636-1936*. Cambridge: Harvard University Press, 1965.

Myers, Gustavus. *History of the Great American Fortunes*. New York: Modern Library, 1936.

Navin, Thomas R. "The 500 Largest American Industrials in 1917." *Business History Review*, 44, Autumn 1970.

Navin, Thomas R., and Sears, Marian V. "The Rise of a Market for Industrial Securities, 1887-1902." *Business History Review*, 29, June 1955.

O'Connell, Shaun. *Imagining Boston: A Literary Landscape*. Boston: Beacon Press, 1990.

O'Connor, Thomas H. *Lords of the Loom: The Cotton Whigs and the Coming of the Civil War*. New York: Charles Scribner's Sons, 1968.

Odendahl, Teresa. *Charity Begins at Home: Generosity and Self-Interest Among the Philanthropic Elite*. New York: Basic Books, 1990.

"Old Colony Trust Company, 1890-1915." Boston: n.p., 1915.

Olmstead, Alan. "Mutual Savings Bank Depositors in New York." *Business History Review*, 49, Autumn 1975.

Ostrander, Susan A. *Women of the Upper Class*. Philadephia: Temple University Press, 1984.

Parsons, Talcott. "A Revised Approach to the Theory of Social Stratification." *Essays in Sociological Theory*. New York: Free Press, 1964.

Parsons, Talcott, and Smelser, Neil J. *Economy and Society*. New York: Free Press, 1956.

Pessen, Edward. *Riches, Class and Power Before the Civil War*. Lexington, Mass.: D.C. Heath, 1973.

Professional and Industrial History of Suffolk County, Massachusetts. Boston: n.p., 1894, 3 vols.

Quincy, Josiah. *The History of the Boston Athenaeum*. Cambridge: Metcalf, 1851.

Redlich, Fritz. *The Molding of American Banking: Men and Ideas*. New York: Johnson Reprint Corporation, 1968, 2 vols.

Rishel, Joseph F. *Founding Families of Pittsburgh: The Evolution of a Regional Elite, 1760-1910*. Pittsburgh: University of Pittsburgh Press, 1990.

Rochester, Anna. *Rulers of America: A Study of Finance Capital*. New York: International Publishers, 1936.

Rothman, Ellen K. *Hands and Hearts: A History of Courtship in America*. Cambridge: Harvard University Press, 1987.

Schumpeter, Joseph A. *Capitalism, Socialism, and Democracy.* New York: Harper and Row, 1950.

——— . "Social Classes in an Ethnically Homogeneous Environment." *Imperialism and Social Classes.* New York: Meridian, 1955.

Scott, John. *Corporations, Classes, and Capitalism.* London: Hutchinson, 1979.

Smith, Bonnie G. *Ladies of the Leisure Class: The Bourgeoisies of Northern France in the Nineteenth Century.* Princeton: Princeton University Press, 1981.

Stetson, Amos A. *Eighty Years: An Historical Sketch of the State Bank, 1811-1865; The State National Bank, 1865-1891.* Boston: printed by the directors for private distribution, 1893.

Stevens, Marshall Wilkins. "History of Lee, Higginson and Company." Boston: n.p., 1927.

Stone, Lawrence. *The Crisis of the Aristocracy, 1558-1641.* New York: Oxford University Press, 1967.

——— . *Family and Fortune: Studies in Aristocratic Finance in the Sixteenth and Seventeenth Centuries.* New York: Oxford University Press, 1973.

Story, Ronald. "Harvard and the Boston Brahmins: A Study in Institutional and Class Development, 1800-1865." *Journal of Social History*, 8, Spring 1975.

——— . *Harvard and the Boston Upper Class: The Forging of an Aristocracy, 1800-1870.* Middletown, Conn.: Wesleyan University Press, 1980.

Sylla, Richard. "Forgotten Men of Money: Private Bankers in Early U.S. History." *The Journal of Economic History*, 36, March 1976.

Taussig, Frank William, and Joslyn, C.S. *American Business Leaders: A Study in Social Origins and Social Stratification.* New York: Macmillan, 1932.

Useem, Michael. *The Inner Circle: Large Corporations and the Rise of Business Political Activity in the U.S. and U.K.* New York: Oxford University Press, 1984.

Wantanabe, Kishichi. "The Business Organization of the Boston Manufacturing Company—The Early Development of Modern Management in the U.S." *Economic and Business Review*, Kyoto, Japan: Sangry University, 1 (May 1974).

Ware, Caroline F. *The Early New England Cotton Manufacture: A Study in Industrial Beginnings.* New York: Russell and Russell, 1966.

Warner, Sam Bass, Jr. *Streetcar Suburbs: The Process of Growth in Boston, 1870-1900.* Cambridge: Harvard University Press, 1978, 2nd edition.

Weber, Max. *Economy and Society.* New York: Bedminster Press, 1968, 3 vols.

————. *General Economic History.* New Brunswick, N.J.: Transaction Books, 1981.

Wecter, Dixon. *The Saga of American Society: A Record of Social Aspiration, 1607-1937.* New York: Charles Scribner's Sons, 1937.

Weeks, Edward. *The Lowells and Their Institute.* Boston: Little, Brown, 1966.

————. *Men, Money and Responsibility: A History of Lee, Higginson Corporation, 1848-1962.* Boston: by the author, 1962.

White, Gerald. *A History of the Massachusetts Hospital Life Insurance Company.* Cambridge: Harvard University Press, 1955.

Whitehill, Walter Muir. *Boston: A Topographical History.* Cambridge: Harvard University Press, 1975.

————. *Museum of Fine Arts, Boston: A Centennial History.* Cambridge: Harvard University Press, 1970, 2 vols.

————. *The Provident Institution for Savings in the Town of Boston, 1816-1966: A Historical Sketch.* Boston: published by the Provident, 1966.

Whitney, David Rice. *The Suffolk Bank.* Cambridge: Riverside Press of Houghton Mifflin, 1878.

Williams, Alexander W. *A Social History of the Greater Boston Clubs.* Barre, Mass.: Barre Publishing Co., 1970.

Williamson, Harold F. (ed.). *The Growth of the American Economy: An Introduction to the Economic History of the United States.* New York: Prentice-Hall, 1944.

Winsor, Justin (ed.). *The Memorial History of Boston, 1630-1880.* Boston: Osgood and Co., 1885, 4 vols.

Zeitlin, Maurice. *The Large Corporation and Contemporary Classes.* New Brunswick: Rutgers University Press, 1989.

BIOGRAPHIES AND FAMILY GENEALOGIES

Adams, Charles Francis, Jr. *An Autobiography, 1835-1915.* Boston: Houghton Mifflin, 1961.

Ames, Winthrop. *The Ames Family of Easton, Massachusetts.* Boston: privately published, 1938.

Bacon, Edwin (ed.). *Men of Progress: 1000 Biographical Sketches and Portraits of Leaders in Business and Professional Life in the Commonwealth of Massachusetts.* Boston: New England Magazine, 1897.

Bowen, Catharine Drinker. *Yankee From Olympus: A Biography of Oliver Wendell Holmes.* New York: Bantam Books, 1968.

Briggs, L. Vernon. *History and Genealogy of the Cabot Family, 1475-1927.* Boston: Charles E. Goodspeed, 1927.

Cabot, Ella Lyman. *Arthur T. Lyman and Ella Lyman.* Boston: privately published, 1932.

Clemens, David Heymann. *American Aristocracy: The Lives and Times of James Russell Lowell, Amy Lowell, and Robert Lowell.* New York: Dodd, Mead, 1980.

Coolidge, Emma Downing. *Descendants of John and Mary Coolidge of Watertown, Massachusetts, 1630.* Boston: Wright and Potter, 1930.

Coolidge, Joseph, and Olivier, Marguerite. *Genealogy of Some of the Descendants of John Coolidge of Watertown, Massachusetts, 1630.* Boston: privately published, 1903.

Crawford, Mary Caroline. *Famous Families of Massachusetts.* Boston: Little, Brown, 1930.

Cunningham, Edith P. (ed.). *Charles Elliott Perkins and Edith Forbes Perkins: Family Letters, 1861-1869.* Boston: privately published, 1949.

Duberman, Martin. *James Russell Lowell.* Boston: Beacon Press, 1966.

Eliot, Samuel Atkins (ed.). *Biographical History of Massachusetts: Biographies and Autobiographies of the Leading Men in the State.* Boston: Boston Biographical Society, 1909-1918, 10 vols.

Emerson, Edward W. *Life and Letters of Charles Russell Lowell.* Boston: privately published, 1907.

Forbes, Ralph E. *The Forbes Family.* Milton, Mass.: privately published, 1934.

Gardner, Frank Augustine, M.D. *Gardner Memorial: A Biographical and Genealogical Record of the Descendants of Thomas Gardner, Planter, 1626-1674, Through His Son, Lieut. George Gardner.* Salem, Mass.: privately published, 1933.

Genealogy of the Lowell Family: The One Hundred and Fiftieth Anniversary of the Foundation of the First Religious Society of Newburyport. Boston: William Huse, 1876.

Greenslet, Ferris. *The Lowells and Their Seven Worlds*. Cambridge: Riverside Press of Houghton Mifflin, 1946.

Gregory, Frances W. *Nathan Appleton: Merchant and Entrepreneur, 1779-1861*. Charlottesville: University Press of Virginia, 1975.

Hale, Susan. *Life and Letters of Thomas Gold Appleton*. New York: Appleton, 1885.

Hall, Henry (ed.). *America's Successful Men of Affairs*. New York, 1896, 2 vols.

Harris, Leon. *Only to God: The Extraordinary Life of Godfrey Lowell Cabot*. New York: Atheneum, 1967.

Higginson, Thomas Wentworth (ed.). *The Descendants of the Reverend Francis Higginson, 1630*. Boston: privately published, 1910.

————. *Harvard Memorial Biographies*. Cambridge: Sever and Francis, 1867, 2 vols.

Hill, Hamilton Andrews. *Memoir of Abbott Lawrence*. Cambridge: University Press, John Wilson and Son, 1883.

Hoyt, Edwin P. *The Peabody Influence: How a Great New England Family Helped to Build America*. New York: Dodd, Mead, 1968.

Hughes, Sarah Forbes (ed.). *Letters and Recollections of John Murray Forbes*. Boston: Houghton Mifflin, 1899, 2 vols.

Hunt, Freeman. *Lives of American Merchants*. New York: Derby and Jackson, 1858.

Jewett, Isaac Appleton. *Memorial of Samuel Appleton*. Boston: Bolles and Houghton, 1850.

Kirkland, Edward C. *Charles Francis Adams, Jr., 1835-1915: The Patrician at Bay*. Cambridge: Harvard University Press, 1965.

Lawrence, Robert Means. *The Descendants of Major Samuel Lawrence*. Cambridge: Riverside Press of Houghton Mifflin, 1904.

Lawrence, William. *Life of Amos A. Lawrence, with Extracts from his Diary and Correspondence*. Cambridge: Riverside Press of Houghton Mifflin, 1899.

Lowell, Delmar. *The Historic Genealogy of the Lowells in America*. Boston: privately published, 1899.

Lyman, Coleman. *Genealogy of the Lyman Family in Great Britain and America*. Albany, N.Y.: J. Munsell, 1872.

May, Samuel Pearce. *Descendants of Richard Sears of Yarmouth*. Newton, Mass.: privately published, 1913, 2 vols.

Meredith, Gertrude E. *The Descendants of Hugh Amory, 1605-1805*. London: privately published, 1901.

Morison, Samuel Eliot. *Harrison Gray Otis: Urbane Federalist*. Boston: Houghton Mifflin, 1969.

———. *One Boy's Boston, 1887-1901*. Boston: Northeastern University Press, 1983.

Morse, Frances Rollins. *Henry and Mary Lee: Letters and Journals, with Other Family Letters, 1802-1860*. Boston: privately published, 1926.

Morse, John Torrey, Jr. *Life and Letters of Oliver Wendell Holmes*. Boston: Little, Brown, 1896.

———. *Memoir of Colonel Henry Lee*. Boston: Little, Brown, 1905.

Peabody, Marian Lawrence. *To Be Young Was Very Heaven*. Boston: Houghton Mifflin, 1967.

Pearson, Henry Greenleaf. *An American Railroad Builder, John Murray Forbes*. Boston, 1911.

———. *Son of New England: James Jackson Storrow, 1864-1926*. Boston: Thomas Todd, 1932.

Perry, Bliss (ed.). *The Life and Letters of Henry Lee Higginson*. Boston: Atlantic Monthly Press, 1921.

Pier, Arthur, S. *Forbes: Telephone Pioneer*. New York: Dodd, Mead, 1953.

Pierce, Frederick Clifton. *Foster Genealogy: Being the Record of the Posterity of Reginald Foster; Also the Record of all Other American Fosters*. Chicago: Press of the W.B. Conkey Co., 1899.

Porter, Kenneth Wiggins. *The Jacksons and the Lees: Two Generations of Massachusetts Merchants, 1765-1844*. New York: Russell and Russell, 1937, 2 vols.

Prescott, William Hickling. *Memoir of the Honorable Abbott Lawrence*. Boston: privately published, 1856.

Putnam, Elizabeth Cabot, and Putnam, James Jackson. *The Hon. Jonathan Jackson and Hannah (Tracy) Jackson, Their Ancestors and Descendants*. Boston: privately published, 1907.

Putnam, James Jackson, M.D. *A Memoir of Dr. James Jackson*. Boston: Houghton Mifflin, 1905.

Representative Men of Massachusetts, 1890-1900: The Leaders in Official, Business and Professional Life of the Commonwealth. Everett, Mass.: Massachusetts Publishing Co., 1898.

Sheppard, John H. *Sketch of Hon. Nathan Appleton.* Boston: D. Clapp and Son, 1862.

Smith, Charles C. "Memoir of John Amory Lowell." *Proceedings of the Massachusetts Historical Society,* January 1898.

Taylor, P.A.M. (ed.). *More Than Common Powers of Perception: The Diary of Elizabeth Rogers Mason Cabot.* Boston: Beacon Press, 1991.

Tharp, Louise Hall. *The Appletons of Beacon Hill.* Boston: Little, Brown, 1973.

Waters, T. Frank. *A Genealogy of the Ipswich Descendants of Samuel Appleton.* Salem, Mass.: Salem Press, 1907.

Winthrop, Robert C. *Memoir of the Hon. Nathan Appleton, LL.B.; prepared agreeably to a resolution of the Massachusetts Historical Society.* Boston: J. Wilson and Son, 1861.

RECORDS, DIRECTORIES, AND MANUSCRIPT COLLECTIONS

The Boston City Directory [Containing Names of the Inhabitants, Their Occupations, Places of Business and Dwelling Houses, with a List of the Streets, Lanes, Wharves, The Town Officers, Public Offices and Banks and Other Useful Information]. Boston: John H.A. Frost and Charles Stimpson, Jr., 1820-1840.

The Boston Evening Transcript. 1830-1930.

Clark, Edward E. *The Boston Blue Book* [Private Address and Carriage Directory and Ladies' Visiting and Shopping Guide for Boston and Brookline, Containing the Names of over 6,000 Householders]. Boston: privately published, 1878-1929.

Codman, Ogden. *Index of Obituaries in Boston Newspapers, 1704-1800.* Boston: n.p., n.d.

Dictionary of American Biography. Edited by Dumas Malone; Supplements edited by John A. Garraty. New York: Charles Scribner's Sons, 1932.

Directory of Directors in the City of Boston and Vicinity. Boston: Bankers' Service Co., 1905.

Forbes, A., and Greene, J.W. *The Rich Men of Massachusetts: Containing a State-*

ment of the Reputed Wealth of About 1500 persons, with Brief Sketches of More than 1000 Characters. Boston: W.V. Spencer, 1851.

Harvard University Graduate School of Business Administration, Baker Library, Special Collections: Appleton-Dexter Family Papers, Higginson Family Papers, Gardner Family Papers. Papers of the Boston Manufacturing Co., the Hamilton Co., the Lawrence Co., Lee, Higginson, and Co., the Lowell Co., the Merrimack Manufacturing Co. The R.G. Dun & Company Credit Ledgers.

Harvard University Graduate School of Business Administration, Baker Library: *Annual Reports*: American Bell Telephone Co., American Telephone and Telegraph Co., 1880-1919, and the General Electric Co., 1893-1901.

Harvard University, Houghton Library: *Class Reports*. Cambridge: various publishers, 1841-1899.

————. *Quinquennial Catalogue of the Officers and Graduates, 1636-1930.* Cambridge: Harvard University Press, 1930.

————. *Sibley's Harvard Graduates.* Cambridge: Harvard University Press, 1873-1972.

Hurd, Henry M. (ed.). *Index of Obituaries in Boston Newspapers, 1704-1800.* Boston: Boston Atheneum Press, 1969, 3 vols.

Index to Obituary Notices in the Boston Transcript: 1875-1899, 1900-1930, 1940, 3 vols.

Leonard, John William (ed.). *Who's Who in Finance, Banking, and Insurance.* New York: Joseph and Sefton, 1911.

"List of Persons, Co-partnerships, and Corporations who were Taxed $25 and Upwards in the City of Boston, 1836-1848." Boston: Assessors' Office, Massachusetts Hospital Life Insurance Co., n.d.

"List of Persons, Co-partnerships, and Corporations who were Taxed on $6,000 and Upwards in the City of Boston, 1849-1852." Boston: Assessors' Office, Massachusetts Hospital Life Insurance Co., n.d.

A List of Stockholders in the National Banks of Boston. Boston: Aldred Mudge and Son, 1866.

Massachusetts Department of Vital Statistics: McCormack Building, Boston: Marriage Records. Death Records.

Massachusetts Historical Society: Anna Sears Amory Letters. Elizabeth R. Mason Diaries. Journals of Hetty S. Lawrence Cunningham, 1876-1878 and 1881, Marian Lawrence Peabody Papers. Lee Family Papers. F.C. Lowell II Papers. Sears Family Papers.

The New England Historical and Genealogical Register. Boston: Samuel G. Drake.

The New York Times Obituaries Index, 1858-1968. New York, 1970.

Our First Men: A Calendar of Wealth, Fashion, and Gentility, Containing a List of Those Persons Taxed in the City of Boston, Credibly Reported to be Worth $100,000, With Biographical Notices of the Principal Persons. Boston: all the Booksellers, 1846.

Ratner, Sidney. *New Light on the History of Great American Fortunes: American Millionaires of 1892 and 1902.* New York: Augustus M. Kelley, 1953.

Rider, Fremont (ed.). *The American Genealogical-Biographical Index to American Genealogical, Biographical, and Local History Materials.* Middletown, Conn.: Godfrey Memorial Library, 1952.

The Social Register: Boston. New York: The Social Register Association, 1890—.

Suffolk County, Massachusetts: Probate Court. Wills of Abbott Lawrence and Patrick Tracy Jackson.

Who Was Who In America, 1607-1896. Chicago: Marquis Who's Who Company, vol.1, 1887-1918.

Wilson, Thomas L.V. *The Aristocracy of Boston: Who They Are and What They Were.* Boston: n.p., 1848.

INDEX